"All employees want to perform exceptionally, they just need a tool to enlighten and motivate their thought process. CPIP was the "light" that ignited core values and teamwork throughout the organization. Moving forward, the entire company thinks in terms of agreements that they are personally able to keep instead of what "projects" they weren't able to obtain. Grades aren't necessary here at Regional Medical Imaging, but trust is essential. Build a bridge of trust and watch your employees reach greater potential then you ever imagined."

Jill L. Fielder RT (R) (M)
Chief Operation Officer
Regional Medical Imaging

"The Values that we created with Wally have helped to define our company culture. They are a constant reminder of how we should treat fellow employees, clients and our community."

Shayne Newman
President, YardApes, Inc.

STOP the Leadership Malpractice

How to Replace the Typical Performance Appraisal

by: Wally Hauck, PhD

Published by Motivational Press, Inc.
2360 Corporate Circle
Suite 400
Henderson, NV 89074
www.MotivationalPress.com

www.wallyhauck.com

Manufactured in the United States of America.

ISBN: 978-1-62865-004-4

Contents

Introduction:
A Breach in the Standard of Care

In the summer of 2001, 15 of the September 11 terrorists completed a simple two-page application at the Saudi Arabian consulate for a visa to come to the United States. According to expert analysis of these visa application forms, all 15 of the applications should have been flatly denied under the existing law. The law holds that the applicant must convince the officer that the visa will be used only for travel, work, or school and not a stepping stone to immigration. (Mowbray, 2002) Under the law, all applicants are to be assumed to be an immigrant unless otherwise established.

According to the experts the consular officers ignored this provision of the law in order to approve the applications. Why? The experts familiar with the visa approvals did not fault the consular officers – *"they fault the policies and guidelines under which the officers were forced to operate."* (Mowbray, 2002)

During 2001 the permissive culture in the consulate in Saudi Arabia had denied less than 2% of visas whereas the average denial rate in consulates was 25%. The rate of approval of Saudi applications was factored into the consular officer's performance appraisal. Consulate leadership sent clear messages of courtesy and permissiveness for Saudi applicants. This message contradicted the guidelines of refusal the consular officers were obliged to follow, denied their freedom to exercise their best discretion, and damaged their willingness to speak the truth. The result, four months later, was 3,000 American deaths. This is leadership malpractice at its worst. The use of the typical appraisal process at the consulate was a contributing factor. It's time for this malpractice to stop.

Malpractice is failure of a professional person to do his or her job. This failure results in some injury to others. Malpractice generally occurs through ignorance, incompetence, neglect, or carelessness. Malpractice can also be characterized by criminal behavior but this book is not about criminal activity or corruption. It's about how the purposeful use of the typical appraisal process is a major cause of malpractice and it won't stop until it is replaced. The aim of this book is to convince leaders of this premise and to offer a proven replacement. Unless this change is made the policy will continue to be a barrier to achieving the results we all want.

During college my daughter worked for a National food service company that served meals to retired Nuns at a convent near her college. She had worked there for two years before she experienced her first performance appraisal. Her boss, Jerry, wanted to give her a raise. To do that, he was required (by policy) to hold a performance review meeting and rate her performance. The rating would determine the amount of the raise. She was consistently reliable never missing her assigned scheduled work. She easily cooperated to trade hours with her colleagues to ensure full staffing. She always put in full effort. In addition, the nuns all loved her. Unfortunately, Jerry was never there to witness any of this. He was always either in his office or at another customer location.

The appraisal meeting lasted about 20 minutes. He explained the rating scale was 1-5 where a "1" rating was "needs improvement" and a 5 rating was "exceeds expectations." He told her, *"Don't expect a 5. No one ever gets one. We don't believe in 5's. When people receive a 5 they are not motivated to improve."*

Jerry rated her 3.5's and 4's in all categories. She let him go through the entire process. After listening carefully and politely (she was taught to respect authority) she said, *"Jerry, may I ask you a question? How did you know what to rate me, you are never here?"* He stumbled and said, *"I have a general idea. Sometimes when I get here at the end of your shift I have seen you mop the floor and you did a good job."*

The level of absurdity and malpractice seems off the chart with this example but this story is true. Absurdity in the typical appraisal process is more the rule than the exception. Can we expect my daughter's performance to improve or decline after that meeting? Furthermore, what impact do the ratings she received have on her performance?

There are clear similarities between a physician who commits malpractice and an organizational leader who commits it. In a malpractice lawsuit there is always a claim that involves the breach of the standard of care by a professional. This breach results in an injury. A leader is a professional who is responsible for a standard of care of the organization and its stakeholders (employees, customers, investors). The breach is the use of the typical appraisal process. The injury is the damage the existence and use of the appraisal creates for employees, customers and investors.

A physician accused of malpractice is part of a very complex medical system. The system has many factors that interact to create the results. The physician is only one part of this complex system. The same is true for organizational leaders. Both the physician and leader are put in a position where they must pretend to be omniscient (all knowing) and omnipotent (all powerful). Just as my daughter's boss Jerry had to pretend he could accurately rate my daughter, leaders are absurdly expected to conduct their daily work responsibilities while "sitting on every employee's shoulder" observing their performance so they can deliver immediate and constant feedback and an accurate and fair rating. It's absurd. It's injurious. It's malpractice. This book will reverse this absurdity by offering replacement thinking and replacement methods that better match the needs of employees who must effectively operate within the complex system and the "new" knowledge economy.

The word malpractice was carefully chosen for the title. It fits the situation because there are clear similarities between a physician who commits malpractice and an organizational leader who commits it. In a malpractice lawsuit there is always a claim that involves the breach of the standard of care by a professional. This breach results in an injury.

A leader is a professional who is responsible for a standard of care of the organization and its stakeholders (employees, customers, investors). The breach is the use of the typical appraisal process. The injury is the damage the appraisal creates for employees, customers and investors.

We have been taught a theory of leadership that is now obsolete and useless for the current age (often called the knowledge age). This deception has created false responsibilities and hidden the true responsibilities of leaders. Some even argue the theory our business schools favor is one void of moral responsibility focusing only on science as its core therefore leaving the spiritual and ethical side to flounder and to cause dysfunction. (Ghoshal, 2005) Furthermore, any injury caused by the malpractice is often too far removed from the leader's actions. For example, if my daughter's performance slipped after her performance appraisal meeting it is unlikely the leaders would look to her boss as a cause.

Most Human Resource professionals (and attorneys) attribute the failure of the typical performance appraisal to poor management skills and or poor training of those managers who must implement it. This is incorrect. Would training have helped Jerry? Perhaps, but the injurious flaws of the typical appraisal are systemic. It's not the techniques it's the very nature of the appraisal itself. It's in the assumptions upon which the appraisal is based.

Appraisals attempt to measure the performance of an individual in a complex system. This book will show it's not possible to accurately separate the measurement of an individual part in a complex system. It is mostly guesswork, opinion, and bias at best. Accurate assessment of a single part's contribution cannot be verified because the system within which people work is too complex.

Many of us exercise. If you exercise, your heart, lungs and nervous system all must work together to make that happen. Which of those body organs is more important? It's impossible to know because the organs are interdependent. The lungs will work only if the heart is pumping blood bringing oxygen to the muscles. The nervous system sends needed messages to the brain which send signals to the muscles etc. Any attempt to rate or grade each of the parts separate from the others makes no sense. It's not useful. Instead, it's the quality of the interactions between the organs that enable the exercise.

Systems thinking is a set of assumptions, a specific language, and a set of tools that emphasizes the importance of improving the interrelationships between the parts (elements of a system) instead of improving the parts. Systems thinking offers new options and enduring solutions to solve the most challenging problems. In short, it provides a more accurate view of reality. Systems thinking is founded upon a set of enduring and universal principles that can easily be detected in nature. An example is cooperation (vs. competition). Cooperation between the parts of a system creates much better results over the long-term than does competition.

Leaders must begin to shift their assumptions from the current thinking to systems thinking. In his book, *The Fifth Discipline*, Peter Senge defines it: *"Systems thinking is a conceptual framework, a body of knowledge and tools that has been developed over the past fifty years, to make the full patterns clearer, and to help us see how to change them effectively."* (Senge, 1990)

The book is organized into four parts: **The Claim, The Causation, The Verdict, and the Settlement.** In a malpractice lawsuit there is always a claim that involves the breach of the standard of care by a professional. This breach results in an injury. The key to eliminate future injury is to uncover the root causes (The Causation) take action to remove those causes (The Verdict) and implement those changes (The Settlement) to eliminate injury in the future.

The Claim describes the injury and the damage caused. It explains why we must change and why the typical appraisal must be part of the change. The Claim describes the serious injuries being caused by the use of the typical appraisal. It helps to create a compelling case for change and provides the foundation of the leader to shift to new thinking and new action.

The Causation explains the reasons why the appraisal is still promoted. It's not the leaders who should be attacked. It's our leadership model that needs changing. We have been deceived with an obsolete model. This book questions the very foundation of our improvement models i.e. our leadership theory. There is no evil intention or criminal corruption behind the deceit but there is serious injury. Our economy has evolved but our leadership model is stuck in the past.

The Causation explains how and why the typical performance appraisal was originally adopted as a management tool and why it remains the most popular management tool to this day. The explanation makes it OK for leaders to change without losing face and without embarrassment because it explains how we have all been deceived and how we all can evolve together.

The Verdict is the description of a replacement leadership model. It offers a replacement for industrial age Taylor Scientific Management model. Dr. Deming's Theory of Profound Knowledge provides the best foundation for a replacement. The advice in this book attempts to be consistent with Deming's System of Profound Knowledge.

The Settlement explains the elements of the replacement appraisal. The replacement appraisal is called the Complete Performance Improvement Process (CPIP). To be an effective replacement it must be able to fulfill the important functions of an appraisal and avoid injury. It must avoid injury to the most important objectives of leaders today such as high employee engagement, attracting and retaining the best talent, high levels of trust, optimum innovation, and the ability to adapt to change (all of the key issues on the minds of leaders). But, it's not enough to just avoid injury. A replacement must help a leader to effectively achieve each of these objectives.

Any alternative must be consistent with systems thinking thereby acknowledging the interdependence of all of the parts. Any alternative must build trust between the parts and not damage it as the typical appraisal does. The alternative must enable the leader and the employees to act as partners and colleagues to solve process issues.

The alternative must heap a greater sense of responsibility on both the employee and the leader. These responsibilities will be of higher quality. The alternative must demand employees be treated like adults and not like children. It will enable managers to behave like facilitators and not omniscient parents and/or arrogant biased judges.

The alternative must provide a process for immediate feedback. It must provide a process to deliver that feedback without fear of retribution and without bias. It must deliver it solely for the purpose of increasing trust or improving learning and it must discourage feedback for the purpose of manipulation and for personal gain at the expense of the system performance.

The alternative will facilitate the creation of joy at work for all employees. It will create an environment that fosters fun, trust, the love of learning, innovation, productivity, continuous improvement, and outstanding results. It will unleash employee engagement. CPIP does all of this and it has the potential to do even more.

Part I
The Claim

A Case for Replacement of the Typical Appraisal

Chapter 1:
What Should an Appraisal Do?

Aim of this Chapter: To clarify the definition, functions, and intended outcomes of a typical appraisal in order to set up the argument for why it is an example of leadership malpractice.

Hurricane Irene was rated the fifth costliest hurricane in United States history. A facilities manager at one of my clients prepared the 20 acres of grounds for Irene which was expected to hit Connecticut on a Saturday night in 2011. He arranged for his employees to dig ditches to move water away from the buildings. Five inches of rain was expected to fall in just a few hours. He had all the generators checked. He arranged for his staff to be on-call over the next 36 hours. He arranged for a back-hoe to be maintained and ready. He scheduled the staff for cleanup duties on the day after the storm. He told his wife he'd see her Monday and made arrangements to sleep in his office.

A member of the Board of Directors of the company came to see the damage two days after the storm. After a brief tour he remarked, *"The grass is too long. When will it be cut and why wasn't it cut before now?"* What did that criticism do for the motivation of the facilities manager? What did it do for the engagement of his employees?

The Design and the Definition

The typical appraisal is designed with good intentions. It also attempts to fulfill important purposes. If we are going to replace the typical appraisal then we must keep the good and get rid of the bad. We must understand the key worthy purposes we want the replacement process to fulfill. We must then redesign the process to be sure it meets those purposes. In the effort to redesign we must be sure to identify any flawed principles upon which the typical appraisal is based and replace those flawed principles with ones more closely aligned with systems thinking. We can then design the replacement process to match the principles and deliver the key functions (outcomes).

The typical appraisal can be defined as a process that judges individual performance. (Coens & Jenkins, 2000) According to Tom Coens and Mary Jenkins, authors of *Abolishing Performance Appraisals*, five key general features or characteristics are shared by all typical appraisals.

First, employees' work performance, behaviors, and traits are judged by someone other than the employee themselves. The employee may also do a self-assessment but the typical appraisal always has a rating or grade that is assigned to the employee by someone other than the employee. Most frequently this person is the employee's immediate supervisor (the person written above them on the organizational chart).

Second, the rating of the employee applies to a specific time period (usually one year) and not a particular project or process. Third, the typical appraisal is systematically applied to all employees and it is mandatory. Mandatory compliance is the fourth characteristic.

Finally, the fifth characteristic is the record keeping feature. The documentation results are filed by someone other than the employee and are kept for legal reasons by a responsible party, usually Human Resources.

This set of features can be summarized into a specific definition:

> *The practice of performance appraisal is a mandated process in which, for a specified period of time, all or a group of employees' work performance, behaviors, or traits are individually rated, judged, or described by a person other than the rated employee and the results are kept by the organization.* (Coens & Jenkins, 2000)

Let's not forget the 360 degree instrument is a form of the typical appraisal. The 360 degree provides opinions of more than just the immediate supervisor. By definition, it requests opinions "all around" the employee. It therefore includes the employee's customers (internal or external), his/her peers, and his/her boss(es). These opinions are most often anonymous and they are often included in addition to the narrative and the rating provided by the immediate supervisor.

The Purposes

The typical appraisal serves specific functions or purposes (outcomes). First, it attempts to improve individual performance and development. To do this, leaders use tools and techniques such as coaching, mentoring, giving feedback, counseling poor performers, setting goals, and measuring goal achievement.

Second, it attempts to improve organizational performance. Leaders communicate strategic objectives, set goals and create measures for achievement of those goals.

Third, it enables leaders to make promotional and career decisions (succession planning). It provides the necessary data for leaders to make decisions about succession planning, promotional screening, career path, downsizing, and pay-for-performance award distributions.

Forth, it attempts to improve the communication and trust between managers and employees. And fifth, it attempts to protect the organization from the legal challenges employees (especially poor performers) might file if they disagree with the ratings on their forms or any of the decisions that were made fulfilling the first four functions.

These five functions are important. It is a huge challenge for the typical appraisal to fulfill all of these with just one process. We want to be sure to fulfill all important functions with any replacement process. The Complete Performance Improvement Process (CPIP) is the suggested replacement for the typical appraisal. CPIP is designed to fulfill four primary functions.

First, CPIP is intended to improve the quality of the interactions between the parts of the system. This includes the interpersonal interactions between individuals (all employees) and the system interactions that occur in the processes employees use to do their work. By improving the interactions it contributes to improving the performance of the individuals, the performance of the organizational system, and improving the level of trust in all parts of the organization (including external customers).

Second, CPIP is intended to improve employee development (the skills and competencies). It encourages all employees to take a greater level of responsibility for their own development. With CPIP the leaders are no longer responsible for the majority of an employee's development. The leaders take the role of a facilitator of the employee development but not the leader of it. The leaders help identify the barriers to development but they are not necessarily active in the removal of those barriers unless requested by the employee. The leader can play the role of the coach. If the employee needs or wants a different coach they can select one. It should be one that best suits the development they desire. The leader is the facilitator of the development not the omniscient creator of it.

Third, CPIP is designed to assist in the alignment of every action with the strategic objectives of the organization. The leader and the employee create a partnership to clarify the organizational objectives and to translate those into objectives in their function and for each position within the function. The leader and employee then agree on the process steps and the agreements needed to accomplish those objectives.

The fourth function is to help all employees to manage their own performance in the context of the system. This includes managing variation. Poor performance must also be managed immediately to avoid wasted time for leaders, employees, and the organization. Things evolve and economic environments change. As those changes occur sometimes new skills need to be developed. Most employees are able to make the adjustments. Most employees are willing and able to ask for help and sometimes employees are unwilling or unable to adapt. Sometimes employees need to change or need training and sometimes they need to move on.

One of my clients, a recently hired manager of health and safety for a school, called me frustrated with the performance of one of her colleagues. She was frustrated that the school principle was either unable or unwilling to confront serious performance issues that were preventing the manager of health and safety from doing her job. An organizational strategic objective was recently adopted by the Sr. Leaders, i.e. improve safety and reduce costs. The health and safety manager immediately could see opportunities for action to achieve these objectives. The school principle was either unwilling or unable to take these actions and this was the source of the manager's frustrations. The principle either didn't see the opportunities or consciously decided to ignore them. The "new" manger thought they were obvious. The principle saw them as the "way we have always done it." This gap in motivation and priority is very common in organizations. As strategies evolve the people require leadership to make the shift in priorities. The typical appraisal does a poor job helping employee to make these types of shifts.

CPIP improves the communication between employees. It improves individual and organizational performance. It enables employees to make valuable career decisions while helping the organization to make succession planning decisions. CPIP protects both the employee and the organization from legal challenges. The only function not fulfilled by CPIP is making pay decisions. In the new leadership model decisions about pay are separated from all CPIP discussions. A separate process is needed for pay decisions and pay-for-performance is discouraged. Connecting pay decisions to performance discussions can create injury to individuals, the organization and customers. A discussion of this topic is presented in Chapter 14.

Chapter 2:
The Injuries are Serious and Often Hidden

Aim of this Chapter: Provide proof (data) the use of the typical appraisal significantly contributes to injury and any benefits are overshadowed by such harm.

The February 1, 2003 disintegration of the Columbia Space Shuttle was a horrific tragedy. The loss of the seven–member crew tore apart the hearts of Americans, damaged the reputation of the Government's space program, and shattered the confidence of the American people in the leadership at NASA. The accident was investigated by the independent Columbia Accident Investigation Board. They issued its findings in August of 2003. The physical cause of the Columbia was the flaw in the thermal protection tiles of the left wing. However, there is never just one cause in a complex system.

According to their report the organizational causes were rooted in the history and the culture that allowed compromises, bowed to bureaucratic decision making, and prevented open and honest debate without fear of criticism or retribution. (Board, 2003) The board concluded the accident was not a random event. It was rather a product of the history, the culture and the management processes. It also stated that a high risk operation, like the Shuttle program, requires a healthy fear of failure to be successful and avoid catastrophic errors. Unfortunately, the airing of professional differences of opinion where blocked by the organizational barriers. These barriers prevented effective communication of critical safety information and therefore stopped the healthy airing of disagreements and conflict that would have brought forth the truth and prevented the accident.

Team members felt pressure to remain quiet unless specifically asked for their input on their particular area of expertise. Engineers demonstrated reluctance to bring their real concerns to the forefront for fear of retribution. These symptoms of poor communication are similar to those seen in all organizations that use the typical performance appraisal process.

It took a highly qualified board of rocket scientists (and others) seven months to see the connection between an event of a small piece of foam hitting a heat tile and the culture of fear that contributed to it. For average leaders who need to deal with problems immediately (and who don't have the resources to investigate every single error) it is difficult to see the connection between the use of the typical appraisal and the horrific results that seem to occur around its utilization. The aim of this chapter is to make that connection and provide data that helps persuade leaders to replace it now.

The Truth is Suffocated

My daughter is a junior in college. She and I always discussed the quality of her professors and one of her psychology professors had just been replaced with an adjunct who was also an independent consultant. My daughter explained how he seemed so arrogant. *"He continually brags about how knowledgeable and intelligent he is. He talks too much and doesn't like tough questions that might make him struggle with an answer."* She explained. *"He always has to be right and I hesitate to ask him any questions. I don't feel I am learning anything, Dad."*

I encouraged her to speak to him and ask a few questions after class to see if he is open to some challenge. I tried to influence her to take action. She refused. *"Dad, he will hurt my grade!"* The use of grades in schools is a policy that is the model for the use of the typical appraisal in the workplace. Without my daughter's feedback (or feedback from other students) it's probably unlikely this teacher will ever see the connection between the grading policy and his ability (or inability) to improve his teaching skills. This lack of effective feedback and his lack of skill is a barrier to optimum learning of the students. He can't hear ways to improve his teaching processes without feedback. The injury to my daughter's confidence, her joy in learning the subject matter, and her love for school probably cannot be measured. The damage to the student learning is also unknowable.

You may have heard the interesting story "allegedly found in a diary in Magellan's own handwriting", which describes how the South Americans he first encountered in the early 1500's could see the boats that his explorers landed in, but they could not perceive the ships anchored offshore. As the story goes, only their Shaman was finally able to perceive the ships offshore because he was somehow (due to his skill as a spiritual being) open to the possibilities of strange things from other worlds.

The story may or not be true but the lesson for Human Resources and for organizational leaders is valuable. Being open to very new ideas from different worlds would be useful for improvement of the typical appraisal. HR and leadership professionals must be open to "perceive" a new model in order to see the injury the typical appraisal causes and the possibility of improvement with a replacement process.

Fear is Increased

My sister worked for a company that was about to be sold to an investor. She called me in a panic. Her performance appraisal was scheduled and she was nervous they were about to fire her right before the sale. I assured her the request to schedule a performance appraisal was not really about her but instead about providing the new buyer with evidence about the performance of the current employees. I was sure her employer wanted to provide the buyer with some evidence about how effective the current employees were in order to make the sale go through without incident. The last thing the seller needed was to address any performance issues with employees. The sale was more important.

The next day she called to tell me I was right. Her original fears were unfounded. Her performance appraisal rating was excellent and met all her expectations. Clearly the seller (my sister's current employer) wanted to convince the buyer the people were excellent. So, was that performance appraisal really about her or about the sale?

Many performance appraisals are not really about the people but instead about some other motivation or intended outcome. This can include things such as a manipulation due to a bias, poor leadership, justification for a raise or bonus, justification for a firing, justification for a promotion or a demotion, or in this case, justifying a sale of the company. Aren't performance appraisals supposed to be about improving the development of the individual? If so, why would leaders misuse the policy for their own selfish motivations?

Leaders often manipulate the appraisal process to serve their own purposes. Just as with my sister, the owner manipulated the process to make all employees "look good" so the new buyer would be impressed. This compromised the opportunity to receive real feedback for improvement. It compromised the truth.

Leaders very often will compromise the process to achieve some short-term goal. The appraisal then becomes more about achieving the goal and less about the person receiving the appraisal.

Motivation is Damaged

That performance appraisal with your name on it is really NOT about you for other reasons besides manipulation. It is really about how you are able to interact with others and how environmental factors outside of your control impact your performance. It may also be about the motivations of the person rating you.

Our microwave burned out one day. My wife and I decided to buy a new one. Before embarking to a particular store I decided to check Consumer Reports. They rated the Kenmore brand at Sears at the very top. I told my wife and she agreed to go with me to the Sears store that day.

Before we left she was smart enough to check the website and found a Sears's outlet store not far from our home. The outlet store sells merchandise that was returned or slightly damaged at discount prices. I agreed we should go there first. We found the perfect microwave (size and color) at a discount of 50% off retail. I picked it up to check it for blemishes and defects. It looked fine. My wife paid for it. I put it in the car and brought it into the house.

Who should get the credit for the purchase, me or my wife? If our home was an organization with performance appraisals, pay-for-performance policy, and a management by objectives policy, we might have to decide who owned this objective and who would get credit for the intelligent purchase. How would deciding who gets the most credit benefit the organization? How does it benefit the individuals? How does it help make decisions in the future? What would a decision do to the relationship between my wife and me? Would trust be improved if one of us received more credit (or bonus) than the other?

In a complex system the question of who should get credit for this objective is irrelevant and impossible to answer. It was the quality of the interactions between my wife, me, the internet, and the store employees that achieved the results. It is impossible to say who should get the credit. We may not have chosen the Sears store without my interaction. We may not have chosen the outlet store without my wife's interaction. We may not have chosen to inspect the heavy microwave unless I was there to pick it up and turn it around.

Right now injury from the use of the typical performance appraisal is often hidden because it is difficult to make the connection between the injury and the appraisal policy or activity. Just as Jerry (my daughter's supervisor) was completely unaware of the impact he had on my daughter's attitude and my daughter's professor was unaware of the impact his behavior and grade policy had, leaders are unaware of the damage the typical appraisal process causes. The damage is probably unknowable. How do you measure the loss of revenue caused by an unhappy customer? How do you measure the loss of productivity by an unhappy worker? Deming once said, *"The most important figures that one needs for management are unknown or unknowable."* (Deming, 1986)

Blame is Rampant

A few years ago I had a Blackberry. I had to sync it with my Outlook files on my computer to avoid missed appointments and forgetting tasks. One day I received an error message during a synch. I got very angry. I didn't have time to call Verizon or Blackberry customer service for an answer. *"Can't they make things right the first time?"* I screamed out in frustration.

I called Verizon and started demanding service. *"Why should it just suddenly stop working?"* I shouted. The customer service person was very cordial and calm. She walked me through a series of steps to back up my data and then wipe clean the devise so it could synch properly. It all took about 45 minutes. She told me it was probably a corrupt piece of data that had caused the problem. I was upset and impatient with her. I wasted 45 minutes on something that could have been avoided. How could corrupt data get into my Blackberry?

After walking through all the steps I was able to synch again without incident. That is when it dawned on me. I had accidently disconnected the devise during a synch earlier in the day. I received a call in the middle of the synch process and, in order to answer the phone call, disconnected the devise in the middle of the synch process. My action actually caused the corrupted files. I was a cause of the dysfunction. My mistake created the injury and wasted time.

Stops the Search for Sophisticated Answers

Often the injury by the leader's use of the typical appraisal is hidden and unknowable. The use of the typical appraisal causes both hidden and assignable injury but it is mostly hidden and un-assignable. Peter Senge calls this the "delusion of learning from experience." Senge explains that the consequences of our actions are often in the distant future or in a distant part of a much larger system and therefore they remain hidden to our experience. He explains that often our actions have consequences well beyond our learning horizon and this makes it impossible to learn from the direct experience. (Senge, 1990) The experience of the injury from the performance appraisal is most often well beyond our learning horizon.

There is the hidden injury and then there are the overt injuries as measured by surveys and studies. For example, we know that most leaders and employees agree that the typical performance appraisals don't really work very well. They don't fulfill their intended purposes. Even Human Resource professionals acknowledge they fail at least ½ the time. The Society for Human Resource Management (SHRM) and Globoforce conducted a survey in the winter of 2012. Ninety-five percent (95%) of the respondents confirmed the importance of performance management but 45% said the typical appraisal is an ineffective measure of employee performance. In the same survey the previous year it was 39%. (SHRM and Globoforce, 2012)

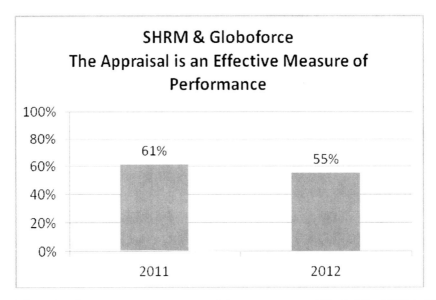

Watson Wyatt is a human resource consulting company. Their WorkUSA 2004 report revealed that only 30% of U.S. workers say the typical performance management process does what it is intended to do. (Watson Wyatt, 2004)

The fifty plus years of intense research for the typical appraisal has not resulted in improvement in the efficacy of the process according to the 2003 Hay Group's Insight Connections Survey of more than 300 organizations. 72% of the respondents said the performance management policy is a recurring burden imposed on them. 56% said they had a clear understanding of how their job performance was judged. Only 53% thought their supervisor effectively let them know what kind of job they were doing. (The Hay Group, 2003) These are failing grades.

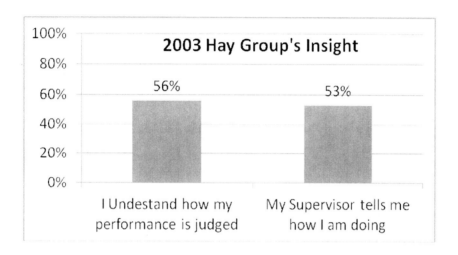

The 2006/07 survey by Salary.com revealed enormous "perception of efficacy" gaps between employees and leaders. (Salary.com, 2006-2007) Here are some examples:

65% of employers claimed the typical appraisal lead to improved performance vs. 39% of employees

55% of the employers claimed they formally meet with employees at least 2 times a year vs. fewer than 30% for employees

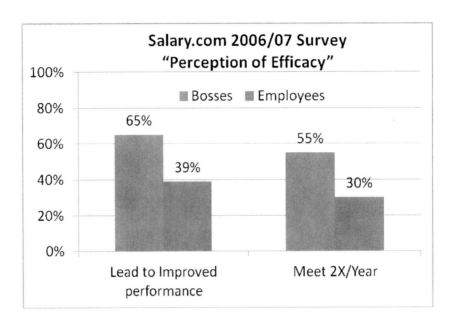

This type of gap appeared in another survey by Accountemps. Accountemps specializes in temporary staffing for accounting professionals. 1,400 Chief Financial Officers were surveyed about the efficacy of the typical appraisal. 95% of the CFO bosses said it was very or somewhat effective vs. only 62% employees who said the same. (Accountemps, 2012)

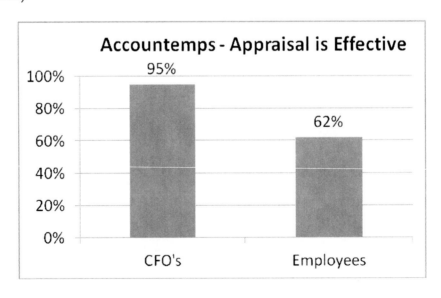

An important function of the appraisal is delivering timely and useful feedback to employees. According to a 2012 poll by Achievers 2,677 people (made up of 1,800 employees, 645 human resources managers, and 232 CEOs) uncovered a serious gap. (Achievers Intelligence, 2012) Only 33% of employees agree or strongly agree that they receive useful feedback with the typical appraisal.

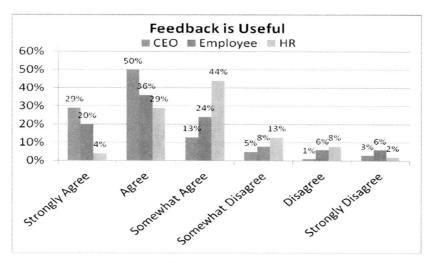

All these gaps are an indication of the poor results of the typical appraisal.

In another study the Hackett Group found dissatisfaction with Human Resources and its ability to manage the typical appraisal process. In this survey 64% of executives were either very dissatisfied or dissatisfied with the job their human resources people were doing to manage performance. (Zappe, 2012)

It is serious to accuse the typical leader of injury through incompetence and/or negligence. It's serious to accuse a leader of malpractice for promoting the use of a process that 85% of organizations use. The claim must be backed by evidence. Fortunately we can summon experts such as Dr. W. Edwards Deming who called the *evaluation of performance, merit rating, or annual review a deadly disease.*" (Deming, 1986) Deming also explained how leaders must remove barriers that rob the worker of the right to pride in workmanship. He explained how fear must be driven out of the workplace for everyone to effectively conduct their work. He specifically mentioned the abolishment of the annual or merit rating and the practice of management by objective (MBO). Despite this sound advice from Deming 26 years ago 85% to 90% of organizations are still using the typical appraisal.

Cripples Innovation

As an example of how serious the injury can be let's look at a set of interviews conducted in 2012 by Author Kurt Eichenwald with Microsoft employees. Using the typical appraisal Microsoft managers were told they must "stack rank" all employees. Eichenwald found that a management system known as "stack ranking" (forces every unit to declare a percentage of employees as either top performers, good, average, or poor) has effectively crippled Microsoft's ability to innovate. *"Every current and former Microsoft employee I interviewed—every one—cited stack ranking as the most destructive process inside of Microsoft, something that drove out untold numbers of employees..."* (Eichenwald, 2012)

Other examples include Connecticut, and other State Governments, recently passing education reform legislation that includes a *"standard and fair model of teacher and administrator evaluation based upon student learning."* (Dannel P. Malloy, 2012) Municipalities continue to "throw" money at the standardized tests scores which have remained flat for more than 30 years. Dropout rates in Connecticut schools are stuck at about 25%. Human Resource professionals continue to put greater effort into employee engagement improvement efforts and yet those same engagement numbers are flat or falling. (Blessing - White Research, 2011)

Why does credible research show the importance of attracting and retaining talent and yet only 20% of people strongly trust the top management and 32% of a worker's desire to stay or go is the result of feeling trust towards the boss? (Murphy, Burgio-Murphy, & Young, 2007) Why do many human resource managers say that respect in the workplace is at an all-time low? (Verespej, 2003)

We have major issues regarding our ability to lead people and to solve our organizational problems. We seem stuck. Are things getting better, getting worse, or staying the same? Are we confident we can lead our way out of these poor results with our current thinking and our current methods? What if everything we have been taught is now obsolete and that obsolescence explains why we are stuck?

There are five important competencies an organization needs to develop in order to be successful in the knowledge economy. I believe responsible leaders are lying awake at night thinking about how to improve each of these competencies while at the same time each of these competencies is injured by the use of the typical performance appraisal. To be competitive every action leaders take must improve these competencies. Leaders can't afford to injure competencies that can help them achieve success. Each competency is injured by the typical appraisal. These competencies are also interdependent and therefore any damage to one negatively impacts the others and thus the injury is multiplied.

The Five Competencies

The first competency is the ability to improve employee engagement. Employee engagement is an important element today for organizational success. Engagement is an emotional connection that energizes the employee to exert greater discretionary effort. This extra effort forms part of the foundation for the other competencies including innovation, learning, retention, productivity improvement, and adapting to change.

The second competency keeping leaders up at night is the ability to attract and retain talent. The typical appraisal creates a barrier to the improvement of this competency. Controlling people drives away good people. Autonomy helps people stay. This section explains how the typical appraisal is a control technique that compromises retention of the best talent.

The third competency is the ability to improve trust with every interaction. Trust is the grease that enables an organization to operate at high speed with the least amount of friction. The typical appraisal damages trust and therefore slows performance. This section explains why and how.

The forth competency injured is the ability to continuously innovate (optimum learning). Critical thinking and innovation are damaged by the typical appraisal.

The fifth and final competency is the ability to adapt to change. To succeed in the knowledge age requires the accelerated ability to adapt. Most organizations rely heavily on planned change. Planned change is often too late or too slow and is dependent on management to design and implement the plan. Furthermore, research by John Kotter claims that planned change fails to achieve intended outcomes up to 70% of the time. (Kotter, 1996) Unplanned change, on the other hand, or "creative destruction" can be constant and instantaneous and every employee can contribute if the correct environment is created. Like flocking birds that move instantly and in unison without dependence on any one leader, a self-organizing system adapts quickly and easily to changing environmental conditions. Creative destruction and self-organizing systems are descriptions of cultures that enable organizations to adapt.

An effective appraisal process should be able to enhance each of these important competencies and not detract from them. Unfortunately, the typical appraisal causes trouble in each. We need to explore the specific explanations about how the typical appraisal causes injury to each of these competencies.

The Injury to Employee Engagement

Employees need a sense of autonomy to feel fully engaged. The typical appraisal damages autonomy and therefore damages engagement.

Employee engagement levels have the attention of many C-Suite executives. The latest research by Towers Watson (2012), a human resources consulting firm, confirms the wide acknowledgement that employee engagement is a critical element for high levels of financial and operational results. Any executive who doesn't pay attention to employee engagement might be accused incompetence and/or malpractice. This is especially true in light of the Tower Watson research which shows the average percentage of employees who are highly engaged comes in at only 35%. We need improvement. What ideas will help us?

There are multiple models about how to achieve engagement. Many of them are very similar. The one outlined here might make some executives uncomfortable because it requires employees to be trusted first. For simplicity these ideas are call *The Three A's of Engagement*.

Anxiety

The first "A" is for **Anxiety**. Anxiety is often considered a negative force (emotion) that causes stress and stagnation. Positive anxiety, on the other hand, is the urgent emotional need to act before an opportunity is lost. Positive anxiety is useful for learning and development. A balance between the challenge a person experiences doing a task and the skills he/she uses to perform those tasks will generate positive anxiety and joy at the same time. (Csikszentmihalyi, 1990) This positive anxiety is required and compatible for engagement and necessary for learning.

Contrary to common belief feeling comfortable (or satisfaction) usually does not generate learning. Neither does negative stress. Unfortunately the stress most employees feel today is negative and caused by the existence of threats or bribes which are designed to provide pressure to perform. Pay-for-performance policies in conjunction with performance appraisal ratings are applied and these result in a reduction in engagement instead of an increase. Positive anxiety is intrinsic (internal), self-imposed, and naturally healthy motivation.

People can use positive anxiety to make positive change. A great example of positive anxiety in practice is seen in the process of learning "speed reading." Many "speed reading" teaching techniques require the student to push themselves to reading speeds 5 or even 10 times faster than their normal pace. This "push" creates positive anxiety and trains the eyes and the brain to adapt to a much higher speed. The push creates positive change even though during this push causes an experience of anxiety.

It is not only permissible for leaders to create positive anxiety in the work environment for employees; it is their obligation if they want to achieve higher levels of performance. Leaders have the most influence over the elements in the work environment. Leaders must therefore be acutely aware of the type of environment they create. Is it positive anxiety or negative anxiety?

Autonomy

The second "A" is for **Autonomy**. Autonomy is the freedom to determine actions and decisions. Autonomy is a higher standard than just empowerment. Empowerment is the act of giving power to someone. Empowerment suggests there must be an authorization by management to perform a task or responsibility. Autonomy is about freedom for self-management. With autonomy the employee decides when and how to act to solve a problem. No authorization by management is necessary. Empowerment requires a list of tasks employees can perform. Autonomy requires a list of principles that employees can act within.

Autonomy is best provided when employees understand the principles under which they can make decisions on their own. This doesn't mean specific processes and/or detailed steps are missing. Toyota, for example, has four principles employees must follow to work toward improvement in their locations.

The first principle states that all hand-offs between internal suppliers and internal customers must have clear steps in a specific sequence and these steps are clearly defined (usually by the customer). The second principle states that every supplier-to-customer hand-off is direct and unambiguous. The third principle demands that the pathway for these hand-offs must be simple and direct. The forth principle states that improvements can be made by anyone and at any time as long as those changes are done using the scientific method. (Stephen Spear, 1999, September - October) Although the four principles work together as a system, this final principle creates the greatest opportunity for allowing employees to demonstrate autonomy. In these principles the decisions are dependent upon what employees want and not on decisions from above.

Advancement

The final "A" is for **Advancement**. Employees need to see how their efforts truly make a difference. This advancement must not just be progress for the sake of progress. It must be in context of a higher purpose and vision. In order for advancement to happen the progress seen by employees must be toward a vision, aligned with the mission (purpose) of the organization, and aligned with the values of both the individual and the organization.

Three elements are needed to achieve advancement. First, employees must understand the aim of their actions. The aim is also often known as the mission or purpose. We must be able to answer the question, "Why are we taking this action? What's the point?" For example, if our task is to clean a table we must know for what purpose the table will be used. Is it a table to clean fish or to perform open heart surgery? The purpose will determine the method we decide to use for our task.

Secondly, we must have feedback from our tasks and that feedback should be immediate (or as close to immediate as possible) and frequent in order to optimize our learning. Without immediate and frequent feedback we will lose motivation because we lose the opportunity to learn.

Finally, we must see progress toward achieving our aim. Without progress frustration will emerge and frustration will damage engagement. The delay between action and information must be as short as possible to optimize engagement and minimize frustration. The other day I planted grass seed. Although I know it takes about 10 days to germinate and to show little sprouts, every day after planting I watered the spots and looked for evidence of progress. It was frustrating for those first 10 days with no feedback. On the other hand, recently my wife and I painted our kitchen and family room. We were able to receive instant feedback during the painting. We could instantly see how beautiful the room was becoming.

The combination of taking action toward a clear compelling purpose, receiving feedback, and seeing credible progress will create the experience of advancement, joy, learning, and engagement.

The experience employees have with these "Three A"'s generates powerful employee engagement. The "A"'s create a recipe for success and will help to achieve the organization results. All three elements work as a system. They must all be present to achieve the engagement and results we all seek.

The Two Stealth Archenemies of Employee Engagement

I needed to use my leaf blower. I plugged it into an extension cord with multiple plugs. It didn't work. I shook it, twisted the plugs and wires to no avail. I decided I needed to take it apart and find the root cause of the problem. I found my electric drill. I wanted to use it to remove all the fasteners more quickly. I plugged the drill into the same extension cord. It also didn't work. I realized one of the extension cord plugs was defective and prevented the use of both the blower and the drill. Once I switched plugs everything worked fine. A hidden flaw in the extension cord stopped me. Sometimes what we think is the root cause of a problem is not the problem at all. We need to experiment.

Many leaders work incredibly hard to improve employee engagement and yet they rarely achieve a significant improvement. The percentage of engaged employees continues to hover around 30% and has for years. Why? Many Human Resource managers believe that poor management practices are the root cause. Just as I chose the wrong root cause so are these HR leaders.

There are two major barriers that continue to prevent improvement in employee engagement, i.e. contingent pay-for-performance and the typical performance appraisal policies. These two stealth archenemies create hidden barriers to improving engagement. Sometimes what we think is causing the problem is not the problem at all. We need to find the tool that doesn't work and stop using it.

Employee engagement is the emotional connection employees have that causes them to want to exert extra discretionary effort and do their best work. (Blessing - White Research, 2011) Because the effort is discretionary it doesn't require extra pay. It naturally emerges from the work environment and the quality of the leadership.

The most damaging type of pay-for-performance is the contingent type where the message is "do this and you will get that." This type of pay-for-performance damages engagement because it converts intrinsic motivation into extrinsic control. It undermines the sense of purpose. It ignores the "why" and instead focuses on the "what" (the extrinsic reward the accomplishment will give the employee).

Risk taking and challenge are also damaged. Rewards connected to tasks will cause many employees to search for the easiest way to achieve the reward. Often in this case quality and customer satisfaction are secondary priorities for the employee compared to the receipt of the reward.

The typical performance appraisal policy damages at least two of the key elements of engagement. First, because it is a grade (or rating) on the employee performance it reduces the desire for risk taking and accepting challenging assignments. Any assignment too challenging will likely cause an average employee to experience fear of failure or fear of a poor grade due to not being able to reach the stretch goal. This fear often goes unnoticed and therefore the damage is immeasurable and hidden.

Furthermore, annual feedback is not enough to meet the "frequent and meaningful" criteria for feedback that creates engagement. A different feedback process is needed. I often hear consultants and managers advise those who deliver performance appraisals that the typical feedback delivered during this meeting must not be a surprise. In order to avoid surprises there must be a different more frequent process that provides that frequent meaningful feedback all year long. Why not just replace the typical appraisal with that process? Fearless Feedback is the suggested replacement process and is described in Chapter 10.

Contingent pay-for-performance and the typical appraisal both undermine a number of critical elements of employee engagement and they do it in ways that remain hidden. Keeping those policies while trying to improve engagement will only cause frustration for both managers and employees. The injuries stay hidden and unconnected to the policies in the minds of leaders because we all have been taught a theory of leadership that is outdated causing the tools to become obsolete. Sometimes we need to find the tool that doesn't work and stop using it.

The Injury to the Ability to Attract and Retain Talent

You will recall how my sister worked for a company that was about to be sold and it appeared the leaders were about to manipulate the appraisal policy for their own selfish motivations to insure the sale went through. There are other types of manipulation of the process that attempt to ensure talent is kept in the organization. This manipulation strategy often backfires. Performance appraisals are a control technique. Manipulation is just another way to control people.

Talent management is practice based on a flawed set of assumptions i.e. the very best performing organizations are the ones obsessed with hiring, developing, ranking, and ruthlessly evaluating the very best talent. Enron was the ultimate "talent management" organization. The demise of Enron cost shareholders more than $11 billion. The stock went from a high of $90/share to a $1/share in just one year.

You might think we could learn from this epic business debacle of Enron but some of us didn't. I am referring to the authors of a new book confirming the value of talent management. I won't give the title because I don't want to promote something I believe is so clearly incomplete and nearly criminally wrong. Smart people can be VERY wrong and I believe this new book promoting talent management confirms it.

McKinsey & Company promoted talent management in the late 1990's and Enron became the poster child for its practices. GE was also a big proponent. Of course Enron and GE were both very successful for a while. We know the story of Enron. GE was also very successful and propelled Jack Welch to celebrity status for management gurus. However, GE has lost its luster too going from a high of around $50/share in 2001 when Jack Welch retired to around $15/share today.

To be fair there are numerous factors for these failures and one could argue that the McKinsey theory of talent management is not the major factor. However, managing talent is not the most effective management theory for today's complex global economy and any book that promotes this practice as the major factor for success has two huge challenges to overcome:

- This is inconsistent with systems thinking and systems thinking must be at the heart of any management orthodoxy.
- Managing talent creates a dependency on managers by employees and that damages the organizations ability to adapt to change and prevents long-term optimization and predictability.

Talent management demands the manager rank the talent and disproportionately reward the "top" performers while "yanking" the poor performers out. Many call this practice "rank and yank." This policy and practice creates a high degree of competition, back-biting, cheating, hiding information, and all around dysfunctional behaviors. In systems thinking everyone must cooperate to optimize the system over the long-term. Systems thinking require total transparency, complete integrity, and optimum cooperation. "Ranking and yanking" is consistent with short-term thinking and it often destroys the cooperation necessary for optimum success.

Our economy is now is more "brain based" than "labor based". The very complexity of the new competitive world requires continuous information exchange. The expansion of competition around the globe has created the need to understand and adapt more quickly. Successful leaders have adopted many different kinds of technology to stay on top of the shifting trends and enormous volume of information they must assimilate. They must increasingly seek more efficient ways to access and process timely, complete and accurate information. Without the latest technology, the competitive advantage is lost. This applies to the leadership of people as it does to every other aspect of business.

The key asset of our organizations is inside the brains of the people. Because operations require diverse and continuous accumulation of knowledge these knowledge workers are less and less interchangeable. Employee turnover must be reduced to a minimum to protect the knowledge inside the heads of these highly skilled employees. The "rank and yank" policy contradicts this strategy.

Successful leaders must increase their organizations' capacity to acquire, generate, distribute and deploy knowledge strategically and operationally. They must do this by creating environments that optimize brain-power. These environments will encourage workers to take risks, come up with new ideas and, even if necessary, to "throw away the rulebook".

In a system the quality of the interactions between the parts is more important than the quality of the parts. For example, imagine you want to own the very best car in the marketplace. Instead of buying one you decide to build it by taking the best parts from numerous different auto manufacturers and building a hybrid car from those best parts. This approach won't work because the parts won't optimally interact with each other and the ultimate purpose and functionality of the car will be lost.

The three primary colors of red, green, and blue interact to make up the full spectrum of light. When equal amounts of all three primary colors are added together they produce white light. It is the interaction between the three that create the white light. The parts alone cannot do it. Only the interaction between the three colors produces the desired outcome. This one example in nature confirms the importance of interactions over the importance of parts alone. Unfortunately there are many examples of how leaders ignore natural law and place too much emphasis on the importance of the parts alone. Talent management is an attempt to manage the parts of a complex system and is another example of leadership malpractice.

When managers need to provide constant evaluations with candor they have little time for anything else. There is never enough time to observe the talented employees to provide an accurate picture. Secondly, if the employees rely on the manager for their feedback then they can become dependent upon the manager for an important element of engagement. The evaluation process therefore becomes manager-dependent and that often leads to disappointment and dysfunction.

Our schools are "manager" dependent as well and very few are fulfilling their intended objectives. Instead of allowing students increased opportunity to self-manage (track and evaluate their own progress) teachers and administrators use standardized tests, standardized curriculums, and teacher dependent systems that take away autonomy and attempt to control learning as if the students were widgets in a factory that need to be fitted with accessories. Schools are therefore failing to deliver results because they inhibit autonomy.

Talent management broke down at Enron and it broke down at GE. When Jack Welch left the GE stock started a continual slide. If talent management was the right strategy wouldn't GE's success continued after Welch?

There is a better way; create system-dependent, not manager-dependent, processes. We can do better if we all employees to self-manage. We can do better if we help all students to self-manage their own learning. Self-management allows an organization to better respond to the accelerated pace of change. We need a different model that not only allows self-management but creates the need for it.

We see self-management in nature. Instead continuous evaluation by a higher power animals and plants operate and thrive in self-organizing systems. Birds flock by self-management to hard wired principles. Fish swim in schools following key principles of survival. Each fish or bird manages itself according to those principles. We need an improvement strategy that aligns with natural law. Talent management is not one of those strategies.

The Injury to Trust

The results of an organization are directly dependent upon the level of trust. Exceptional leaders recognize this and behave accordingly. They recognize their behavior must demonstrate trust first before they can expect trust in return. Exceptional leaders purposely put people in situations where they will be challenged to utilize their skills to the fullest extent. An exceptional leader will make him or herself available but they won't micro-manage. Ernest Hemingway once said, *"The best way to find out if you can trust somebody is to trust them."*

With this in mind one of the most important responsibilities of a leader is to manage the variation in trust in their organization and/or within their team. This requires a keen understanding of the right definition of trust. The International Association of Business Communicators defines trust as: *a willingness to be vulnerable because of the presence of integrity, concern, competence and shared objectives.* The theory is by managing each of these four elements a leader can become vulnerable and by making themselves vulnerable, they bring out the best in the employees. They foster autonomy and with autonomy comes growth and engagement.

In the movie *The Horse Whisperer* Robert Redford plays a middle aged expert horse trainer/cowboy in Montana. He is introduced to a young girl and her mom who ask him to help rehabilitate their horse. The girl and the horse suffered near fatal injuries in an accident with an 18 wheeler on a snowy morning. The girl and mom wanted to avoid putting the horse down even though its injuries was so severe. The horse was obviously not the only casualty. The girl lost her leg in the accident. She was only 14. Her emotional well-being suffered long after the physical injury healed.

Redford realized he needed to help the girl before he could help the horse. In one scene he and the girl find themselves out on the range alone with an old pickup truck.

Redford asks the girl to drive him back to the ranch while feigning fatigue. He challenges her to use her skills. He trusted she would be able to drive him even though she had never driven a truck let alone a standard shift and her prosthetic leg was needed to work the gas pedal and brake. He trusted her first, provided support, and allowed her autonomy to give it a try.

Although nervous and uncertain at first the plan worked. She did it. By putting her in a position to use her skills, trusting her, and encouraging growth she became an engaged participant in the process of helping to rehabilitate the horse. By trusting her, giving her training and allowing her to use her skills (providing autonomy) she became engaged. This is the strategy often underutilized by leaders. It works for employees. It works for students.

Our schools are in trouble. The documentary *Waiting for Superman* demonstrates this conclusion well. Some say the film blames unions and teachers for the problem. Although certainly unions play a role in the dysfunction those who say that it's the unions alone that cause the problems miss a major insight. The real root cause is how we are all taught to think about students, how we assign responsibility for learning and how we have set up the school system. Our school systems send the message, *WE DON'T TRUST YOU* therefore we need a strict curriculum because we can't trust you will study what you need to know to be successful. *WE DON'T TRUST YOU* therefore we must standardized testing to drive improvement and reward or punish students and schools to perform at high levels. *WE DON'T TRUST YOU* therefore we must have grades to attempt to motivate students to do better. These messages deliver a damaging result namely a manager-dependent environment where students will ask, "Is this information going to be on the test?" If not, I won't study it and I won't make an effort to learn it.

What would happen if we changed the message to **WE TRUST YOU**? Isn't it true that students naturally want to learn and teachers naturally want to do a good job? If so, why not trust them to do just that? If so, we can create an environment of autonomy. We can then expect engagement and optimum learning.

Successful leaders trust people will do the right things. Therefore, why not create a system that sends a message of trust instead of distrust? Why change the entire system because occasionally there appears a few bad apples who can't be trusted? Instead trust people and give them the tools.

In 2008 I approached the management of my local Chamber of Commerce in Bridgeport Connecticut to help me conduct a survey that would answer a number of questions for my dissertation. These questions included, "what impact does the typical performance appraisal have on trust" and "how is the quality of the performance appraisal discussion impacted by the level of trust between the leader and the employee?" (Hauck, 2008) The participants for this survey were all graduates of a leadership training facilitated each year by the Chamber.

The results of the survey confirmed what most of us intuitively know already i.e. when the employee and manager bring a high level of trust to the typical performance appraisal meeting, the meeting is effective. If they don't have trust it backfires. Furthermore, the typical appraisal meeting does little or nothing to improve trust between the manager and supervisor.

The participants were asked to rate (on a scale of 1 to 10) the current level of trust with their immediate supervisor. They were also asked how well the typical appraisal meeting helped improve individual performance. The analysis of the results of these two questions gives us an important insight. When trust was high between the employee and the manager, the performance appraisal meeting was significantly more effective in helping improve individual performance. When trust was low, the appraisal meeting was a waste of time. Nearly 80% said the meeting either made individual performance worse or kept it the same.

It's interesting to see confirmation of something we already know namely that trust is an important foundation of a performance discussion. What is much more important is the impact the typical appraisal has on trust. In their book Driving Fear Out of the Workplace, Kathlene Ryan and Daniel Oestreich explained how interviews with hundreds of employees revealed the top things people were most afraid to lose at work. The loss of credibility or reputation, the loss of career or financial advancement, and possible damage to the relationship with their immediate manager topped the list. (Kathlene Ryan, 1998) The typical appraisal meeting negatively affects each of these.

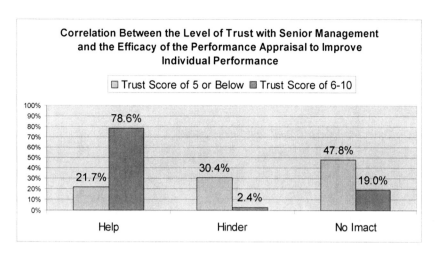

Correlation Between the Level of Trust with Senior Management and the Efficacy of the Performance Appraisal to Improve Individual Performance

In the typical appraisal the manager gives the employee a performance grade or rating. The very existence of this grade creates the possibility of loss of reputation and or loss of personal credibility. Any possibility of a negative rating will increase the probability the employee will experience fear. This probability increase in fear is subtle and powerful.

In summary, without trust a performance appraisal meeting is a waste of time. Without trust the meeting will yield little or no improvement ideas or actions. To make a performance meeting worthwhile participants (especially the leader) must understand the key elements of trust and how to manage the variation in each.

According to the author Pamela Shockley-Zalaak (Pamela Shockley-Zalaak, 2010) the willingness to speak up is an indicator of the level of fear in an organization. According to her research the experiences feared most are the loss of credibility, loss of career advancement, and damage to the relationship with their immediate supervisor. The possibility of these three experiences alone was enough to stop people from being open and honest in their communication. This reluctance to speak for fear of repercussion will most frequently occur during performance appraisal meetings. The appraisal meeting is supposed to be the place to be open and honest and yet the very nature of the appraisal meeting feeds the top three fears that cause people to shut down.

The employee receives a grade during the typical appraisal. For most employees, the presence of the grade (or rating) increases the same three fears (loss of credibility, loss of career advancement, and damage to the relationship). The supervisor's role as the judge of the employee performance increases the probability of these fears. The supervisor's role as the judge is a barrier to open and honest communication. The lack of open and honest communication is a barrier to having trust. It is a vicious dysfunctional cycle.

The Injury to Innovation

"He that innovates and is lucky will take the market."
W. Edwards Deming

A higher level of fear and a lower level of trust will damage an organization's ability to innovate. In the new knowledge economy innovation is needed more than ever to create a competitive advantage. The industrial age economy with large corporations conducting massive research and development efforts is giving way to smaller more nimble ones that can create knowledge with increased collaboration and with every employee interaction. This sets a new standard where every interaction needs to be an innovative opportunity.

The typical appraisal often morphs into a one way communication dominated by information about th employee because the fear of repercussion holds most employees back from sharing open and honest communication about the manager's behavior. To become competitive in the global marketplace organizations must be able to make every interaction safe and open. To enable the best ideas to surface and to encourage synergy (the creation of ideas that can only occur with two or more people effectively communicating and cooperating) all parties must be free to speak their truths.

The capacity to create trusting partnerships must become an organizational competency in order for innovation to be optimal (Pamela Shockley-Zalaak, 2010). The ability to learn together during every interaction is the high standard necessary today for sustainable competitive advantage. The typical appraisal is a barrier to optimal innovation because the rating stops the manager and employee from being trusted partners.

As discussed, fear is an emotion better off being avoided. Negative emotions and poor attitude of workers impact productivity, quality, service, revenue, profit, turnover etc. The leader's ability to positively manage their own emotions and their ability to manage the emotions of others positively influence the social interactions and therefore the success of the organization. Although most people view work as primarily a financial transaction between the employer and the employee everyone is influenced by the social interactions that they experience at workplaces are primarily social networks.

Numerous scientific studies have demonstrated how a negative work environment negatively impacts our brain function and therefore impacts our ability to be productive and innovative. Naomi Eisenberger, a leading social neuroscience researcher at the University of California at Los Angeles (UCLA), studied what happens in the brain when people feel rejected, reprimanded, criticized, given an assignment that feels worthless. Her work demonstrated how the brain registers the same experience it does when the body experiences physical pain. (Rock, 2009)

When the brain registers pain it also registers a threat. A threat impairs the individual's ability to process complex information. This threat response impedes productivity. This threat response uses up oxygen which is therefore diverted from other parts of the brain including the portion that holds memory and the portion that processes new information. *"This impairs analytic thinking, creative insight, and problem solving; in other words, just when people most need their sophisticated mental capabilities, the brain's internal resources are taken away from them."* (Rock, 2009)

Daniel Goleman's research confirms this dysfunction. The limbic system of the brain is an open loop system. It is influenced by outside moods and feedback. A closed loop system, like the circulatory system, is a system that is self-regulating. A self-regulating system can obtain feedback independently of others whereas an open loop system creates a link with others. In groups, people "catch" feelings and moods from one another. Although most people believe attitude is a choice, Goleman's research clearly shows a strong connection to others when choosing an attitude. It is the leaders' moods that has the greatest impact on the attitudes of employees! (Daniel Goleman, 2002) *"While mild anxiety (such as over a looming deadline) can focus attention and energy, prolonged distress can sabotage a leader's relationships and also hamper work performance by diminishing the brain's ability to process information and respond effectively."* (Daniel Goleman, 2002)

The problem with negative emotions being unchecked is that they "flood" the consciousness and attention. This is the primordial response of our ancient ancestors that helped keep them alive. The "flight or fight" response helped protect us in ancient times. When the "flight or fight" response occurs, no creativity, strategic planning listening or focus on a task can occur. Unless a leader has the ability to control these emotions, the staff picks up on them and they too become immobilized. The typical performance appraisal can, and often does, solicit this type of response and so the very tool that is supposed to build productivity and problem solving actually prevents those very outcomes it was designed to produce.

Research by David Rick confirms Goleman's work. He takes it one step further by actually mentioning the performance appraisal process. When a person is criticized part of their brain shuts off narrowing their focus and diminishing creativity. (INFORUM, 2013)

Intelligence of the individual employees is not enough to create a strategic advantage. What is needed is the ability to use that intelligence to process information into knowledge and wisdom. The only optimal way to accomplish this is with cooperation between the employees to fully utilize the potential that is the intelligence of the individuals and the collective intelligence of the entire organization.

Edward de Bono explains this in his book Teach Your Child How to Think. (Bono, 1992) De Bono explains how intelligence is potential and potential can sometimes be under-utilized. Just becomes someone own s fast sports car does not mean he/she is a good driver and can win a race. It is the combination or interaction of the ability to drive and the potential of the car that makes the difference. So it is with creative thinking. Intelligence alone will not do it. It takes a combination of the ability to use the potential which includes the skill of the thinker and the environment which allows and/or encourages the thinking.

The Injury to the Ability to Adapt to Change

Numerous articles explain how planned change is difficult, expensive, and 70% of the time fails to achieve its original intended objectives. (Scott Keller, 2012) Perhaps it is time for a new approach. Perhaps we need to embrace an additional type of change called self-organizing change (instead of planned change). Since change is accelerating and shows no sign of slowing any time soon leaders must hone their ability to manage change but we are hand-cuffing ourselves if we only use one type of change i.e. planned change.

Skylar Capo, 11, of Fredericksburg, Va., saw a little bird on the ground in her dad's backyard. (News, 2011) She then noticed the family's cat eyeing it, too. Skylar scooped up the woodpecker and looked for the bird's mother. Her search turned up empty. She asked her own mom, Alison, to help her decide what to do. Her mom suggested they take care of the bird until it was strong enough to survive on its own. Being an avid nature lover and animal rescuer, Skylar was thrilled. She had saved the bird from an untimely death at the paws of the cat and she was going to learn how to care for it.

The Capos put the bird in their car to drive to a Lowes Home Improvement Store to search for materials they may need to care for the bird. Bringing the bird inside in a cage so it wouldn't suffer in the summer heat while they shopped they began their search when a shopper stopped them. The shopper claimed to work for the U.S. Fish and Wildlife. She explained they were in violation of protected species act. Two weeks later the Capo's were fined $535 because the law prohibits the capture or transport of any protected species. A State Trooper, even though she was told the whole story, threatened Skylar's mom to 1 year in jail if she ever did it again. Thankfully two weeks later the ticket and the threat was cancelled and apology was given.

The typical appraisal process is frequently used to enforce policy and procedure. Policies are designed to control behaviors and they virtually always have positive intentions. However, as with little Skylar, policies often don't fit every situation and therefore can cause unintended consequences (the cat killing a baby bird). Because it is used as an enforcement tool it often stops new creative action. What will little Skylar do next time she sees a baby bird in danger?

The typical appraisal holds many employees back from taking risks and this prevents the organization from achieving incremental change. The typical appraisal reinforces the status quo and places full responsibility upon management to achieve change. Employees are taught to wait for management to tell them what is allowed and not allowed. They are taught to wait for policy. They are threatened with the penalties of criticism and/or lower performance ratings if they don't follow the rules. They are taught to stand and watch the cat eat the baby bird.

In a world of constant change, increasing competition, and evolving customer needs can a tool like the typical appraisal, which is designed to enforce existing policy, give organizations the flexibility they need to survive and or thrive? We need a different tool that enables employees to have more autonomy, to encourage risk taking, and to increase engagement not damage it. The typical appraisal helps keep us all still in a world that is revolving and evolving.

Part II
The Causation

Chapter 3
The Industrial Age: What in the World Were (are) We Thinking?

Aim of this Chapter: To explain how we have outgrown the need for the typical appraisal

Often management acts like a flea on an elephant. The flea barks out commands and sometimes the flea guesses correctly when it shouts, "Left, right, or stop". Sometimes it doesn't. The flea is either happy or upset based on the outcomes. The elephant is indifferent and unaware.

Anonymous

There is a saying that seems to explain how our subconscious beliefs can influence us. It states something like this: *"Fish don't know they are in water."* Similarly, most people don't know who Frederick Taylor was even though some say he remains today one of the most influential people in history. His theory and practices surround us like "invisible water."

His process of Scientific Management has influenced everyone's belief system about management and about how the world works. His beliefs about people and work are still embraced today and we can see examples in our school systems and organizations. Unfortunately his beliefs, and the policies that follow from them, have reached their limit in their ability to improve productivity and performance in the knowledge age. Taylor methods are a barrier to employee engagement and that can explain why we are performing so poorly on that front.

Frederick Taylor's Scientific Management model embraced certain assumptions and principles. The main assumption was the view of the world where organizations seen as large machines. In his model each part needed to be as efficient as possible in order for the entire machine to be efficient. This assumption caused him to analyze each job into small segments that could be performed within certain time limits with certain quality outcomes. Once analyzed into the most elementary segments these tasks could be timed and evaluated according to the perfect standard as set by management. Management's job was to evaluate the individual parts on their ability to perform those tasks according to the specific standard. In the Taylor view of the world productivity and quality of organizations are the creation of the management team.

Taylor saw the management of people like an engineering problem. (Wheatley, 2006) This approach ignores the intrinsic motivational factors that contribute to innovation, creativity, and joy at work. Tremendous effort was exerted by Taylor and his colleagues to not just ignore this intrinsic dimension but to squelch it for fear of the people messing up their engineering plans. People were seen merely as "cogs" in a great big machine that needed to be either completely efficient by doing their job perfectly or being replaced quickly.

Although this view of the world is a bit extreme and its rigidity has been reduced somewhat, the thinking and structures of its essence still remain. We can see examples in our school and university systems. Students are seen as "raw material" that enters the "factory." It needs to be controlled and molded with specific curriculum as dictated by the "genius" management of the schools and it needs to be kept in line with rigorous testing otherwise those "parts" might actually demonstrate they have a mind of their own and vary off the path they are designed to be on. The thinking is the students must be molded by the greater minds that designed the system i.e. school leadership and the curriculum builders.

This is the "water" most of us are all immersed in while growing up. How can we choose anything else when we enter the workforce? How can we possibly know there is another world view out there that works better when we have had this immersion for 12 to 20 + years?

C. L. Sholes created the prototypes of the first typewriter in Milwaukee, WI in the 1860's. The top line of our keyboards reads "QWERTY" but that was not the first design. When first built Sholes arranged the letters in alphabetical order in two rows. This first typewriter was sluggish and would often jam.

The letters were arranged in a circle and were each perched on "type-bars" which would fly up and strike the paper when the typist hit the corresponding key on the keyboard. Sholes significantly improved the performance of the typists by re-arranging the letters with "QWERTY." At the time some accused Sholes of deliberately arranging his keyboard to slow down fast typists who would otherwise jam up his sluggish machine. He had the opposite motives. He wanted to speed up typists' performance and avoid the type-bar jams.

The QWERTY arrangement was created in cooperation with educator Amos Densmore who studied the letter-pair frequency. It seemed if two type bars were near each other in the circle, they would tend to clash into each other when typed in succession. So, Densmore and Sholes figured the most common letter pairs such as "TH" and separated them at safe distances in the circle. Still today our keyboards use QWERTY and yet the last typewriter factory on the planet (in India) closed its doors on April 26th 2011 having been replaced by computers now. (Hawkes, 2011) Furthermore, electric typewriters, which began to dominate the market in the 1960', eliminated the concern of dreaded type-bar jam. Still today we have QWERTY. We are stuck with it for the foreseeable future and yet it is obsolete in that it does nothing for our ability to type on our computers.

Frederick Taylor's Scientific Management was also developed in the late 1800's with also the very best of intentions. Today it is as outdated as much as QWERTY and yet we are addicted to it. It is part of our thinking as much as QWERTY is part of our keyboards.

The unconscious embrace of Taylor Scientific management is one of the root causes of the adoption of the typical performance appraisal. Once leaders understand this it is hoped they can shed this theory like an "out of style" suit and clothe themselves in a new philosophical wardrobe that fits the knowledge age. Systems thinking asks different questions and this is the key to solving these problems. Taylor Scientific Management focuses on improving the performance of the individual based on a specific standard. Systems thinking focuses on improving the system in order to improve the performance of the entire organization so everyone wins.

Leaders need to be aware of the impact of their behavior. A leader's number one job is to create a functional and respectful context. Leaders who continue to embrace the Taylor thinking and methods, even though it is unknowingly and unconsciously, create injury.

What if Everything We Learned is Wrong?

It is essential to challenge our own and our leaders' fundamental beliefs about people that have been embedded into our brains since the late 1800's through our educational system. Here are some challenging questions we must answer to begin to challenge those fundamental beliefs:

- If people are the most important asset why do we insist on creating fear by rating them with performance appraisals and pay-for-performance?

- If people are emotional beings and employee engagement is an emotional reaction why do so few organizations encourage the respectful expression of emotion in the workplace?
- If giving grades to students is a good idea why do 50 to 80% of high school students admit to cheating? (Noguchi, 2012)

A leadership theory is the model (or paradigm) that helps us to decide how we think about people and problems. How we think is significant because it leads to the actions we choose to take in order to solve problems we face. For example, if you don't trust certain people you will create more rules and policies that attempt to control those people and/or avoid (or minimize) the consequences of their actions. Furthermore, you will set up policies to "ding" them when they wander off plan.

A leader's paradigm creates an impression because it creates an environment that influences certain behaviors. When I was very young, my mom's attitude toward me and her resulting behaviors were unpredictable. I never knew when she was in a good mood or a bad mood. I would "walk on egg shells" until I knew it was safe to "be myself." If I knew she had a bad mood, I would be very cautious about what I said. Her mood and her way of thinking influenced my behaviors. I needed to protect myself from any retribution by "reading her moods" and behaving (or hiding) accordingly. I have developed an ability to read people quickly and accurately. I developed this very naturally in order to survive in the environment of unpredictability created by my mom.

We need a revolution in the leadership in schools that gives students more freedom to learn and teachers freedom to facilitate that learning. We need a revolution in our organizations (one leader at a time) that significantly boosts employee engagement through autonomy. That shift will improve innovation, productivity, and performance and it can be found with Systems Thinking and the embrace of W. Edwards Deming's System of Profound Knowledge. Both will be explored in detail in chapters 5-8.

The typical appraisal process and rewards and recognition policies are a form of control that is left over from the industrial age and Taylor Scientific Management methods. Like the South Americans in 1500's, HR professionals are having trouble seeing a world without these outdated management tools. Like QWERTY the typical appraisal has found its way into our everyday life and is part of how we operate in our organizations and our schools, it is impacting our performance, our relationships, and our organizations. It is entrenched into our world and is very difficult to adopt something different because of how we have been taught to think about the world. To make a change we must begin to question the foundations of this thinking. We must question with boldness the principles and beliefs being embraced and ask are those principles and beliefs consistent with natural law?

There are consultants today making a great living claiming the Millennial Generation is very different and the workplace must adapt to their special needs. I can agree that their behaviors and beliefs may be different because the context within which they grew up was different. Those of us who grew up in the 1960's can remember how the generation felt unique. We expressed ourselves in new ways from the way we wore our hair, the way we dressed, and our language because of the context of the 1960's. We had different music, lots of love, drugs, and anti-war sentiments. The Millennial Generation has computers, iPods, iPhone, iPads, the Internet, multi-tasking, social consciousness etc. It's this context that influencing their behaviors and their thinking. Each generation is entitled to its own behaviors but these are largely the result of the context within which they were observed.

The principles upon which the typical appraisal and pay-for-performance policies are based are flawed. The shift from the menial task Industrial Age workplace to the complex knowledge age is shedding the bright light of truth on why and how these polices no longer add value. They don't work anymore, not necessarily because of the generational differences per se but because the nature of work has changed. We perform fewer menial tasks today than in the industrial age. Menial tasks can be done by computers. We can shop and checkout at the grocery store without even contacting a human being.

The current performance appraisal process really doesn't work well because it is consistent with this view of the world. This will be explored more and clarified in chapter 6. Furthermore the appraisal process is most often manipulated to justify some motivation other than its original purpose e.g. justifying a raise (or bonus) to keep a high performer happy or justifying the firing of a poor performer.

The main assumption of the current appraisal process is that improving the quality of the parts of the system (people) will improve the organizational performance. This describes our desire to analyze the parts of a whole in order to understand the whole. Therefore most leaders now assume that poor organizational performance is rooted in poor employee performance. This belief is a dysfunctional yet sophisticated form of blame. As Jack Welch has stated, *"You've got to be rigorous in your appraisal system. The biggest cowards are managers who don't let people know where they stand."* In Taylor the rules and structure of the organization control the employees to drive them toward performance. Additional assumptions that follow from this are:

- Individuals have control over the results of their work and the factors that allow them to achieve their goals. This too is false because there are always many factors that contribute to the success of a goal.
- Managers can evaluate individual performance separate from the contributions of others and the influence of the work tools, environment etc. This too is false. Managers cannot separate their bias (either positive or negative) from their evaluation.

These assumptions are false because they are inconsistent with natural law and systems thinking. A better assumption is: *"the quality of the interactions between the parts (employees and departments) is more important for improvement of the organization than improving the quality of the parts."* In other words, you can't separate the evaluation of the person from the quality of the interactions that person has with their co-workers and the working environment. We must conclude that the typical appraisal doesn't really evaluate the individual at all but instead evaluates the quality of the interactions between the employee and the system within which they work. Therefore, to create improvement, we must focus on improving the interactions in that particular environment.

At the end of the 15th century in America the hunter-gatherer Native Americans first became exposed to the European immigration. The explorers and the farmers attracted to the new world brought a new age that clashed directly with the Native American nomad culture. The Native Americans were the victims of the age of agriculture evolution.

No less dramatic is the clash of ages occurring in today's workplace. The Age of Knowledge and the leadership of the Industrial age are clashing but this time the casualty is employee engagement. Leadership policies such as the typical appraisal are still stuck in the Industrial Age while the economy and employees are struggling to adapt to the Knowledge Age. Recent studies by two independent human organizations highly this.

Both SHRM (Society of Human Resource Management) and Aon consulting asked their respective client networks to identify the top issues facing HR professionals in the future. Coincidentally they both ended up identifying the same top three issues:

- Attracting and retaining talent
- Building employee engagement and trust
- Aligning employee goals with organizational goals

These issues have been around for years and we still have difficulty addressing them because our leadership models and skills have not evolved at the same rate as our macro-economic conditions. In 2004 a Harris poll of 23,000 employees confirmed that we have a leadership evolution problem. (Covey S. R., 2004) Harris reported only 20% of employees felt their organization did a good job clarifying and aligning goals. Only 20% said they did a good job with engagement, and only 15% did a good job with trust.

In 2011 Aon reports similar results. According to the 1,328 employees surveyed, only 12% of leaders very effectively clarified business goals and only 7% very effectively managed their talent.

Our leadership skills have not evolved to catch up to the need for knowledge creation and knowledge management. Our leaders are not changing policies. They still embrace the current performance management and pay-for-performance policies consistent with the industrial age while all the research continues to show them to be ineffective.

Management by Objective is like Frankenstein: Good Intentions that Turn Into a Monster

Frankenstein started out with good intentions. The Dr. lost his brother to a tragic accident and vowed to bring him back to life. With all the best of intentions to create life, his work led to the creation of a monster. Management by Objective (MBO) is much like a Frankenstein monster. I am sure Peter Drucker had the best of intentions when he created the idea of MBO but injury has been the result.

MBO is a tool to align all actions in an organization around a set of objectives by first identifying the objectives, giving employees objectives consistent with those of the organization, monitor progress, evaluate the employees and the performance (usually through performance appraisals), rewarding the achievers, punishing the slackers, and then revising the organization objectives again.

MBO is an outgrowth of those same Taylor assumptions we have already discussed. It adds one more: Employees won't put in extra effort unless they are constantly reminded, rewarded, and threatened to work on what is most important. The pay-for-performance portion of MBO is supposed to deliver this.

The unintended consequences of MBO (the monster) have just recently been confirmed thanks to the "No Child Left Behind" legislation passed by President Bush in his first term. A recent series of articles by USA TODAY uncovered frequent cheating by teachers and principals. (Upton, 2011) This is not the first time cheating has appeared since No Child Left Behind was implemented. A study by the Wall Street Journal[1] uncovered purposeful tampering of the Regents exams in New York. (B. Martinez, 2011) I think they should re-name the program: No "Cheating" Left Behind: MBO Fails Again!

Holding people accountable to results when they can't control (or even influence) all the factors necessary for success will cause either manipulated numbers or cheating. As Deming said, *"Fear invites wrong figures. Bearers of bad news fare badly. To keep his job, anyone may present to his boss only good news."* (Deming, The New Economics - Second Edition, 1994) The environment created by pay-for-performance and MBO encourages manipulation because of the pressure for results.

Some may be thinking that these are isolated instances. Why did Bausch and Lomb executives fabricate sales data and hide inventory to meet stretch goals? Why did Auto repair managers in Sears bilk customers with unnecessary repairs to meet monthly bonuses? Why did Jiffy Lube managers sell unnecessary parts to customers to meet weekly goals? Why did Enron executives manipulate projects? I could go on.

Pressure to perform damages employee engagement. It robs employees of pride and encourages breaks in rules to achieve the results. It puts results in front of ethics.

With the best of intentions your senior leaders may be creating a monster with MBO, stretch goals, pay-for-performance, and performance appraisals. This monster will damage employee engagement and stunt performance improvement. These are the exact opposite of the original desired outcomes. It is time to eliminate the growth of MBO and to reverse its course before it consumes more employee engagement and valuable resources. We must especially protect the engagement of employees and must especially protect our children. We must kill this monster now.

---

1 *Agreement: Something specific, measurable and time sensitive. All factors are in your control because of a predictable method.*

Is Bad Behavior In The System or in the Person?

We have two dogs and a cat in our family. The dogs are always hungry and if we leave anything on the floor or drop anything by accident they will devour it. They are normal.

When we first got them we already had our cat and we were used to leaving the cat food on the floor. Once the dogs arrived that proved a big mistake. Any leftover cat food was devoured when we weren't watching.

When I fed the cat I had to watch carefully and scold the dogs if they attempted to eat her food once the cat was finished. It was a waste of my time and I was often annoyed because the dogs just didn't seem to learn the command, "NO CAT FOOD FOR YOU!"

It finally dawned on me that I could feed the cat on top of the washer in the laundry room. She could easily jump up and I could leave it out in case she wanted to finish later. It was out of reach of the dogs. I realized the cat food on the floor created an environment that encouraged poor behavior. It's the very nature of a dog to eat food available. By changing the system of feeding the cat the bad behavior stopped. I could trust the dogs again. I stopped yelling at them. My relationship with them improved. They trusted me more. They didn't shirk away whenever I came into the room.

I am not suggesting we treat people like dogs. As leaders we can often set people up for failure and unknowingly create opportunities for bad behavior. Our decisions and policies can create an environment that increases the probability of poor behavior and then act surprised and even punish the employee when they behave poorly. Performance appraisals and Pay-for-performance are two examples of policies and practices that often unwittingly create an environment of dysfunction.

Pay-for-performance

Pay-for-performance is coercion and coercion damages employee engagement. Pay-for-performance attempts control behavior and sends subtle message, "We don't trust you to do the right thing and we don't think you will work hard unless you have a reward."

Studies by Deci and Ryan have shown how typical pay-for-performance schemes can backfire. The purpose of offering a reward for certain behaviors or outcomes is to create motivation. According to numerous studies over the past 50 years the opposite occurs. Those coerced with incentives end up less interested in the activity once the reward is removed. They stop performing when no one is looking and when no reward is offered.

Rewards can also encourage cheating. Employees who know their pay is determined by goal achievement can be tempted to manipulate the results. A recent study by the

New York Regents exam board is a good example. Teachers who are evaluated based on the number of students who pass the Regents exams manipulated the scores to allow those students missing the passing grade by a point or two to pass anyway. The statistics showed an enormous bulge of scores right on the passing line which could not be explained by normal statistical variation.

Just as I continued to yell at the dogs for their poor behaviors, leaders cling to policies that create dysfunction and they blame the employees for the poor behaviors. Isn't it time we "put the food up on the washer" and stop these dysfunctions? Wouldn't it save us time as leaders? Wouldn't it improve our relationships and the performance of the organization? Wouldn't new processes that avoid these dysfunctions improve employee engagement?

Dr. W. Edwards Deming's theory of Profound Knowledge offers our best hope for improving our thinking and to realize how we have been immersed in Taylor "water" for over 100 years. Deming's theory helps us to understand that a system has interdependencies and interactions. His theory teaches us that the qualities of the interactions in a system are more important than the parts of the system. It teaches that there will always be variation and we must be able to manage that variation with knowledge of the system. It helps us to appreciate how to accumulate knowledge and we must appreciate the differences between people and not treat them as widgets in an assembly line. We will explore this in detail in chapter 7.

Chapter 4
The Seeds Continue to be Sown – Stop Please

Aim of this Chapter: To provide evidence about how our institutions and our leaders continue to perform malpractice by teaching and using Taylor Scientific Management practices despite the evidence it causes harm and despite the presence of more effective replacement practices.

Taylor Scientific Management thinking is everywhere and, if you know what to look for, you will see it in action nearly everywhere because it is still embedded in our minds, our habits, our policies, and our culture. This embedding makes it nearly impossible to reverse. There is hope to replace the ineffective policies and practices if they are clearly identified first.

Stop Reliance on Policy and Start Living Principles

I facilitated a training in Kansas City. I was unable to catch the last flight out to New York that day. I had a reservation for the first flight out at 7 AM the next day. Kansas City was expecting a blizzard that evening. Only a few inches was expected but the wind and cold was to cause the blizzard conditions.

I awoke and saw the few inches of snow that morning and after walking outside I could see the snow blowing horizontally. The meteorologists were correct. This was a blizzard.

The conditions prevented the ground crews from clearing the runways fast enough and it prevented them from deicing the planes well enough to make it safe for take offs. The airport closed. I was re-booked to a flight leaving in two days. It was the weekend before Christmas and so everything was booked up. I was upset and worried I might actually get stuck.

I kept calling customer service at Delta and I ended up being scheduled for flight out on Friday (not Saturday) at 5:59 PM. I had been re-booked by the Customer Service people over the phone. They had also assured me I was on the stand-by list for the flight at 7 AM on Friday. Although I was assured I was on the stand-by list, I was not very confident in my chances. After all, 100's of people had been stranded there for at least 24 hours. I was determined to try to get on the flight anyway.

I arrived at the airport at 5 AM waiting to be cleared. The 7AM flight was delayed to 8 AM. When I saw most passengers had boarded I went to the desk and asked if all stand by s had been cleared. The Agent said she didn't have any stand-by's. I complained bitterly explaining I had been promised by Customer Service that I would be put on the stand-by list. I had been assured by them at least twice that I was on that list. The agent said, "My paperwork is complete and there is no way I can get you on the flight."

I felt I had been misled. I was angry and complained with the gate agent to no avail. I sat back down and planned my revenge when she emerged from the jet way and paged me. She quickly punched the computer key board and exclaimed, "You'e in 9A." She had put me on the flight.

After boarding I then learned that there were 5 seats open on the flight, Robert and Holly, the two flight attendants on the flight had complained to the agent that the flight had five empty seats. They insisted it should not leave with empty seats if there were people waiting to go to New York. They insisted she let me on the flight.

Holly and Robert explained how the agent complained about her paperwork, how it would have to be revised and that this action the flight would surely delay the flight if she processed this change and let me on the flight. Both Robert and Holly insisted and explained the flight was already late. What would a couple extra minutes mean?

Why did Robert and Holly fight for me? Why did they insist on the change and why were they so committed to influence the agent? They were acting out of principle and values not policy. The agent was acting based on policy. They felt empowered to insist on a different action than that which was described in the Delta policy. Their instincts told them customers needed more flexibility in the policy because of the context. The frustration caused by the blizzard could never have been anticipated by the policy makers.

The gate agent could have anticipated this but she didn't. She also could have realized that the reservation system had broken a promise. I was promised to be on the stand-by list and there was not stand-by list according to her. A promise had been broken. Keeping promises with customers is also a principle that organizations must follow if they are to expect customer loyalty. Clearly, for the agent, it was more important to keep the policy "don't re-open the paperwork once it is closed" and/or do whatever it takes to keep the departure on-time. Policies don't always apply if you want to create optimum customer value. Principles always apply.

What principles did Robert and Holly apply? Possibly it was "always keep your promises with your customers if you can." Or perhaps, "Always fill the seats if people are waiting and seats are available." I can't be sure they were acting out of the principles of keeping agreements, telling the truth, and the need to serve the customer or "you must fill every seat!" They were unspoken and unwritten but it's my guess the agent and the flight attendants were not aligned on the same principles.

This is a classic example of Taylor Scientific Management in action. The policies are created by management. Why? Because in the Taylor Scientific Management world the manager who creates the policy is omnipotent and omniscient. They know what is best for the company, the employee, and the customer. They dictate and they must not be questioned even if they make no sense.

When employees are empowered to act based on principle they have autonomy to make a judgment. They judge what is best for the customer, the company, and themselves. Ideally their decisions are based on thinking for the long-term not the short-term. They decide what is best because they are in the best position to make the best decision for all concerned. That is what the two flight attendants seemed to do despite the policy the agent tried to follow.

I wrote a note to the airline on their website. I explained what had happened regarding the airport closure, the missing stand-by list that I was promised to be on, the gate agent responses to me, and the behaviors of the two flight attendants. I wanted the airline to know how their system had not worked well to serve the customer because of the errors, the lack of alignment of the personnel, and how appreciative I was for the two flight attendants insistence I be put on the flight. My intention was mainly to compliment them. Here is the response I received:

Thank you for sharing your positive comments regarding the service provided by our employees. On behalf of "our" airline and all its affiliates (names purposely excluded), I also apologize for your disappointment with the customer service provided by our counter agent.

We appreciate your kind comments regarding the service received from our flight attendants, Robert and Holly who assisted you to get on the flight. I recognize due to their efforts you were able to travel. We believe our team members are our most important assets, and I am happy to learn our flight attendant exceeded your expectations. Please know I will be sharing your comments with our In-flight leadership team so this flight attendant receives appropriate recognition, on your behalf. Thank you for sharing your thoughtful remarks.

Also, we appreciate your comments regarding the unsatisfactory customer service you encountered at our counter. After reading your remarks, I certainly understand why you wanted to bring this matter to our attention. I can imagine your disappointment with the service provided by our counter agent who displayed a rude behavior and showed lack of concern. I am truly sorry you did not receive the service you expected and should have received, as we expect our employees to be helpful and professional at all times. Please know I will be sharing your comments with our Airport Customer Service leadership team for internal follow up.

Dr. Hauck, I hope I have been able to resolve any concerns you have about our customer service. As our valued "frequent flyer" member, your business is important to us and given the opportunity of serving you in the future, I am confident "our airline" will not only meet but exceed your expectations.

I subsequently responded to her as follows:

Thank you for your response.... I would please be gentle with the gate agent. I do not fault her for her response. My guess is she has been told in the past by management to NOT change the flight status if it will cause a delay and/ or if the paperwork is already done. I assert it is leadership's job to create an alignment about customer service and how and when to prioritize and resolve any conflicts between policy and customer needs. Clearly the gate agent was more concerned about the flight being late. My guess is there is some incentive, by management, to get flights out on time and that, in part, caused her to respond the way she did. Clearly she and Robert and Holly had different priorities. Well run organizations are aligned on priorities especially those that can affect the customer directly. This means leadership must do a better job first and we must not blame the individuals. Any reprimand of the gate agent I believe is inappropriate and will make no positive difference in the future. Leadership must change at "your airline" first.

Taylor Scientific Management theory embraces certain assumptions about the root causes of problems. This correspond illustrates a typical response and a typical set of assumptions about people and problems. My note to the airline merely identified the missing stand-by list for that flight, the behaviors of the gate agent and the behaviors of the flight attendants (for which I was extremely grateful).

The response from the airline placed the blame for the poor service squarely in the lap of the gate agent. The customer service person who wrote the response assumed the gate agent could have provided better service and she also assumed I would agree with that assessment. This is a typical unsophisticated assumption to a complex situation and is consistent with Taylor Scientific Management thinking. Taylor theory oversimplifies. It assumes it is the individual who made the errors. It easily separates employee behavior from the context within which it occurred.

We can assume there must have been some good reason why the gate agent refused to put me on the flight after the paperwork was completed. I doubt it was just an inconvenience. I doubt she was just being difficult or argumentative. It must have been other factors such as instructions from management or possibly a competing goal such as on-time departure. Taylor Scientific Management frequently ignores these factors and over simplifies to find just one root cause and that cause is often the act of an employee(s). This assumption is not only unsophisticated but the blame it expresses is severely damaging to the engagement of the employees and the loyalty of the customers. Furthermore, the blame on one employee will create fear in all the others who hear it. Even though they did not make the mistake(s) they assume they're next on the list of those to be blamed.

Blame is Driving While Systems Thinking Takes a Back Seat

A nurse, in an Ohio Hospital, accidently discarded a kidney that was awaiting a transplant and had been provided by a living donor. The nurse had been on break, had been replaced by a different nurse, and was therefore unaware the kidney was submerged in an ice filled sludge. She purposely disposed of the contents into a disposal hopper thinking the kidney was still in the operating room because "that's what usually happens."

The hospital suspended the two nurses after the incident; one was later fired, and the other resigned. Furthermore, a surgeon was stripped of his title as director of some surgical services. What a tragedy on many levels.

The nurse who discarded the kidney had walked past a doctor and other nurses carrying the container. Should someone have noticed? Should someone have said something? How was she to know? She was fired! Does that make sense?

In the light of our typical industrial age model of management that focuses on holding people accountable for results it makes total sense. Why? Because, someone must be at fault! That's the philosophy with which we were raised. That's the philosophy that dominates our schools and our organizations, i.e. someone must be held accountable for the results.

In 1950 Dr. W. Edwards Deming explained his philosophy of systems thinking to the Japanese leadership. The Japanese proceeded to implement Deming's philosophy of Profound Knowledge. By the late 1960's Japan was dominating the manufacturing of electronics including televisions, radios, and stereos. By the end of the 1970's the gap in quality between Japan and the USA was reaching a crisis. The philosophy of focusing on the improvement of the system was winning the competitive edge. Costs were lower and quality was higher. The age of blaming people for mistakes was dead. At least it was in Japan. Unfortunately it is still very much alive today in America.

Today we still tend to blame people for mistakes. Unfortunately, according to Dr. Deming's philosophy probably 94% of all mistakes come from the system and processes and only 6% from the people. There were probably a dozen or more hand-offs that occurred in that operating room between the surgery preparation time and the time the nurse returned from her break. Each of those hand-offs (or system interactions) was an opportunity to have good quality or poor quality. Information about the location of the kidney was a hand-off. What to do with the slush was a hand-off. Each of those hand-offs was a process that could be improved. To blame her does nothing to improve those hand-offs and therefore, nothing to prevent a reoccurrence.

Today our children are failing to learn reading and math skills at their respective grade levels, yet we continue to embrace standardized testing and performance evaluations for teachers. We continue to attempt to improve the individuals by judging, grading, blaming, and firing them. We fail to fully recognize that our system of grading students destroys their passion for learning and steals their willingness to take responsibility for their own learning progress. We continue with the same flawed processes and hand-offs that make up the entire dysfunctional system. We blame and then expect different results.

If we fired every nurse and every teacher in the country and replaced them all with highly trained substitutes would we improve anything? Couldn't we expect a similar number of students would fail and a similar number of kidneys would be discarded? Unless we embrace a systems view of the world and stop blaming we will continue to see these tragedies. If blame is driving systems thinking takes a back seat.

I Won't Trust You and So You Won't Trust Me

In a discussion about how to improve sales performance a sales manager clearly articulated her major frustration. Her source of frustration was the sales representatives complaining about being criticized for having too much telephone talk time with new prospects. Management tracked the total time for each call and set goals for the sales reps based on that total talk time.

The sales manager was upset because she caught many reps cheating. She explained how she "caught" reps artificially boosting their talk time to increase their averages. Management wanted shorter talk times in order to reach more prospects. The sales reps wanted longer talk times to achieve greater flexibility in the sales process in order to close the sale. In an effort to control the sales reps, who in the minds of management clearly could not be trusted, rules and policies were created and the reps were evaluated based on those rules.

According to research by DecisionWise only 46% of employees have confidence in senior leaders. (Maylett, 2012) This lack of trust of employees is another Taylor Scientific Management calling card. Polices and rules are what's most important in the Taylor world. Innovation is for management. The rules and policies, created by management, are for the employees. Why would the sales reps manipulate the talk-time? Are they lazy? In management's eyes they might be. After all, why else would the sales manager be so frustrated? But, more likely, they just want to do a better job and the policies and/or rules are actually barriers to performance not enhancements for performance. Taylor thinking doesn't take innovation, pride, and creativity of employee into consideration. I know this sounds harsh but Taylor thinking assumes the employees are wrong, lazy, or cheaters. Like the Pygmalion affect it expects employees can't be trusted and therefore they behave in ways that lowers trust. The result of course is employees have little trust of management. It is a vicious cycle of dysfunctional thought with continuing poor relationships.

I visited a client this past week. I conducted leadership training for a Human Resources team in a large organization. I asked them to give their impressions about their employees. I was astonished at their answer. I can summarize with this statement, *"You can't fix stupid."*

Why would a professional organization that must provide service to its employees feel they are stupid? Are they? Certainly not! Is the HR department flawed? Have they hired the wrong people? Certainly not! This belief (feeling) is a symptom of the quality of leadership at the top. The senior leaders have failed to include one of the most important things managers need to do a good job, to feel joy in work and to be engaged. They failed to fully empower employees to manage their own processes. They are attempting to manage from the top instead of leading from the top.

Empowering employees to solve their own problems is only paid lip service and rarely fully implemented. That is one of the key root causes of the *"You can't fix stupid"* attitude. If leaders truly trusted employees to study and improve their system interactions, this poor attitude would quickly disappear and would be replaced by joy in work, improved productivity and profitability. It is the lack of trust leads to lack of empowerment which causes frustration which leads to blaming the employees.

Why do senior leaders only pay lip service to empowerment and how can important responsibility be shifted to the employees? Again, these results relate back to Taylor Scientific thinking and the assumptions it encourages. We have all been taught that the person(s) in authority is omniscient (all knowing). It all starts in school where we think the teacher has all the answers because they are the ones who tell us what to study, what questions to ask, how to think, and the answers to all the tests. They are the ones who grade us. This naturally follows into our organizations. It is consistent with the approach of managing from the top and not leading from the top.

The policies that continue to reinforce this idea include the performance review and pay-for-performance. The managers grade our performance and control how much we get paid because they are "all knowing". This role played by our teachers and our managers is thoroughly ingrained into our brains, reinforced in our language, and supported by our structures and policies.

The key lies in making a shift in thinking toward Dr. W. Edwards Deming. We need his *Theory of Profound Knowledge* more than ever. We can embrace his appreciation for *systems thinking*, his theory of how *knowledge* is accumulated, and his *theory of psychology*. *Profound Knowledge* is the most effective way to think about the workings of an organization.

Leaders can also begin to build trust with each and every interaction. This requires trusting employees first. It requires the realization that employees really want to do a good job and they want to develop trust and pride. They are not, in their hearts, looking for shortcuts. They only look for shortcuts when they are encouraged by flawed policies.

A good way to show trust is to stop the typical policies of performance reviews and pay-for-performance. These can be replaced with policies that reinforce trust and systems thinking. Building trust and embracing *Profound Knowledge* is an example of leading from the top (not managing from the top).

Making Leaders – Not Victims – How Taylor Scientific Management Has Ruined Our Schools

Parents and teachers face daunting challenges. As of 2011 students in the USA rank 14th in reading, 25th in math, and 17th in science skills in world education rankings. Bullying is rampant with 77 percent of all students are being bullied verbally in some way or another including mental bullying or even verbal abuse, 56 percent, of all students have witnesses a bullying crime, 15 percent of all students who don't show up for school report it to being out of fear of being bullied and, 71 percent of students that report bullying as an on-going problem.

Tools that were supposed to work have failed. The policy of *No Child Left Behind* has failed with waivers being provided to 19 of 50 states. Standardized testing has failed as measured by world rankings and by the achievement gap being the highest in history.

Our school system is creating victims not leaders, dependency not autonomy. A dependence on specific curriculum, grades and standardized testing is killing autonomy of both teachers and students. This approach is translated into our workplace. The University of Sheffield conducted studies in the past few years finding, for example, the top time-waster for managers is dealing with poor performance of people. Nearly 30% of the average manager's time is spent on poor performers. Nearly 20% of a manager's time is spent correcting mistakes causes by poor performers.

Other than developing an effective strategy (business model), the ability to manage people issues is the most important skill a leader can develop. This skill can accelerate an organization's success. When this skill is missing everything slows down. Because change is occurring at hyper speed, global competition is growing fiercer and the need for innovation and knowledge accumulation is increasing, leaders need fully engaged people to address today's challenges. Because we have created victims in our schools and universities we inherit them in the workplace and begin to believe we must continue to control them because that is what victims expect.

The current leadership model used in both schools and in most workplaces is proving ineffective because it focuses on things that send a message of mistrust and the need for bureaucratic control. This message causes employee engagement levels to stall and innovation to disappear. The victims from the school system enter the workplace and cause managers to cling to the skills they were taught i.e. giving direction and judging people. Employees therefore cling to their victimhood by waiting to be told what to do and remaining fearful of making mistakes (victims). It's a vicious perpetual cycle. For today's challenges we need a new model. We need self-management and self-management tools. We need leaders not victims. We need autonomy not dependence.

We know that self-managing employees working in collaborative environments produce superior results. Leaders must know how to engage and develop self-managing teams in order to create more adaptable, innovative, and productive organizations. There are 3 steps leaders can take to reverse this perpetual dysfunctional trend that's damaging our global competitiveness.

First, leaders must begin to take a risk and truly trust employees. They must expect them to behave like adults and therefore treat them like adults. They must expect them to care about each other and about their customers. Leaders must expect them to be trustworthy. This is not just empowerment. Empowerment means management is still in control and they are merely giving employees something that the managers can always take away, i.e. power. A leader who truly trusts people is acknowledging that employees already have the power and the leader knows it.

Second, we must rely on principles and less on policy. We must clarify operating principles and stop relying on following more and more bureaucracy. Today it seems the typical Human Resource professional must either be an attorney or be totally familiar with laws, regulations, and policies. Last year I made a presentation at a three day HR conference. The agenda was devoted to legal issues and government regulations for two out of the three days.

Here are some examples of principles that can be clarified, "every action must be aligned and consistent with a specific vision and aim." A second is, "every action is consistent with specific values behaviors." Another is, "everyone is responsible for identifying and delivering excellent interactions (both interpersonal and process hand offs). The quality of these interactions will be defined by their internal and external customers."

By following principles instead of policy, employees are able to make quick decisions to improve their performance without a reliance on manager oversight and performance appraisal bureaucracy. They are also able to adapt to quickly changing customer needs and market changes. When we tell employees they must follow policy they are restricted, their creativity is stunted, and their sense of autonomy is lost. Lost autonomy creates victims.

In March of 2013 a nurse at a retirement community in California called 911. A resident of the independent living community had collapsed in the dining room. The 911 operator asked a few simple questions about the woman's condition. It was clear she would not survive long without some assistance. She needed CPR (cardio-pulmonary resuscitation). The operator requested the nurse take action immediately. The nurse refused. The operator was incredulous and began to argue with the nurse suggesting the woman would not survive without her help. The nurse refused again explaining it was the policy of the independent living organization to not provide CPR. They were not legally obligated. The operator argued. The nurse refused. The woman died. It's a sad example of how following policy and not principle can often result in tragedy.

Creativity is needed more than ever today to solve problems and keep up with the competition in the context of rapid change. Unfortunately, as we have already discussed, our public school system still embraces Taylor Scientific Management and that approach systematically damages the engagement and creativity of our young people. The loss of creative skill is often referred to as "the 4th grade slump." The term "the 4th grade slump" was coined by Professor E. Paul Torrance one of the founders of Psychology of Creativity. This "slump" is characterized by a significant drop in the willingness to take risk, a significant reduction in natural playfulness, and a huge drop in creativity sometimes known as divergent thinking. (Eger, 2010)

A 1968 study by George Land and Beth Jarman confirm this conclusion. (Eger, 2010) Land and Jarman gave 1,600 3 – 5 year olds a creativity test (one used by NASA to measure divergent thinking in engineers). The retested the same children at 10 and again at 15. 98% of the 3-5 year olds scored at genius level while only 32% of the 10 year olds scored that high and only 10% of the 15 year olds scored that high. When 25 year olds were tested, only 2% showed genius level divergent thinking. We are clearly damaging our children's genius and we continue that same approach in the workplace when we continue to embrace Taylor Scientific Management methods.

Employees and students must be allowed to experiment to optimize learning. Trusting them to follow principles and to experiment creates an entrepreneurial environment that optimizes innovation, quality improvement and productivity gains. We must move away from command and control. We must embrace a different philosophy and a different relationship with employees. We must break this cycle of creating victims. The new model and environment must be based on trust and learning. It must acknowledge and expect employees to be adults with autonomy who experiment.

Typical Managers Unknowingly Stop Innovation

The manager dependent environments send subliminal messages about the difference in status between an employee and a manager. The message is "the manager is the parent and the employee is the child." Naturally if you treat someone like a child it increases the probability they will act like one. Organizations need adults who are innovative not children who comply. The typical manage stifles risk taking and innovation because they are responsible for evaluating their employees. Manages are also evaluated by their managers and so on all the way to the top.

This hierarchy of criticism makes the reward for being truly creative small in comparison to the damage one mistake might make to a career or reputation. Furthermore, that mistake becomes part of the employee's permanent record and everyone who considers that employee for a future position will be able to read it and know how and why they messed up. This fear of failure, and the label the employee might carry, stops innovation in its tracks.

Managers are told to evaluate employees. They do it and unknowingly damage the very thing that could improve the organization's competitive advantage. Criticism is often viewed by many employees as incivility because it feels disrespectful. A recent study in Harvard Business Review confirmed the damaging costs of incivility. The targets of incivility very often hide their true feelings but they exhibit their dissatisfaction in very damaging ways such as intentionally decreasing work effort, intentionally decreasing time at work, intentionally decreasing the quality of their work, and taking their frustration out on customers. (Christine Porath, 2013)

Porath and Pearson go on to explain that innovation and creativity are also damaged by this incivility. (Christine Porath, 2013) Simply witnessing (or hearing about) the incivility is enough to damage team spirit, creativity, and risk taking. The typical performance appraisal policy offers many opportunities for employees to hear horror stories of incivility, disrespect, and criticism.

Typical Managers Accidentally Impede Adaptability

Today increasing the capacity for change is necessary to match the speed of change in the global economy. For example, just a few years ago Research in Motion dominated the cell phone market. Today they are dwarfed by Apple and Google. The ability to adapt is probably more important than ever before yet our managers accidentally slow the pace because they are focused more on themselves and less on the elements that create adaptability.

When Steve Jobs was asked why he had located all the iPhone manufacturing in China he denied it was due to labor costs. Instead he explained the ability to quickly change direction and manufacturing specifications was the major factor. He relayed the story about a change in the IPhone cover from plastic to glass. To test the efficacy of the IPhone Jobs carried a prototype in his pocket the way he might expect any executive to do. After just a few days the plastic cover showed scratches.

Knowing this would create an impression of poor quality he demanded the covers all be changed from plastic to glass. With only weeks left before launch suppliers needed to be found, molds needed to be built, shipments of covers needed to be made overnight. Thousands of workers were awoken in the middle of the night, fed an early breakfast and put immediately to work to replace the covers and meet the demands. Jobs explained he could have never made that change in the USA. There would be too many complaints and too many barriers. The speed of change was more valuable than the other costs.

The war for talent contributes to this inability to adapt. Focus is given to improving the parts of the organization (the top talent) while the adaptability of the organization's system suffers. In the war for talent managers compete with each other for attention and success. These intelligent individuals are often able to manipulate their own success while creating unintended negative results in another part of the organization, e.g. selling more than the operations can deliver or over promising to meet a performance goal. Usually the setting of numeric goals that must be achieved to receive either a pay-for-performance bonus or a "results oriented reputation" are the root causes of this behavior.

The focus by senior leadership on attracting and retaining talent can accidentally damage the organization's ability to adapt because the focus is on those individuals and not on encouraging the cooperative effort to detect the subtle important changes that need to be made to continuously respond to changing customer needs and wants. Focus on the individual parts of the system take focus off the cooperation between the parts of that system which unknowingly damages adaptability.

Managers are consistently rated poorly by employees and employee engagement scores are stalled. Why? It's because managers are being asked to play a role that is irrelevant for the current needs of employees and the needs of the organization. The typical manager unintentionally damages engagement scores, stops creativity and prevents adaptability. Senior leaders need to recognize that the typical manager must be replaced with a facilitator who understands how to lead people to greatness while optimizing a system. Managers need to be supportive facilitators not bureaucratic overseers because bureaucratic overseers are now irrelevant.

Does Your Team Have Communication Gangrene?

When the blood supply is significantly reduced or even completely cut off for a period of time the body tissue can die. This is a potentially life threatening condition. Often the affected tissue needs to be removed to prevent death. The condition requires immediate attention.

The Problem

Lack of communication in certain functions in organizations is similar to lack of circulation in a body part. This lack of communication is also a life threatening condition for performance, employee loyalty, employee engagement, and productivity. The presence of this "communication gangrene" can "kill" these results. This is true for not only the select employees (body part) but for the entire system (the entire individual). Just like the entire body can die if the gangrene goes untreated, the entire organization can die unless an organization has a way to treat any gangrene and has a process to prevent it in the first place.

Very often certain individuals are affected more than others in communication breakdowns. What is your current process for managing communication breakdowns and for preventing them? Do you ignore them until the body part begins to die and needs to be cut out? This is the equivalent of waiting until an employee has an emotional outburst and then holding a performance review meeting or even a corrective action meeting to either punish or threaten that employee. It is treating the symptom not the root cause. Just as amputation is treating the symptom, performance management is treating the symptom by blaming the individual for the poor communication. The problem is more complex in both the body and in the organization. They are both complex systems and need to be cared for and treated as such.

In the organization, if these are your major options now, it is the equivalent of ignoring pain in your foot and waiting until it turns black before you take action. At that point usually the only option available is removal of the infected tissue or amputation of a portion of the limb. The equivalent would be the removal of the "infected person" and the reprimand, or removal, of the management in the function.

Communication breakdowns in organizations manifest with lower employee engagement. The employee stops participating and sharing information. He/she will have confusion, general ill feelings, anxiety, emotional outbursts, poor attitude, lack of co-operation, others making an effort to avoid the infected employee and working around him/her.

Employee Engagement is essential for survival in the new knowledge economy. Taylor Scientific Management won't do it. Clinging to attorneys and bureaucracy won't do it. Continuing to embrace the policies of Taylor like the typical performance management and the typical pay-for-performance processes won't do it.

Part III
The Verdict

A replacement leadership model

Chapter 5
Systems Thinking, What is it?

Aim of this Chapter: To provide an answer to our problem by clearly describing a replacement leadership model that forms the foundation for a replacement performance appraisal.

A verdict is a decision. It's a judgment about a situation or matter given to a jury or judge to come to a conclusion. The purpose of the first four chapters is to create the case for a different way of thinking and therefore, a different way of behaving. With the evidence presented at this point ideally the members of the jury (you) have come to the unanimous conclusion that the current leadership model is incomplete and "guilty" of tremendous injury to organizations, employees and society. Verdicts are based on evidence. This evidence is not just proof of injury but it provides reasons why the guilty leaders could have made a different choice. They could have chosen a different path that would have avoided the injury. They could have chosen "systems thinking."

Apparently there are an entire series of quotes that take the form, *"There are no bad [something], only bad [something else]."* For example, *"there are no bad dogs, only bad owners"*; *"there are no bad foods, only bad diets"* etc. I want to add a new one, *"There are no purposely disengaged workers only leadership malpractice."*

I am not suggesting employees should be treated like dogs. My point is dogs are naturally motivated and happiest when they are treated consistent with "pack mentality." Dog trainers who treat dogs consistent with pack mentality have the happiest and best behaved dogs.

Similarly, people are naturally motivated by "engagement psychology." Leaders who understand engagement psychology and create an environment consistent with it will have engaged employees. Unfortunately, most leaders have not been taught the correct engagement psychology thus many organizations (if not most) consistently have low trust, high disengagement, poor productivity, and poor performance.

Leadership malpractice typically takes the form of sophisticated ways of blaming employees for poor results. Leadership malpractice uses phrases like "a leader must drive performance" or "we must drive results" because, the assumption is, employees can't do it without the leader pushing, pulling, driving, supervising, overseeing, and evaluating.

As we discussed in the previous chapter, many leaders are not yet "thinking in terms of systems." Most leaders still believe an improvement in the parts in an organization (the employees) will improve the organization. This is a false belief that actually damages employee engagement and performance improvement.

General Motors provides a good example of this. In 1982, GM closed its Fremont, California plant in 1982 because, of all of its plants, it had the worst record for: employee absenteeism, productivity, quality and morale. Then in 1983, Toyota and GM agreed to re-open the plant under two major conditions: one, that the plant would be managed by Japanese-trained leaders; and, two, 85% of all previously employed United Auto Workers would be re-hired.

By 1991, that same plant, renamed NUMMI (New United Motors Manufacturing Inc.) had catapulted from having the worst track record to having the best in all the areas in which it had previously failed. What made the difference? The change simply cannot be explained using conventional management theory, which typically blames the people for poor performance. As the example illustrates, the people, who were once part of the failure, became part of the success. The explanation lies in new a leadership style that used influence to change the methods that in turn changed the environment to produce positive results. The explanation lies in the different type of thinking.

What Type of Leader/Manager Are You? – Train-Wreck or Systems?

I recently read a story about large multi-location national organization and an improvement project facilitated by a well know consulting firm. A recent safety accident had taken the life of a production worker. This triggered the intensive and comprehensive initiative.

The consultant did due diligence and found that the standards of work were not being followed. In addition there was no pay-for-performance reward system in place nor was the performance appraisal process being followed consistently. They immediately recommended that managers be trained to develop specific safety goals and hold their people accountable to those goals by conducting frequent review of their work. They reduced the number of people each manager had reporting to them in order to make them easier to manage.

The supervisors under each manager were also trained to hold their people accountable to the specific goals. To reinforce this structure and motivate the workers, the consulting firm designed a "pay-for-performance" policy that rewarded workers (including managers) only if they achieved their assigned goals, and took additional action with those who didn't. Furthermore, the performance appraisal process was simplified and mandated. The meetings were to be held every 6 months instead of every 12months. This policy was added to the performance goals for each manager and supervisor.

What struck me was the date on this report was October 1841. Months earlier two Western Railroad passenger trains had collided between Worchester, Massachusetts and Albany, New York, killing a conductor and a passenger and injuring seventeen passengers. This story was recanted in Peter Scholtes' book, The Leader's Handbook. The consultant was the Prussian Army. This means our management model is formatted based on the Prussian Army and it has not significantly changed for at least 170 years.

"On October 5, 1841, two Western Railroad passenger trains collided somewhere between Worchester, Massachusetts and Albany, New York, killing a conductor and a passenger and injuring seventeen passengers. That disaster marked the beginning of a new management era." (Scholtes, 1998)

The Train-Wreck Manager

Train-wreck managers look for someone to blame. They assume the root causes of problems are to be found in the actions and decisions made by people. This manager assumes improvement in the individual behaviors alone will reduce the errors. Train-wreck management is a very narrow and unsophisticated view of the world. These managers ignore two very important ideas. First, they ignore the idea that there are performance factors (possibly unseen or unknowable) outside an individual's control. Secondly, they ignore the concept of variation. They view the world in black and white terms. Either a mistake is made by the individual or it isn't. The world tends to be "gray" (because of variation) not "black and white."

There is variation in everything. Train-wreck managers look for those who caused the errors and bring the mistakes to their attention. Train-wreck managers damage employee engagement.

The Systems Manager

A system is a series of interdependent processes working to achieve an aim. Systems managers firstly appreciate the concept of systems. Systems managers look for opportunities to synergize with a team and brainstorm the real root causes of problems. They recognize and appreciate the interrelationships between the parts in a system. System managers acknowledge that performance of an individual will be influenced by the interaction between the system and the individual.

A baseball team is a system. Each player is interdependent with the others members of the team. The pitcher who tires toward the end of a game might throw with less power. A hitter on the opposing team can then hit the ball more accurately and past the 2nd baseman that dives for the ball, touches it and makes an error. The permanent record shows the 2nd baseman made an error. It doesn't show how the pitcher had tired.

Perhaps sending a relief pitcher in sooner would solve this problem. This acknowledges that the interaction between the pitcher, hitter, and second baseman all combine into a complex process. Systems are complex and require special thinking and special tools for study. Systems managers improve employee engagement. Train-wreck thinking requires a great deal of work but very little thinking at all.

Evaluating individuals alone and attempting to control individual behaviors is an incomplete and ineffective strategy for performance improvement. Train-wreck managers' approach creates more variation and less effective solutions.

Note the thinking here: problems are caused by people who don't do their job well, so finding someone to blame is the first step to correcting problems. Scholtes notes: "The era of management that began in the mid-1800s can be characterized as "management by results"....Since managers could no longer do the work themselves or direct others in the doing of the work, managers exercised their authority by holding people accountable for results....In the 1950s, management by results reached its epitome in MBO (Management By Objectives) and performance appraisal, the Harvardization of train-wreck management." (Scholtes, 1998)

Studying the parts of a system will not help develop knowledge about the results of their interactions and the emergence of new knowledge that is the result of those interactions - One property of a system is "emergence." Emergence will not spring from the application of parts of a system taken separately. No matter how much I learn about hydrogen and how much I learn about oxygen, studying them separately will never allow the property of "wet" to emerge. Wetness emerges from the system of two hydrogen atoms and one oxygen atom (water) – emergence comes from interactions.

Is Bad Behavior In The System or in the Person?

We have two dogs and a cat in our family. The dogs are always hungry and if we leave anything on the floor or drop anything by accident they will devour it. They are normal.

When we first got them we already had our cat and we were used to leaving the cat food on the floor. Once the dogs arrived that proved a big mistake. Any leftover cat food was devoured when we weren't watching.

When I fed the cat I had to watch carefully and scold the dogs if they attempted to eat her food once the cat was finished. It was a waste of my time and I was often annoyed because the dogs just didn't seem to learn the command, "NO CAT FOOD FOR YOU!"

It finally dawned on me that I could feed the cat on top of the washer in the laundry room. She could easily jump up and I could leave it out in case she wanted to finish later. It was out of reach of the dogs. I realized the cat food on the floor created an environment that encouraged poor behavior. It's the very nature of a dog to eat food available. By changing the system of feeding the cat the bad behavior stopped. I could trust the dogs again. I stopped yelling at them. My relationship with them improved. They trusted me more. They didn't shirk away whenever I came into the room.

As leaders we can often set people up for failure and unknowingly create opportunities for bad behavior. Our decisions and policies can create an environment that increases the probability of poor behavior and then act surprised and even punish the employee when they behave poorly. Performance appraisals and Pay-for-performance are two examples of policies and practices that often unwittingly create an environment of dysfunction.

How to Encourage Accountability

I love my 14 year old Acura. Although it has 280,000 miles it runs beautifully. Of course, with a 14 year old car one must expect to replace parts occasionally. One morning the front left ball joint failed and I was stranded at a park with my dogs.

Luckily I have AAA membership. I called and requested a tow. The nature of the breakdown caused the front end to be nearly touching the pavement. I cautioned the AAA agent to send the right kind of tow truck to handle such a situation. She assured me *"all our service stations are knowledgeable professional shops"*. Of course, you guessed it, when the truck arrived the driver proclaimed, *"I brought the wrong kind of truck. I will need to get a different one."* He suggested I call AAA and report the error and gain approval for him to implement the new action.

I took his advice and called AAA. When a woman answered, a different person from the original customer service representative, I realized the explanation was going to be challenging and the accountability for the error was non-existent.

It took a while but the driver returned with the correct truck and I was off to have my car repaired. On the way to the shop I was wondering how and if AAA could learn from this situation. I tried to warn the first customer service person to avoid a mistake. The mistake still happened and it caused wasted time for AAA, the tow truck driver, the towing company and the customer (me). What was the root cause(s) of the error and how could AAA learn to avoid it in the future? Unless accountability is set up into the system the answers to these questions will be elusive and the mistakes will likely reoccur.

Accountability means to be responsible and it requires four elements. First people need to be aware of the situation or problem. Second, they must understand a specific process to follow. Third, they must agree to follow the process. Finally, there must be feedback (data or consequences) which includes a measure of variation which might be described as the process failing (has more variation than expected). It is a leader's responsibility to set up the environment (or system) so that all four elements are present. Without these elements a leader just ends up blaming people for mistakes and learning is compromised.

In my story all four elements were missing. The initial customer service person was clearly un-aware of the need or the meaning of the information I provided her regarding the condition of the car and the type of truck needed. In addition, she had no clear process (I am guessing because of my impression) to handle this information or request. Third, she obviously made no agreement to follow such a process. Finally, my impression was there was no feedback loop to either her or any other customer service person regarding the mistake (of course I am guessing).

Are you setting up accountability or just blaming people for mistakes when they occur? Without accountability we steal the opportunity to optimize learning. Perhaps if there was a process to escalate the call to a supervisory level when a puzzling or challenging question was asked that might have begun to set up the accountability system in AAA. Perhaps if the telephone system was set up to quickly escalate the call, as needed, to a knowledgeable technician. Perhaps if the customer service person was trained to recognize the opportunity and to transfer the call, the second element of accountability would be met. Perhaps if there was a feedback loop to report wasted time for tow truck drivers it would create the forth element of accountability. Perhaps if there was a team of knowledgeable process experts who could study the root causes and therefore modify the process or change the training processes (consequences and feedback) the mistake would not be repeated.

It is a leader's job to set up the accountability system. In the 15 years of consulting I have rarely seen an organization with robust accountability. Instead, leaders tend to look for mistakes, guess at root causes on their own, and use a performance appraisal process to punish the employee who unfortunately found him or herself in the middle of a dysfunctional system.

Train Wreck managers use phases like, *"we need to better manage our people; we need to drive improvement, or drive change; we need to manage employee performance every day."* These are all consistent with the Frederick Taylor model which holds that employees need to be managed. Let's change our paradigm. To begin to do that let's change our language. Let's start encouraging and facilitating self-management.

Self-management means helping everyone to focus on the improvement of their interactions. There are two steps to start facilitating self-management. First, we must draw a distinction between interpersonal interactions and system interactions. Interpersonal interactions are one-on-one communications with co-workers and/or customers. System interactions are the bits of information that pass between people in a process. I call these "hand offs." Discussing issues or having a conflict with another is an interpersonal interaction. A new sales order is a hand off between a sales person and operations. Employees can manage both their interpersonal interactions and they can manage their individual hand offs. They don't need a manager to help them with either one. They can manage the quality, speed, efficiency, effectiveness of all their interactions. They can take responsibility for their behaviors and for the quality and speed of information they process. Some employees may not be fully ready to manage these on their own. This is where managers can help them by facilitating and coaching. They can facilitate improvement by identifying and removing barriers to self-management. They can coach by providing feedback on specific behaviors for the purpose of learning new behaviors and breaking old habits.

Therefore the second step in self-management is to give "Fearless Feedback." Instead of "working on employee performance" we need to provide immediate, respectful, and accurate feedback. When employees are behaving in ways that damage trust or in ways that prevent learning, they need to know. If they are building trust or learning, they need to be appreciated. It sounds so simple and it is not easy because it requires discipline.

Dr. W. Edwards Deming said 94% of the problems are in the system. If this is true we should spend at least 94% of our time on improving the system if we want to optimize.

Furthermore Deming encourages cooperation between the parts of the system and discourages competition. We can assume that people will naturally cooperate if we set up an environment that encourages it. We can also assume when people have poor behaviors (those that damage trust and learning) it is probably because they are experiencing frustrations because the system is not optimized and they are not able to experience joy in their work. The system that creates barriers to achieving joy in work will create frustrations. These frustrations increase the probability of poor behavior. It becomes a cycle of dysfunction but the root cause is in the system not the people.

There are numerous consultants making a very good living helping employees to deal with "difficult people." These consultants teach techniques that address the symptoms of the dysfunction and not the root cause. They are like drug dealers who sell pain killers for migraines. The pain goes away temporarily but the root cause of the headache remains.

The behaviors of the "difficult people" are "red flags" indicating problems in the system interactions. The key is to deliver and receive fearless feedback at all times. Fearless feedback can create total responsibility and accountability to improve and correct both interpersonal interactions and system interactions.

Leaders can begin to facilitate self-management by helping everyone understand the distinction between interpersonal interactions and system interactions and then encouraging respectful feedback on both. It is estimated the average manager spends nearly 30% of their time managing poor performers and correcting their mistakes. Imagine how much more profit could be generated if we freed up this valuable management time. We can do that if we stop trying to manage employees and begin to facilitate self-management. We can change our language first. We can stop looking for flaws in people and start looking for the flaws in the system.

I was facilitating a train-the-trainer program for a client. He was to be trained to deliver a two day customer service program. A requirement of the training process is to deliver a series of presentations of the materials. He had about 3 weeks' time to study the materials. Hus first presentation to me I would rate as average in delivery, knowledge, and enthusiasm. As we watched the video together I could see glimpses of exceptional skills but there was a barrier. There was something holding him back. There was something that didn't seem authentic in his delivery.

After asking him a series of questions he and I were able to determine that his method of studying of the materials and his method for accessing the information during the presentation were not serving him. These two methods were distracting him from his main purpose of facilitating the learning for the students. The material required high quality facilitation skills and did not require memorization. He assumed it did. The materials, when sent to him originally, left the impression that the presentations needed to be memorized. In my opinion it's too difficult to memorize the material and deliver it with authenticity. We discussed his method of study and his method of accessing the materials. His attitude was transformed from hesitant to enthusiastic.

He agreed to use the new methods to prepare that very evening. The next day he delivered a professional, compelling, and authentic presentation. Our synergistic discussion of the video recording of his first presentation uncovered the real root cause. The flaw was not in him, his character, his personality, or his characteristics. It was in the way the material was originally presented by us and interpreted by him. That flaw led to a flawed method of study and an inadequate method of accessing the materials during the presentation. Once these insights were uncovered he was able to make a huge improvement and went from discouragement to engagement and enthusiasm. The key is to begin to look for the flaws in the system and to stop looking for flaws in the people.

Dr. W. Edwards Deming's theory of Profound Knowledge offers our best hope for our future. He taught us that there will always be variation and we must be able to manage that variation with knowledge of the system. He helped us to appreciate how to accumulate knowledge. He helped us to appreciate the differences between people and not treat them as widgets in an assembly line. I believe we have learned an outdated leadership model and we need to learn a new one.

The Values and System Leadership Model (W. Edwards Deming-Based Model Focusing on Trust and Engagement to Support Six Sigma / LEAN Organizations) forms the foundation for the replacement performance appraisal. The replacement appraisal moves the organization to move closer to self-organization and self-management.

Self-management means helping everyone to focus on the improvement of their own interactions. For self-management to begin everyone must understand the distinction between interpersonal interactions and system interactions. Everyone must then receive fearless feedback on those interpersonal interactions and system interactions.

When I was young I had a reading disorder that held me back in school and reading at high rates of speed. I was a very slow reader. I could get by with a little extra effort and re-reading some books over and over. Today, with the flow of information growing exponentially, it is practically impossible for me to stay fully informed unless I can read at high speed with high comprehension. To survive in this new world of information I had to develop new skills. I had to evolve.

Our leadership skills today are in a similar place. In the industrial age we could use command and control skills. They served us well. In his time, Henry Ford needed to hire people with little or no education. Those were the only people available. Our management systems were created to deal with people with little or no education. We needed to tell them what to do. We needed to command their commitment and control their actions. The world has change. We need to grow up. We need to evolve to survive and thrive.

As we have already discussed in chapters 3 and 4 our schools are based on this outdated model. Teachers, administrators, and curriculum developers know what is best of our children. Recently this way of thinking has gotten to the level of the ridiculous where even parents' discernment is less valuable than school administrators and bureaucrats. Schools have zero tolerance policies for drawing guns in art class. The bureaucrats decide that teaching sex education and tolerance for alternative life styles to grade school children. Even the reporting of pregnancies and requests for abortion services are hidden from parental advice in some schools. Aren't these examples of Frederick Taylor Scientific Management i.e. the school bureaucrats know what is best for your children?

A better approach is offered by W. Edwards Deming and the System of Profound Knowledge. Deming offers the opportunity for everyone to participate in the improvements in quality and speed. Deming is our evolution for business and management.

Chapter 6:
It's Like Night and Day: The Very Different Beliefs that Lead to Very Different Methods

Aim of this Chapter: Clarify the typical assumptions which justify the use of the typical performance appraisal and offer alternative assumptions (beliefs) to be more effective and avoid future malpractice.

The east coast was buried in a large snow storm in 2011. New Jersey Governor Chris Christie was lucky enough to be on vacation with his wife and children in Florida. Of course Florida was cold that week as well but I digress. Christie came under sharp criticism for being away from the state during this 5th largest storm in the state's history. Why would someone criticize the Governor for this? It takes a certain mindset. It takes a "Manager Dependent" mindset. We need more people with a "System Dependent" mindset.

A "Manager Dependent" mindset assumes problems can only be solved by certain people and if those people are not around problems will not be solved. This mindset is the genesis of the Talent Management movement in HR circles today. Talent Management claims *"that teams with the best people perform at a higher level."* This mindset is not only incomplete and unsophisticated it is also inconsistent with systems thinking. To be consistent with systems thinking these HR professionals would have to say instead *"teams with predictable processes and people trained to fulfill their specific roles and responsibilities within those processes can manage the variation better than any other teams."* It's not as sexy but it is more accurate in the systems It is the leader's job to create the environment to accomplish this. It is NOT the leader's responsibility to "drive the plow" in a large snow storm. If the predictable processes are clear and if people are trained to manage their roles and responsibilities doesn't the leader need to step back and let people do their jobs? Won't the people just do their work and be self-managed vs. manager dependent? This begins to describe a "system dependent" environment.

We love heroes and heroines. It is exciting to see a person step up and solve a problem in an emergency. It is dramatic. It is fun to celebrate the success with rewards and parades afterward. Let's just be clear, when emergencies occur it is often an indication of poor leadership, poor management, and/or poor planning. Dr. W. Edwards Deming defined management as "prediction." This means to me that if a manager can't predict his/her results within a relatively narrow range then they are not using tools available to them. They are not doing their job.

Evidence of a Manager Dependent environment:

- Decisions are delayed waiting for the boss and/or the boss is a micro manager.
- Training is seen as a waste of money and time (or secondary to the work that needs to be done now).
- People look for others to blame for mistakes or problems.
- People are more concerned about looking good and taking credit for quick solutions (they run from problems or hide them). This is where the heroes and heroines either emerge or disappear.
- The "favorites" are almost always those who look good or who are the heroes and heroines.
- Meetings are wasteful and seem to last forever.
- People hoard information and/or knowledge to protect their jobs or to look good.
- Customer service suffers and is secondary to what is easiest for employees to do.

Evidence of a System Dependent environment:

- Decisions are made quickly at the lowest level possible
- Employees take action to solve problems before the boss even asks
- People admit problems or mistakes to ensure the damage done is limited
- People know what to do and don't need to ask permission
- Customer Service is not only excellent but is often ground breaking and innovative
- Managers talk about systems improvement and avoid criticizing people

The environments are very different and the behaviors are therefore very different. We can therefore assume that the top talent in one environment will behave differently in the other. Therefore, it's not the talent alone that matters it is the system that matters too. In fact, it is the interaction between the talent and the system that makes the greatest difference.

Those who think Chris Christie should have been in town (or come back from vacation) to solve the snow clean-up problem are processing the situation in the "Manager Dependent" mindset. Like any mindset it creates limits or rules. Unfortunately this particular mindset also limits outcomes of performance, engagement, and creativity. It's system dependent management that can deliver the improved outcomes.

During a strategic planning process with a client I suggested the possibility the management team could improve their ability to improve processes. In an employee focus group the day before I asked the employees how they solve problems. *"What is your method of solving problems here in your organization?"* I asked. They gave me the "deer in the headlight look." During the strategic planning session with the management I asked them the same question. The CEO thought for a second and replied, *"We don't use the word process around here. We just get it done."* He continued. *"My daughter works for a large company and they have committee after committee and they never make any decisions. We make decisions. We get it done. Don't use that word 'processes' around here. We don't like it and we don't use it."* His tone was firm and somewhat harsh. He clearly assumed that "process" was not important but action was. This is a classic example of a manager dependent system based on Frederick Taylor Scientific Management thinking. Managers get things done and employees do what they are told. Furthermore, employees are evaluated based on how mangers see how well they have carried out the demands of management.

The CEO's assumption was that process improvement and process management was an example of bureaucracy and was to be avoided. Systems thinking managers know that bureaucracy and process improvement are on opposite sides of the quality improvement continuum. Employees who have the authority and autonomy to manage their own processes and to experiment using the Shewhart PDCA learning cycle (plan, do study, act) will be engaged and will reduce costs while improving quality. (Deming, The New Economics - Second Edition, 1994) Those employees who are "hand-cuffed" by bureaucracy will avoid innovation and risk taking bowing instead to waiting to see what management decides is best.

After some verbal banter with the CEO and his team, the team admitted that they had applied the PDCA to a process and it yielded positive results. Although the PDCA worked for them they had never considered the option of giving the employees autonomy to facilitate improvement with other processes without one of the managers approving and initiating it. We have all been taught a manager dependent mind set with a specific set of assumptions about people, and problems. It all starts in our schools as we have discussed in chapters 3 and 4.

Management makes policy and program decisions based on its assumptions about people. These assumptions or beliefs lie within the psyche of the managerial mind. Though not often verbalized, they leave a trail of unintended consequences. The following assumptions are the typical ones found in organizations and are the result of years of reinforcement of Frederick Taylor Scientific thinking.

These assumptions are consistent with what could be termed a command-and-control culture. This is where management attempts to control behavior and performance of individuals in order to control the performance of the organization.

Typical vs. Alternative Assumptions

To accept the replacement performance appraisal process leaders must be willing to become aware of and then examine their set of assumptions about the world, about people, and about the source of problems. Those assumptions are influencing their actions and decisions. It is important to have a clear distinction between the typical assumptions that justify the use of the typical performance appraisal and those that can allow for a replacement such as "The Complete Performance Improvement Process" (CPIP). Without this clear choice leaders will continue to avoid change and will continue with the typical appraisal.

Typical Assumption:

People are naturally lazy and therefore, need to be "motivated."Most people can't really be trusted to do their best or to put in their best efforts without some kinds of incentives to keep them moving.

Alternative Assumption:

People love learning and are therefore naturally motivated to be challenged, improve, be productive, have pride in their work, serve a higher purpose, and desire excellent relationships. Attempting to replace naturally occurring intrinsic motivations with management imposed extrinsic motivators will damage long-term engagement and quality improvement.

Descriptions of Theory X and Theory Y were introduced by Douglas McGregor in the 1950's. (Kenneth Cloke, 2002) McGregor, a professor at MIT, began to articulate a theory of management that contradicted Taylor Scientific Management. For so long

Taylor theory was predominant that psychologists began to think that the typical worker lacked the desire for decision making and natural desire for work. McGregor proposed a new theory (Theory Y) which assumed workers wanted to be useful, productive, and were motivated by things other than just job security and a living wage.

The traditional Theory X McGregor explained the average worker as naturally lazy; interested in mostly money, status, and rewards; productive only because of the presence of fear of loss of security; naturally dependent on leaders for decision making, praise for good work, and proper instructions on how to do the work (like children are dependent upon parents).

Theory Y, McGregor's new management approach, explained how people are naturally active and enjoy a challenge; they seek to build pride, achieve satisfaction, make a contribution to a higher purpose, and stimulate new challenges. Their natural desire is to learn, to achieve goals, and to make progress toward their higher purpose. They are happy to achieve extrinsic rewards and that may be part of their desire but it is usually not their main focus. They have a natural desire to seek meaning in their work and they care about improving their methods of working. To achieve those lofty goals they seek environments that provide them with choices and autonomy.

For over 60 years at least, organizations have been struggling to adopt Theory Y yet Taylor Scientific Management practices, especially in public schools and Universities, continue to perpetuate Theory X.

Typical Assumption:

People work mostly (motivated by) for money, status or rewards. To get people to be productive, to do the right things, and to be interested in the correct tasks some kinds of rewards are required. Fear is a good motivator.

Alternative Assumption:

Extrinsic cause a loss of interest in the task. Intrinsic rewards that stem from doing purposeful work are much more powerful motivators than any extrinsic reward program could possibly offer. Fear is a "mover" not a motivator.

A very common misconception is that "employee engagement can be created with extrinsic motivators." It can't. Extrinsic activities or rewards can enhance the engagement experience but they can't create it. Only the five intrinsic elements do.

In a recent online discussion with colleagues we were brainstorming all the activities needed for an engaged team. The list included almost exclusively extrinsic motivators such as offering rewards, showing movies, holding blood drives, and attending sporting events. Although these can be fun and interesting activities, they are not substitutes for the key elements of engagement which are based on intrinsic motivators. Engagement is a result of a great environment not a set of goodies doled out by management. This engaging environment cannot be created with extrinsic tricks. It requires a consistent and disciplined approach consistent with intrinsic rewards and a full commitment to values behaviors.

Typical Assumption:

The very best organizations have leaders who are obsessed with attracting and retaining the best talent

Alternative Assumption:

The very best organizations are those that continuously improve the quality and speed of the interactions between the people, departments, functions, and parts of the organization.

In the article The Talent Myth Malcolm Gladwell explains the assumptions behind the search for talent: *"The deep-seated belief that having better talent at all levels is how you outperform your competitors. This "talent mind-set" is the new orthodoxy of American management."* (Gladwell, 2002)

In our schools we are all encouraged to be working on your own. We discourage collaborating especially on tests. Collaborating on tests is considered cheating by most. However, once you get out in the "real" world, everything you do involves working with other people. Talent management is about becoming the very best through the hiring, developing, ranking, and ruthlessly evaluating with candor the very best talent. The very best parts, it is assumed, will create the very best whole.

The alternative assumption involves a very different focus. The alternative says "the very best companies are those who are obsessed with continuously improving the relationships and interactions between the parts (people)." The interactions between the parts are at least just as important, if not more important than the quality of the parts.

Enron was the ultimate "talent management" organization. The demise of Enron cost shareholders more than $11 billion. The stock went from a high of $90/share to a $1/share in just one year.

One might think we could learn from this epic business debacle but many didn't. McKinsey & Company promoted talent management in the late 1990's and Enron became the poster child for its practices. GE was also a big proponent. Of course Enron and GE were both very successful for a while. We know the story of Enron. GE was also very successful and propelled Jack Welch to celebrity status in the world of management gurus. However, GE has lost its luster too. Its stock price has gone from a high of around $50/share in 2001 when Jack Welch retired to around $15/share in 2013.

Of course there are numerous factors for these failures and one could argue that the McKinsey theory of talent management is not the major factor. However, the case can also be made that managing talent is not the most effective management theory for today's complex global economy and management guru who tries to communicate this might be mistaken for two important reasons:

- Talent management thinking is inconsistent with systems thinking and any management orthodoxy must have systems thinking at its heart to be successful in this complex world.
- Managing talent creates manager dependency which then hinders an organization's ability to adapt to change and is a barrier to optimization over the long-term.

Talent management often demands the manager rank the talent and disproportionately reward the "top" performers while "yanking" the poor performers out. They often call it "rank and yank." This policy and practice creates a high degree of competition, back-biting, cheating, hiding negative information, and all around dysfunctional behaviors. In systems thinking everyone must cooperate to optimize the system over the long-term. System thinking requires total transparency, complete integrity, and optimum cooperation. "Ranking and yanking" is consistent with short-term thinking and that often destroys the cooperation. Many say that this policy is part of the reason for Enron's demise.

Imagine building the very best car by taking the best parts from numerous different auto manufacturers and building a hybrid car from those best parts. It won't because the parts don't properly interact and therefore the car cannot operate. Therefore, as we have stated earlier, the quality of the interactions between the parts in a system is more important than the quality of the parts.

Leaders that embrace talent management assumptions believe in cultivating heroes and heroines. Heroes are needed in a chaotic system to swoop in and solve problems. Organizations who have leaders with this mind set find it difficult to be pro-active. The heroes thrive on the chaos. In a chaotic system heroes have more opportunity to shine in front of peers and management. They have more opportunity to be heroes. They perpetuate the myth of talent by solving the unexpected. Some even look for opportunities to create chaos so they can continue to "solve and shine" in front of others.

Typical Assumption

Individuals have control over the results of their work and the factors that allow them to achieve their goals.

Alternative Assumption

In a system the parts are interdependent and therefore one part can significantly influence the performance of other parts.

Water's properties of "wetness" are the emergence of the interaction between hydrogen and oxygen. These properties can only be observed when just the right amount of hydrogen interacts with the right amount of oxygen. The same is true for people in a system. Their interactions will create results that could not have been seen without the interactions that occur between them. These results emerge from the interactions and the quality of those interactions. The results cannot be accurately evaluated and interpreted without an understanding of how these interactions occur.

Typical Assumption

Managers can evaluate individual performance separate from the contributions of others and separate from the influence of the work tools and environment over an entire time period without stereotyping and not focusing on specific or recent events.

Alternative Assumption

It is impossible to accurately evaluate any part of a system outside the influence of the system because the interactions are complex and some can't be measured.

When problems seem on the surface to be "people problems", the related systems must be investigated carefully; and most often the real root causes will be found. A common travel experience is another good example of how problems with systems manifest themselves as people problems.

Not long ago, while I was traveling out of state, I received the gift of a golf club. When it came time for me to fly back home, I had forgotten to consider that post-9/11 restrictions for airplane carry-ons would not allow me to take the golf club with me on to the plane. Instead, my choices for getting it safely home were either to check it as baggage or to ship it. I chose to check it.

At the airline counter the attendant tagged the club and placed it on the baggage belt. My first thought was, "I'll never see that club again!" And just as I had anticipated, when I arrived in New York there was no golf club. I went immediately to the lost baggage department, where I waited and waited while the agent searched for the claim forms. When he finally found the forms, he asked me to fill them out describing the club in detail.

Again, I was asked to wait. At one point, the agent actually said to me, "Why didn't you ship it?" To which, my very first reaction was anger, fueled by suspicion that the club had been stolen by the baggage handlers. Also angry at his unhelpful attitude, I snapped back at the clerk. Then with claim form in hand and nothing more that I could do, I went on my way without the club or satisfaction.

Two days passed without any word from the airline, so I called the phone number on the claim form. Not surprisingly, no one answered the phone, so I left a message. No call-back came, not even the next day. At that point, I was totally convinced that the club would never be returned. To my surprise, the very next day the club arrived via FedEx delivery.

The golf club story demonstrates that when the airline's baggage handling system is unreliable, the people inside and outside of the organization suffer the consequences and waste time. So in this case, thinking in terms of the system means uncovering the reasons that the golf club did not arrive on time. Was it a common or unusual occurrence? Checking baggage today is a complex process. Checking a single, lone golf club stresses the system even more.

Learning how to think in terms of a system requires practice and patience. Once mastered, this skill allows leaders to stop blaming the people for problems. I had lost my patience and blamed the baggage handlers for my missing golf club even accusing them of theft. If I had continued to think in terms of a system, I would not have uttered disrespectful accusations.

Typical Assumption

Employees need to be motivated to do good work.

Alternative Assumption

People are naturally motivated to learn and to do good work and they just need an environment that encourages those behaviors.

The typical performance appraisal attempts to control behavior through a set of responses from a combination of rewards and punishments (the carrot and stick) and this suggests managers can't really trust employees to do the right thing without these control practices. Performance management is really just a sophisticated procedure for creating the "correct" responses.

Typical Assumption

Managers know the answers and make the decisions. They listen to problems and find solutions.

Alternative Assumption

Managers are facilitators. They create environments that allow employees to regularly experiment to find new solutions on their own.

Many organizations still depend upon management to create solutions for problems and many employees have been trained to ask for permission to take action instead of asking for forgiveness for taking actions that turn out to be mistakes. Toyota's four principles employees follow to work toward improvement create an environment of experimentation. (Stephen Spear, 1999, September - October) Managers in this type of environment are facilitators not inspectors. They are servants not bosses.

Adopting the alternative assumptions creates a safe environment for open and honest communication. A safe environment encourages people to naturally cooperate. As a result, blame and negativity are reduced and people tell the truth. People feel trusted and respected and individual behaviors change.

General Motors provides a good example. In 1982, GM closed its Fremont, California plant in 1982 because, of all of its plants, it had the worst record for: employee absenteeism, productivity, quality and morale. Then in 1983, Toyota and GM agreed to re-open the plant under two major conditions: one, that the plant would be managed by Japanese-trained leaders; and, two, 85% of all previously employed United Auto Workers would be re-hired.

By 1991, that same plant, renamed NUMMI (New United Motors Manufacturing Inc.) had catapulted from having the worst track record to having the best in all the areas in which it had previously failed. What made the difference? The change simply cannot be explained using conventional management wisdom, which typically blames the people. The people once part of the failure became part of the success. The explanation lies in new a leadership style that used influence to change the methods that in turn changed the environment to produce positive results.

Many organizations approach improvement as follows:

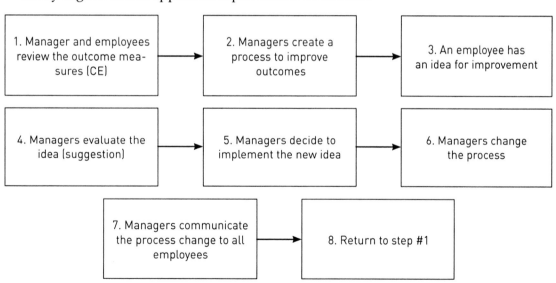

This approach perpetuates a manager dependent environment. It keeps the power at thee top but it comes with serious unintended consequences namely lower employee engagement.

An alternative approach is:

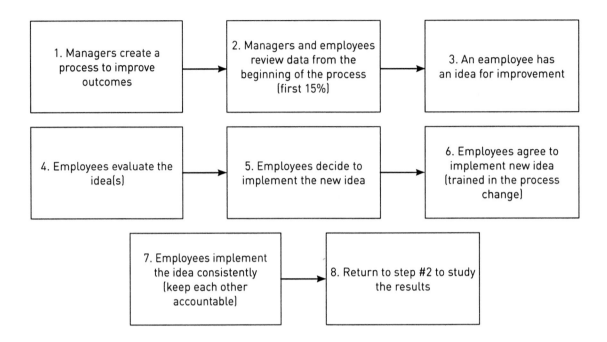

Here employees directly participate in the decisions that impact their work. Furthermore, by asking them to take an active role in changes in the process there is a higher probability they will own the changes and therefore be more con0sistent (less variation) in their actions. By owning the decisions they will also have a higher probability of holding their peer accountable to the decisions they make as a team.

A summary of thoughts about optimization and the assumptions:

- Even if a mistake was human error, if any other person could have made the same mistake, then correcting or punishing that person still does not solve the problem and prevent it in the future.

- An example of a system-dependent method of preventing errors (not a memory dependent method) – *The little screen that pops up when you delete a file on a computer. It asks you ..."Are you sure you want to delete this file?"*

- Optimization is an orchestration not a state of being. By optimizing the system or working on the system you are collecting data to identify the variation so you can predict what will happen and you choose to act in a way that offers the best probability of success. It is all about probabilities not certainties.

- Treating everyone the same to achieve fairness is patently unfair because everyone is different and individuals have different needs and desires. You might have someone who is brilliant and who does not have to put in effort to achieve their goals. You might have another person you works very hard to achieve only part of their goal. What are you really measuring?

- The interactions in a system are very complex. Your heart needs the muscles of your body to be in good shape so you can exercise to keep your heart in good shape, yet the heart must be in good shape to allow the muscles to be exercised to keep the heart in good shape.

When organizations begin to recognize the ineffectiveness and damaging effects of their appraisal system, they usually embark on fixing it. Usually the "fixing" focuses on one of two areas: (1) improving the design of the process (e.g. new criteria, new scales, more interaction, more raters, and more frequent appraisals) or (2) improving the implementation (e.g., better training, stricter rules to ensure timely execution, checking raters for consistency and bias tendencies). These improvement initiatives do little to help because the problem with appraisal is neither in the design or implementation. Rather, it is beneath the surface in the form of underlying assumptions. Unless the underlying assumptions change, there is no hope for any typical performance appraisals process to actually work with predictable results.

Chapter 7:
How Deming Was a Top Steward for Systems Thinking

Aim of this Chapter: Add credibility for the replacement leadership model by demonstrating how Dr. W. Edwards Deming set the stage for all of us to avoid this leadership malpractice.

The word "manager" in the dictionary is explained as someone who is responsible for controlling or administering activities. When we think of "manager" we tend to think about the management of people. This definition of manager is consistent with Frederick Taylor Scientific Management. For Taylor "people" were to be controlled or administered.

Pay-for-performance and performance appraisal policies are designed to control behaviors. People really can't be controlled. We can make laws and policies and yet still see poor or illegal behaviors. In my State of Connecticut it's illegal to drive and talk on a cell phone. Every day I see someone breaking this law. The existence of the law alone will not control this behavior. Something else needs to happen.

According to the research of Kenneth Cloke and Joan Goldsmith managers' role and responsibilities emerged from the rise of slavery. (Cloke & Goldsmith, 2002) Managers were needed to force action of because of the lack of their motivation of the slaves. Managers were needed to safe guard the owners" property and to "motivate" the slaves to perform tasks. Without managers there was no control and without control work was not accomplished. With slavery comes manager dependency.

Dr. W. Edwards Deming had a different way of thinking about the role and responsibilities for managers. He wanted us to use the word "prediction" to describe their role. A process facilitator will, if he/she does their job, will be able to make predictions and predictions are very valuable to a successful organization. Unpredictability is much more costly and much more challenging for delivering good customer value.

For Deming control was not a strategy, it was an outcome. Deming's manager must identify and influence factors that impact the variation. Deming would say a manager's job is to be able to predict what a process(s) will do. A manager therefore improves predictability and reduces drama. A manager is therefore a proactive "Process Facilitator" and makes processes easier and more predictable. A facilitator makes tasks easier or removes barriers preventing the desired results. The Deming manager is part of a team which cooperates to achieve a shared purpose and shared objectives.

If the Deming manager does not control he/she must therefore become a leader. This is why Deming discusses a transformation of management in The New Economics. (Deming, The New Economics - Second Edition, 1994) Deming managers create an environment where people can manage themselves and where they cooperate to manage the variation in the system or the organization. A Deming manager/leader helps people achieve their full potential through inspiration, vision, and intrinsic motivation. Therefore, a Deming manager facilitates a release in human potential or organizational effectiveness.

In 1847 Hungarian-born physician Ignaz Semmelweis, while working at an obstetrics unit in Vienna was astonished and concerned with the frequency of child fatalities that occurred after birth assisted by medical students. The rate of child death was 10-20 time s higher than those that occurred with births assisted by midwives.

Semmelweis' concern motivated him to do a meticulous examination of the clinical practices. He discovered that the medical students who assisted in childbirth often did so after performing autopsies on patients who had died from bacterial infections. The medical students were unknowingly passing on the bacterial infections to the mothers and the children. Semmelweis instituted a strict policy of hand-washing with a chlorinated antiseptic solution and the mortality rates dropped by 10- to 20-fold within 3 months.

Semmelweis used a problem solving process that exemplifies Deming's System of Profound Knowledge Theory. He had a theory. He collected data to test the theory. He made a change to the processes. He generated significant improvement. He didn't blame people. He didn't try to control people. He didn't threaten, evaluate, or criticize people. He used a sound scientific problem solving method. This is exemplary of a Deming manager. Deming wanted management to work on improving the system in order to optimize that system over-time. He wanted managers to provide joy and pride for employees while they continuously adding value to customers. He wanted managers to question prevailing theory. He wanted management to be able to predict. Deming created his System of Profound Knowledge (SoPK) to help managers to accomplish this.

Deming believed that management needed a transformation and that first step in that transformation was the transformation of the individual. (Deming, The New Economics - Second Edition, 1994)   He explained how a manager who understands the key elements of SoPK could then apply those same principles to achieve significant positive results just as Semmelweis did.

There are four parts to SoPK: 1) Appreciation for a System; 2) Understanding Variation; 3) The Theory of Knowledge; 4) Theory of Psychology. All four parts work together as one system to produce the significant results. Taken separately they may help managers make some improvements but they will never produce significant results unless they are applied together as a system. Managing the parts of the system destroys the purpose, or aim of that system.   It takes tremendous discipline to apply all four parts. It requires a transformation. Many are unwilling to put in the effort.   Here is a description of the different parts of SoPK.

The Theory - Deming's Profound Knowledge
The Foundation for Transformation with a Summary of Principles

#1 Appreciation for a System description: *A system is a network of interdependent components that work together to try to accomplish an aim. A system must have an aim - management sets the aim with input everyone must understand the aim. At least 94% of troubles and possibilities for improvement belong to the system not the people. Improving the system is management's responsibility because employees cannot do it while they are working in the system. Management's job is to optimize the entire system over time through innovation and continuous improvement. To improve a system one must focus on the first 15%. 85% of the impact is in the first 15%. Loyal customers are the ideal outcome of the optimized system.*

#2.Theory of Variation description: *There is variation in everything. Variation is the "voice" of the system or process. One must use statistics to make the variation visible (patterns and types of variation). Managers must use control charts to distinguish between special causes and common causes of variation in order to know when to act and when not to act. Managers must manage the variation in the different processes in the system to improve quality and to optimize the system over time*

#3.Theory of Knowledge description: *Management is prediction. Managers must take time to ask, "What theory am I using to address this problem." It's often not what we don't know that holds us back; it is what we know for sure that is totally useless that prevents us from solving problems. Information is relative so we need to continually align on specific definitions. Learning happens with the use of the scientific method of Plan, Do, Study, Act.*

#4.Theory of Psychology description: *Managers must drive out fear and build trust. Managers must recognize differences in people and use such differences to optimize the system. People want to do a good job, to contribute , to have pride and joy in their work and they deserve those things. We must teed to tap into intrinsic motivation (self-esteem, dignity and desire to learn) and de-emphasize the extrinsic motivators.*

SoPK is holistic which means it has a greater value when implemented as a system. The whole is greater than the sum of its parts. Each part is necessary and inseparable if we want to achieve optimum results. The aim of SoPK is to optimize the system over the long-term. SoPK provides a "lens" through which management can view an organization and therefore better understand the interrelationships between the parts of the system. By understanding the interrelationships in an organization we can better optimize the results and optimize the parts.

Deming's SoPK is comprehensive and is a much more useful leadership model than the Taylor Scientific Management model for our current knowledge economy. Without SoPK the Complete Performance Improvement Process (CPIP), the replacement for the typical performance evaluation, would probably not have been created. SoPK can help leaders to avoid malpractice and it forms the foundation for CPIP.

Appreciation for a system

I was asked to conduct training in Dallas on a Friday. I needed to take a flight Thursday evening in order to start the training on time early Friday morning. Because the training was all day (9-5 PM) the only return flight I could take was at 7 PM Friday night and it was the last flight out. The time difference (Dallas is Central Time and Connecticut is Eastern Time) prevented the airlines from having a flight out later than 7 PM.

The training location was 30 minutes from the airport. I was concerned about leaving the training and dealing with Friday night traffic. I needed to return a rental car, have time to clear airline security, and run to my gate. It was going to be close. I called the client, explained my challenges, and asked if we could start the training earlier that Friday (8:30 AM instead of 9 AM) to alleviate some of my concerns. He agreed.

I arrived at the training location 7:30 AM Friday morning to set-up the room and materials. I was expecting 20 attendees. At 8:30 I had only one person. I called the client and asked him what was happening. Where were the other attendees? He called me back and apologized. Apparently the other manager told everyone to arrive by 9 AM not 8:30.

The participants arrived at 9 AM. Now I am 30 minutes behind. The "other" manager arrived and wanted to make announcements and also chit chats. By the time we started it was almost 9:30. Now I am nearly 1 hour behind. The original program was for 2 full days. I had already compressed it into one day to accommodate their budget and their logistics. Now I am one hour behind on a program that has already been significantly shortened. I knew this would impact the quality of the training (the expected behavioral changes of the participants) in ways that could not be measured.

I facilitated the training day and covered all the material . I finished cleaning up at about 4:45 PM and realized I better hustle. On the way to the airport I hit some Friday night traffic and at that moment decided I did not have time to put in the fuel even though I knew I would suffer a $50 penalty for not returning the car with a full tank. I knew the traffic was going to delay me. I knew I needed extra time to return the rental car and take the shuttle bus to the terminal. I also knew I needed extra time to clear security. I was extra nervous because missing the flight would not only cause me stress at home, it would cost much more for the client if I needed to expense another hotel stay.

I skipped the re-fueling, caught the bus, cleared the security and caught the plane. I put the $50 penalty charge on my expense report to the client. Two weeks later I received a call. The client refused to pay the $50 charge. They told me I should have planned ahead to have more time to re-fuel. What is the root cause of the extra $50 re-fueling charge? Was it my lack of planning or the lack of communication within the client organization? The lack of effective communication in the very beginning of the entire planning process created a chain reaction which resulted in greater cost and lower quality.

Managers who do not appreciate how a system works will look at events and assign blame. The accounting department in my client's company looked at the $50 charge and saw me being irresponsible. Actually, I was optimizing the situation and I could make the case that I avoided a probable higher cost because I caught the flight and avoided a hotel night which would have been even more costly.

Managers who don't appreciate a system use linear thinking to assign a cause. Those who appreciate a system will understand that the first 15% of the process generates 85% of the results. The result was an extra $50 charge by the car rental company but the first

15% of the process that led to that charge was the poor communication between the two managers. In this case, the first 15% included my conversation with the client about the planning of the training day. He and I both failed to realize there were other people other than the participants who needed to be involved with our planning process. We failed to include the other manager who remained uninformed about the importance of the 8:30 AM start. If we had included her she would have communicated the 8:30 AM start correctly and all this "waste" would have been avoided.

The typical manager, with the typical performance appraisal, will look at events in a linear way and grade the employee for the results (assign blame for the extra $50). Managers who appreciate a system (systems thinking) ask different questions including, what is the first 15% of this poor result, what process(s) was involved, and what can we do together to learn and change the process?

I was able to convince the client to pay the $50 fee. It took time to explain. This entire experience was wrought with wasted time and wasted effort. Furthermore, the quality of the learning experience was impacted by the mistakes made in the first 15% of this planning process. There is way to measure this loss.

A powerful tenant of SoPK is that 94% of the results come from the system and not from the effort of the people. We can see how this concept applies in this story. The quality of the discussion with the client needs to improve. A question in the planning process that reads, "Are there any others who need to be involved or communicated to about this plan?" would have helped avoid this waste. One small change to a planning check-list might have avoided this issue. To "grade" an employee on their performance appraisal is a management technique that makes no sense when we begin to appreciate a system.

In 1950 Deming was invited by the Japanese Union of Scientists and Engineers (JUSE) to lecture on quality to engineers and top management. (Aquayo, 1990) In his first lectures over 80% of all the top leaders of organizations were in attendance. He presented his famous flow diagram which was a visible representation of how an organization works as a system. It was a stark contrast to the typical organizational pyramid chart which was often shown in the United States. It demonstrates how desired outcomes, such as customer loyalty, are dependent upon the cooperation of all of the inputs. Instead of relying on central command and control a leader needed to appreciate how the system cooperates and integrates.

Japan's leaders were ready to listen. Deming predicted the Japanese would be economically competitive in 5 years. Significant results were seen in 18 months. Even today Dr. Deming's picture hangs in the lobby of Toyota headquarters in Tokyo acknowledging the significant contribution his ideas made to the success of Toyota and all of Japan.

Management's Job:
"Optimize The Entire System Over Time"

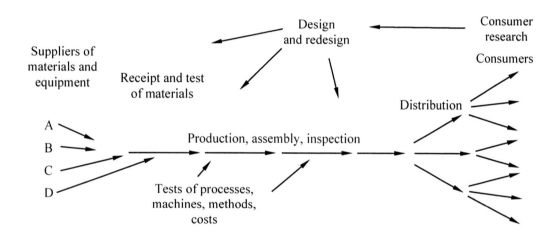

The famous flow diagram Dr. Deming took to Japan

This chart was first used in August 1950 at a conference with top management at Hotel de Yama on Mount Hakone in Japan (*Out of the Crisis, Page 4*)

Theory of Variation

Medical malpractice is rife with misdiagnosis. Leadership malpractice is as well. Below are data for 8 workers making the same product, all working at about the same rate, for 12 weeks. Imagine you are the leader in this plant (doctor) of these workers, what do you make of these data? What would you prescribe? What is your diagnosis? (Tribus, 1990)

Flaws per worker/week

	Week 1	Week 2	Week 3	Week 4	Week 5	Week 6	Week 7	Week 8	Week 9	Week 10	Week 11	Week 12	Sum
Mary	0	0	0	0	0	0	0	0	0	0	0	0	0
Joe	0	0	0	0	0	0	0	0	0	0	0	0	0
Eva	1	0	0	2	0	0	3	0	0	1	0	0	7
Fred	0	0	0	1	0	0	2	0	0	0	0	0	3
Jim	0	0	0	0	0	0	0	0	0	0	0	0	0
Ed	0	0	0	0	0	2	0	0	0	0	0	0	2
Kate	0	0	0	0	0	0	0	0	0	0	0	0	0
Carl	0	0	0	1	0	0	0	0	0	0	0	0	1
Sum	1	0	0	4	0	2	5	0	0	1	0	0	13

What would you do? How would you go about reducing errors? What would be your approach?? Myron Tribus explains how he has presented this table to audiences across the USA, in Mexico, in Canada, in Australia, in the UK and he always got about the same reaction. People almost always suggest one of the following regarding Eva: a "good" stern talk; have Eva work alongside Mary and learn; to fire her; give her more training. In this true life example that answer is consistent with the Frederick Taylor approach of blaming an individual for a system issue. All the variation came from the system and not the people. These errors are caused by the overall system and not the people.

Deming describes two types of mistakes that leaders can make, 1) to act when they should NOT act and 2) NOT act when they should. We can know when to act if we collect data and create a control chart. A control chart is a method to display data to help managers predict when to act and when not to act. Data points that fall between the control limits in the control chart are called common cause variation. This variation in data all comes from the system itself. Data points that fall outside the control limits indicate special causes of variation. These indicate some special or unique event of factor that causes excessive variation in the process.

Think about how long it takes you to travel to your office everyday (drive, walk, ride your bike etc.). What is the average time? Is there a great deal of variation in this process or can you predict (with accuracy) how long the trip will take? If you can predict the amount of time with fair accuracy, the process (or route you take) is probably stable. A stable process is one that has a specific capability. It can be used to make a prediction. By collecting data and plotting it onto a "control chart" a leader can begin to manage the variation in a process. A Control chart is used to monitor the variation in a process. Properly collected data are plotted on a run chart and certain limits are calculated. Data points that fall within the limits (upper and lower control limits) indicate common cause variation or random variation. Any points that fall outside these limits indicate a major change to the system.

Let's assume it takes a person 41 minutes to travel from home to his/her work in the morning. It is not always exactly 41 minutes, 41 minutes is the average. There is always going to be some variation. This variation comes from various factors that occur in the route that person takes. These cause common cause factors might be, traffic, the time he/she leaves the house, the number of lights he/she catches as green, the weather, accidents, the day of week, holidays celebrated, etc. These common causes create expected variation. If all times fall between the upper control limit and the lower control limit the process is referred to as "stable." Being stable doesn't necessarily equal "good." It just means predictable (within the limits). Here is 30 days of travel data going to work in the graph "Travel Time to Work."

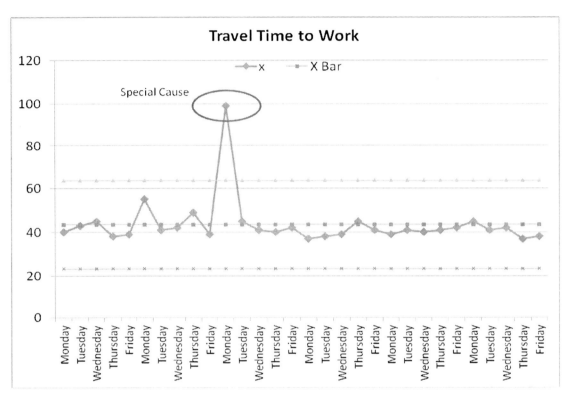

Here the upper control limit is 63 minutes and the lower limit is 24 minutes. If the system was stable we could expect all days of travel to take between 24 minutes and 63 minutes. But, on the third Monday the time was nearly 100 minutes. Ouch! This is a "special cause." Something must have influenced the time, something outside the system, something special. Perhaps it was an accident on the highway and the State Police shut down the highway to clean up the oil spill caused by the overturned truck.

It's the manager's job to create a control chart to identify special causes and common causes especially with the management of people. Deming explains that the most important contribution control charts can make is with the management of people. (Deming, The New Economics - Second Edition, 1994) To avoid this special cause in the future requires special action. Perhaps the worker might want to check with the State Police each morning in order to avoid any future road closures.

Assuming there are no overturned trucks (or special causes) the only way to create a consistent shift in travel time is to change something about the system. Any attempt by the driver to reduce the individual daily times will not create significant improvement and will NOT produce significant improvement (value will remain within the control limits) and may create a safety issue.

Now, let's discuss Eva and the "Flaws per Worker/Week" data. Remember, most viewing this data suggested Eva was the problem. However, when we review the control charts we see a different perspective. There are NO special causes. Eva is NOT a special cause. The errors are all common causes which mean the factors creating the errors all came from the system and not the people.

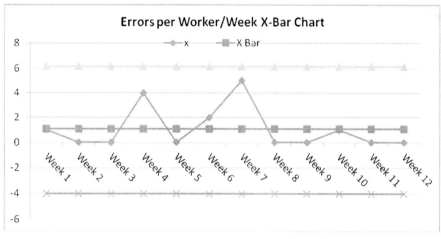

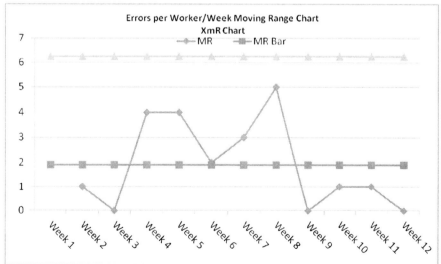

All data points are within the control limits. Any attempt to help Eva to change is probably a waste of time and effort because all the factors that cause the errors come from the overall system within which all the people work. The system influenced Eva's performance harder than the others. She is not a "special cause." Treat her differently makes no sense with this system perspective.

This is a transformational insight for most managers. The typical manager wants to create a linear connection between the errors and Eva. They want to pair Mary with Eva in an effort to re-train Eva. These actions reveal an inability to understand variation. When we use the typical performance appraisal we are also demonstrating our inability to understand a system and our inability to understand variation.

Why do we need to manage variation?

There is variation in every process. The key is to manage the variation to minimize waste, reduce losses, lower costs, and optimize overall performance. The greater the variation from the desired values in a process the greater the loss. This is elegantly represented best by the Taguchi Loss Function.

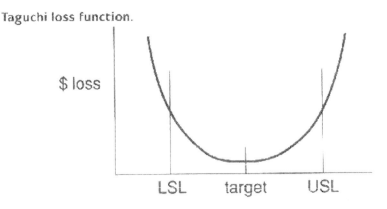

Taguchi loss function.

Consider the number of high-school dropouts. Over their lifetime they typically will earn hundreds of thousands of dollars less than high school graduates. Over 50% of the prison population is high school dropouts. The obvious desired result is 100% of the students graduate in order to reduce prison populations. Any variation from that outcome increases the loss and cost to society. The target is 100% graduation rates. Any variation from that target will create great loss to society. The Taguchi Loss function has a steep curve upward indicating that sharp increase in loss as the variation from target increases.

Leaders who continue to use the typical performance appraisal without the use of control charts get stuck. They remain unwilling or unable to recognize that variation occurs in every process and they continue to see all mistakes (or any variation from their expectations) as avoidable.

Common cause variation is not caused by any one special event. Instead it is the "voice" of the system the way the system is currently operating. If a leader wants to improve common cause variation he/she must study the process using quality improvement tools and make decisions based on knowledge of the system. This often requires a process improvement team because processes are complex and they are interdependent with other processes in the system. A change in one process can cause an impact (unintended negative consequences) in another process. Leaders that make small changes to process with the intention to make improvements can actually make things worse unless they take the time to study the entire process.

Changing situations can create a special cause. Those who do not appreciate the need to manage variation will often make demands on the system that cannot be achieved. For example, the Federal Government has demanded certain automobile mileage standards to the automobile industry. Just demanding the new standards does not take into account how the system must change to improve the mileage standards. Recent demands by State Governments in New England to reduce green-house gases by meeting specific emissions goals has failed. Why? The leaders did not understand the system and did not understand variation. Furthermore, some studies have shown how these CAFÉ standards actually have increased the loss of human life. (Coon, 2001)

As a trainer I know that a training process can deliver certain outcomes if the process is followed correctly and if the venue supports the training. If a client asks (or demands) that I deliver the usual one-day process in one half day I have to evaluate my ability to generate the same outcomes. Very often I must say "no" to the client request unless they wish to settle for less of an outcome or unless I have enough time to redesign the training process. Even if I redesign the training I cannot predict the outcomes until I conduct a test and measure the success.

The key is to make every attempt to become aware of the variation in the processes and manage that variation. This requires the collection of data and the presentation of that data in a control chart.

Managing variation improves quality, profitability, and, shareholder value. Companies that manage variation well can bring new products to market more quickly, with minimal errors, can produce high-quality products with minimal rework, and can grow customer loyalty faster. Variation can increase all eight types of waste as detailed by Toyota:

1. Waste from over production.
2. Waste from waiting time.
3. Transportation waste.
4. Processing waste.
5. Inventory waste.
6. Waste of motion.
7. Waste from product defects.
8. Waste of under-utilization of people skills and capabilities

Waste in any form damages profitability, employee engagement, and customer loyalty. The ability to manage variation in work is a critical competency for all managers and leaders. This skill must be taught to all employees to enable an organization to survive long-term.

Most companies talk a good game about the importance of producing high-quality products and services at a low cost, but few use control charts effectively and very few use control charts to help manage people.

Too often, managers are reactive by fixing problems after they have already been created instead of using control charts to make predictions and thereby knowing when to act and when not to act. The typical managers pretend to be "omniscient problem solvers" deciding quickly what he/she thinks are the answers to the variation. This approach often makes things worse.

For example, a superintendent of a school might decide to invest resources to minimize variation. He/she will want 100% of grade school students to go home with the correct parents, the correct authorized care-giver (such as grandparents etc.), or board the correct bus back home. Minimizing variation to ensure all children arrive home safely is one of the most important things a superintendent can do.

On the other hand, a superintendent may not wish to invest resources to minimize the variation on the percentage of grade school students who attend gym class each week. Once the percentage reaches 98% the resources required to improve this number may not be worth the investment. It is all about optimization. Optimization means you are managing the variation to the best of your ability with the resources available and with the minimal amount of waste. Optimization means the process is as effective as possible with the existing variation.

Without an understanding of variation and without the use of a control charts the actions taken (or not taken) by leaders can cause injury and become malpractice.

Theory of Knowledge

Once we understand the difference between information, knowledge, and wisdom it is amazing how much confusion we see in others. I prefer to use the definitions put forth by Russell Ackhoff and Daniel Greenberg in his book *Turning Learning Right Side Up*. (Russell L. Ackhoff, 2008) Here are some of the key definitions.

- Data: symbols that represent properties of objections and/or events
- Information: data processed to make it useful
- Knowledge: answers "how-to" questions which enable predictions
- Understanding: answers "why" questions or explanations giving reasons for behavior
- Wisdom: takes into account the short-term and long-term consequences of actions. (Russell L. Ackhoff, 2008)

We are in the knowledge economy. We are evolving out of the industrial age economy and evolving into the knowledge age economy. The industrial age was labor based. The knowledge age economy is rising to dominance based on the new ways it creates and exploits knowledge; in other words, it is brain based rather than labor based. (Toffler, 1995) SoPK explains how knowledge is necessary to make predictions. It explains how knowledge is built on theory and without theory there can be no knowledge. This is an enormously important point for leaders and this is why this issue was described with some detail in Chapter 6 where we discussed the different beliefs between systems thinking and Taylor Scientific Management thinking. A set of beliefs can represent a theory. If we change the theory we change the methods which change the results. The new theory will yield new knowledge.

Studying the parts of a system will not yield knowledge about the system. Studying a tire will tell us little about the performance of the automobile system because we can't study the interactions in the automobile system when the tire is separated from it. The typical performance appraisal attempts to study and evaluate the individual employee separate from the system interactions. It does not include a study of the interactions between the individual and the system.

One property of a system is "emergence." Emergence will not occur during the evaluation of one of the parts of a system. Emergence of new knowledge can only occur during the evaluation of the interactions between the individual and the system. The emergence of this new knowledge is a competitive advantage for the entire organization. No matter how much I learn about hydrogen and how much I learn about oxygen, studying them separately will never allow the property of "wet" to emerge. Wetness emerges from the system of two hydrogen atoms and one oxygen atom (water). The emergence of "wet" comes from interactions between the parts. So it is with individuals in a system. Knowledge emerges when we study the system. Knowledge remains hidden when we study only the parts of the system.

We need shared operational definitions in order to have knowledge

I was fortunate enough to land a training job in Hawaii a few years ago. After the training was completed I wanted to play golf and so started out early one morning to the famous golf course resort Kapalua. I was anxious to get to the course because I was so excited and appreciative to be in Hawaii. How many times does one get to be in Hawaii and in addition, play golf at one of the most beautiful courses in the world? As luck might have it I got stuck behind a driver who was traveling at 23 miles per hour in a 25 mph zone. I grew impatient quickly.

After about 10 minutes of frustration I was delighted to see a sign ahead reading 45 mph. Furthermore, the road was widening from 2 lanes to four. Jubilation! As soon as there was enough room I sped around my "slow friend" and accelerated to 45 mph. At the top of the hill a policeman holding a radar gun waved me over. What could he possibly want? I was doing the speed limit? Was he reading my mind when I was thinking the bad thoughts about my "slow driving friend?"

He asked for my license and registration and I asked, *"What's the problem officer?"* He said, *"You were speeding."* I protested saying I was sure I was doing only 45 mph in a 45 mph zone. He said, *"You were doing 45 mph before you reached the sign."* I continued to complain. *"Officer, I could see the sign. Isn't that enough to allow me to do the limit."* He said, *"No! In our State you have to physically reach the sign and pass it before you accelerate to the limit. That will be $85 please. Have a nice day."*

The officer and I had different definitions for the term speeding. In his definition any acceleration to 45 mph prior to reaching the sign was speeding. In my definition, as soon as I could read the sign I was allowed the 45 mph. Which definition was right? In this case, his was of course. He had the knowledge. He could predict. I had an incorrect understanding and a different theory. My knowledge was flawed.

Deming called evaluation of performance a deadly disease. (Deming, Out of the Crisis, 1986)

> *It nourishes short-term performance, annihilates long-term planning, builds fear, demolishes teamwork, and nourishes rivalry and politics. It leaves people bitter, crushed, bruised, battered, desolate, despondent, dejected, feeling inferior, some even depressed, unfit for work for weeks after receipt of rating, unable to comprehend why they are inferior. It is unfair, as it ascribes to the people in a group differences that may be caused totally by the system that they work in. (Deming, Out of the Crisis, 1986)*

Because the appraisal is based on a different theory, to those who embrace Taylor Scientific Management the typical appraisal is an effective management practice. In the mind of a manager who embraces SoPK it is a deadly disease. A different theory will give a different perspective. A more useful theory for the knowledge age will support the replacement of the typical performance appraisal.

Theory of Psychology

I use Google Alerts to search the web and send me articles about performance evaluations. Nearly every day I receive an article or blog entitled something like "How to Conduct an Effective Appraisal Meeting." It usually starts out with a sentence explaining how everyone dislikes conducting an appraisal but if the reader will only follow the author's advice everything will work great. The author then typically goes on to describe his or her "secret solutions" for making the appraisal meeting effective. These articles are a complete waste of time because, as stated in the previous few paragraphs, the theory upon which they are founded is flawed.

One could write an article about "how to effectively drive a car that has two flat tires" but no one would read it because no one would want to do it? It's not safe, it's not relevant, and it's not necessary to learn that. No one wants to conduct a typical performance appraisal meeting either mostly because it also has "two flat tires" (metaphorically speaking). These two flaws include the grade given to the employee by the manager about his or her performance and the pay-for-performance policy tied to that grade. Giving advice about how to conduct a meeting that is systemically flawed, like the typical performance appraisal, makes as much sense as learning how to drive a car with two flat tires.

A new client told me how he nearly quit his new job twice in the past month. Furthermore, in that same time frame, he had talked two of his colleagues "off the quitting ledge" as well. It seems his sales department is under tremendous pressure to perform by meeting a nearly impossible stretch sales goal. The boss was referred to, by the sales people behind his back, as "Captain Bligh". "Captain Bligh" set a very high end-of-year performance goal for the entire team. He translated this end-of-year goal into a weekly sales target for each sales person and then calculated the number of "weekly sales appointments with presentations" each salesperson needed to deliver to meet that revenue goal.

Each week "Captain Bligh" would swoop into the office, review the sales performance and the number of appointments for each sales person. He would loudly remind everyone of the goal and chastise those who were behind (in either or both the number of presentations and sales closed). He would remind them all that their bonus would be determined by their total performance and their performance appraisal rating would be determined by their weekly performance. He would them swoop back out the door.

These sales people are extremely talented, had been recruited from a list of top talent from the competition, were all highly compensated (high six figures) and yet were treated like children who needed to be threatened and prodded to "clean their rooms" and "eat their vegetables" or go without dinner. This management style usually makes performance worse over the long-term. It creates negative anxiety, reduces creative problem solving, and takes the focus off the real issues which relate to how the overall sales and marketing process is working. By focusing on the individual performance of each sales person "Captain Bligh" was actually making performance worse damaging motivation and increasing variation in the sales process. He was "flattening two tires on the sales force car" but expecting the sales people to drive at higher speeds.

Managers who use pay-for-performance to attempt to motivate highly skilled people who perform highly skilled responsibilities are applying industrial age techniques in a knowledge age world. They are making serious mistakes because these policies attempt to control behaviors and control techniques with highly educated talent are malpractice.

The Interior Department's Mineral Management Service had planned to present two safety awards at a luncheon in 2010. The ceremony was scheduled approximately one month before the Deepwater Horizon rig exploded and sank to the bottom of the Gulf causing the largest oil spill in US history. The nominee for the safety awards was non-other than British Petroleum (BP) which operated the Deepwater Horizon oil rig. Deepwater Horizon sank in the Gulf of Mexico and spilled millions of barrels of oil into the pristine Gulf. The awards ceremony was supposed to recognize "outstanding safety and pollution prevention performance by the offshore oil and gas industry." BP was nominated for its work on the outer continental shelf. The big winner of the 2009 SAFE award (the year before) was Transocean, the owner of the Deepwater Horizon rig that exploded under BP's management. BP was also a finalist at the 2009 conference. Apparently the award did nothing to prevent the disaster. Awards do not guarantee quality. Awards do not create prediction. Only knowledge creates prediction.

In 1975, Congress enacted Corporate Average Fuel Economy (CAFE) regulations to reduce gasoline consumption. Current CAFE standards require an average of 27.2 miles per gallon (mpg) for cars and 21.6 mpg for light trucks. Recent legislation signed by President Obama raises these standards. This seems like a good idea if you want reduced oil usage, a reduced dependence on foreign oil, and a reduction in greenhouse gases. These were the three major reasons to adopt the CAFÉ Standards.

Unfortunately, when you consider two unintended negative consequences you can conclude it was not worth because it made things worse in other areas. The reduced cost of operation of a vehicle causes people to drive more miles. This actually does nothing to reduce oil consumption nor does it reduce greenhouse gases since the same miles driven cause the same amount of gases to be emitted (these were the two major intended outcomes of the legislation). Dependence on foreign oil has actually increased since 1975. Furthermore, to meet the CAFÉ standards, the auto industry lightened the vehicle weights causing greater damage during collisions. This caused approximately 2,000 additional deaths every year since the standards were adopted. (Coon, 2001)

Deming's SoPK is a system that works together to create significant transformation. All four elements of SoPK must be incorporated to significant influence the system. We can't leave any of the parts out or we get unpredictable results at best. Many organizations have implemented parts of his system and their results have been mixed. General Electric has implemented Six Sigma which was designed to accelerate process improvement and generate cost reduction with corresponding profit improvement.

Six Sigma efforts focus mainly on the technical and statistical side of quality improvement. Six Sigma efforts tend to ignore the non-technical elements that are included in SoPK such as the theory of psychology, and the theory of knowledge. Six Sigma efforts have therefore delivered mixed results as measured by stock and profit appreciation. Some claim that better results would have been achieved if SoPK was employed because SoPK is a holistic system whereas Six Sigma is limited. (William J. Bellows, 2003)

The use of the typical performance appraisal in conjunction with Six Sigma quality improvement efforts is a good example of what many organizations do today. They choose certain elements of SoPK and reject others. This is a good example of leadership malpractice. The addiction to Frederick Taylor Scientific Management thinking prevents leaders from being willing to implement all of SoPK. This lack of commitment to the full theory can begin to explain why those same organizations experience mixed results when they implement only some of the key elements of SoPK. It can also explain why the typical performance appraisal has survived as the most popular management tool yet it achieves poor results. The typical appraisal is a barrier preventing superior performance and quality improvement results. This is why it must be replaced.

Deming's 14 Points of Management and the 7 Deadly Diseases outline the key principles that form the basis for the transformation and the foundation to justify the replacement of the typical performance appraisal.

Deming's 14 Points of Management

1. "Create constancy of purpose towards improvement". Replace short-term reaction with long-term planning.

2. "Adopt the new philosophy". The implication is that management should actually adopt his philosophy, rather than merely expect the workforce to do so.

3. "Cease dependence on inspection". If variation is reduced, there is no need to inspect manufactured items for defects, because there won't be any.

4. "Move towards a single supplier for any one item." Multiple suppliers means increased variation between lots.

5. "Improve constantly and forever". Constantly strive to reduce variation.

6. "Institute training on the job". If people are inadequately trained, they will not all work the same way, and this will introduce variation.

7. "Institute leadership". Deming makes a distinction between leadership and mere supervision. The latter is quota- and target-based.

8. "Drive out fear". Deming sees management by fear as counter- productive in the long term, because it prevents workers from acting in the organization's best interests.

9. "Break down barriers between departments". Another idea central to TQM is the concept of the 'internal customer', that each department serves not the management, but the other departments that use its outputs.

10. "Eliminate slogans". Another central TQM idea is that it's not people who make most mistakes - it's the process they are working within. Harassing the workforce without improving the processes they use is counter-productive.

11. "Eliminate management by objectives". Deming saw production targets as encouraging the delivery of poor-quality goods.

12. "Remove barriers to pride of workmanship". Many of the other problems outlined reduce worker satisfaction.

13. "Institute education and self-improvement".

14. "The transformation is everyone's job".

7 Deadly Diseases

Lack of constancy of purpose. Instead take the long-term view and have a clear purpose (aim)

Emphasis on short term profits, "creative" accounting, focus on quarterly profits: Instead take the long-term view.

Annual Performance Appraisals – management by objective, management by fear

Mobility of management. Instead operate on different principle where the leadership stays for decades (Toyota)

Running a company on visible figures alone – many important factors are "unknown and unknowable." Instead take action based on sound principles and theory.

Excessive medical care costs. Instead take the long-term view and help employees focus on wellness care.

Excessive legal damage awards swelled by lawyers working on contingency fees. Instead have tort reform and take the long-term view.

Chapter 8:
One Way to Continue Deming's Work – The Values and System Leadership Model

Aim of this Chapter: Describe the leadership model that is consistent with Dr. W. Edwards Deming's System of Profound Knowledge, acts as the replacement for Frederick Taylor's Scientific Management, and forms the foundation for a replacement of the typical performance appraisal process.

Over a three year period my teenage daughter applied to four part-time jobs. Emily has had great "luck" getting each of these jobs. In all four cases she was hired "on-the-spot" right in the interview. She exudes confidence, integrity, competence, and a "willingness to help" attitude. How can one explain her immediate and consistent success with all employers enthusiastically offering her the job immediately? I believe there is one major factor. It's a "great foundation".

After Emily's eighth grade graduation, we held a family meeting. We decided as a family that Emily would benefit from attending a private college preparatory school. My wife and I agreed that the school and the total experience would be a great opportunity to develop her confidence, poise, study habits, positive attitude, and sense of responsibility. Emily's success in being hired "on-the-spot" came in part from our recognition of the key elements that would create a solid foundation for becoming an asset for any organization and society in general. Specific classes that helped Emily with a job search and with conducting an effective interview all contributed to her success.

What do Chief Executives want from their people?

According to a recent survey[1] of 4,700 executives in 83 countries, the top two "people issues" that emerged were managing talent and improving leadership. (Group T. B., 2008)

Executives see talented people as one of the keys to organizational success. Talented people alone will not deliver the results executives seek, yet their belief in the need for talent continues to emerge as a desired success factor.

Successful leaders must also begin to recognize the key elements of the foundation of a successful organization and ensure that elements are provided.

Step 1: A useful metaphor for building a high performance organization is to imagine an organization as a house.

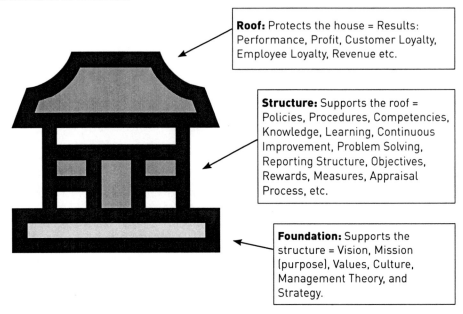

Roof: Protects the house = Results: Performance, Profit, Customer Loyalty, Employee Loyalty, Revenue etc.

Structure: Supports the roof = Policies, Procedures, Competencies, Knowledge, Learning, Continuous Improvement, Problem Solving, Reporting Structure, Objectives, Rewards, Measures, Appraisal Process, etc.

Foundation: Supports the structure = Vision, Mission (purpose), Values, Culture, Management Theory, and Strategy.

The Foundation = Vision, Mission, Values, Strategy, Management Theory etc.

Just as a house needs a solid foundation so too does an organization In a high performance organization, the foundation includes the Vision (an ideal picture of a future state), the Mission (purpose or aim i.e. why the organization exists), the Values (intrinsically important priorities), Management Theory (how the senior leadership thinks about problems and people), and Strategy (the long-term plan of action). If each of these is clear and communicated to all employees, it helps everyone to make decisions quickly while building and managing "the structure" within which the employees "live."

The Structure = Policy and Procedure

The structure (framing and walls of the house) of an organization is made up of all those things that put the items in the foundation into action. The structure is supported by the foundation. The more solid the foundation, the more stable the structure. The structure includes the policies, procedures (processes), competencies (skills), knowledge, learning, continuous improvement, problem solving, objectives, rewards, and measures. The performance appraisal process is one of the policies and procedures. As we have argued in previous chapters, the embrace of Frederick Taylor Scientific Management theory continues to support the policy of the typical performance appraisal. A shift in that theory to Deming's SoPK will justify a shift in the policy.

The Roof = Results

The roof is the results. The stronger the structure and the roof the more the house (organization) is protected from the threatening elements of the environment. For an organization these threatening elements include competitors, economy, government regulations, changing market conditions, changing customer expectations and demands, etc.

Precious resources will be wasted by trying to fix the roof when the real root cause of the problem is a weakened structure caused by a flawed foundation. This is why organizations frequently revise their performance appraisal process (on average every two years). The results are poor and so they "repair the structure" in an effort to "repair the roof" over and over. A better strategy is to reinforce the foundation, and then repair the structure.

A lack of alignment on the elements of the foundation can create barriers to growth and quality improvement. Just as a house with a faulty or shaky foundation would be of poor quality and have major flaws in its structure, an organization with a lack of alignment in the elements of the foundation will be prevented from achieving optimum results.

Clarifying the elements of a solid foundation is not enough to achieve predictable results. There also must be an alignment of the people behind these elements. There must also be a culture that reinforces these same elements. Leadership is both an art and a science. It is just not possible to automate alignment, coaching, persuasion, facilitation of creativity, etc. A successful leader must also know how to align people behind these ideas and capture both their hearts and minds.

Alignment of hearts and minds are necessary prerequisites of commitment to ideas. The typical manager focuses only on the minds of the employees through the use of extrinsic rewards and the typical performance appraisal. True alignment means people are happily willing to take action, be creative, solve problems, be pro-active and have all the other characteristics and behaviors that CEO's are looking for without bribes or threats.

The foundation must have all of the "bricks" in place (Vision, Mission or Purpose, Values, Culture, and Management Theory). These are all interdependent. Any weakness in one of these elements will create a weakness in the entire foundation. The Vision tells us where we are going. The Mission (or purpose/aim) tells us why we want to get there. The values and culture tell us how we are to behave and how we make decisions along the way. The management theory helps us to think clearly, to solve problems quickly, and to remove barriers encountered. Together, these things help us answer the basic questions: Where, How, Why, When, with Who?

The Values and System Leadership Model:

The Values and System Model: What is it?

The purpose of a leadership model is make useful decisions quickly to achieve results toward a purpose. Ideally the model provides everyone the opportunity to make decisions quickly which will optimize employee engagement and operational results which lead to customer loyalty. Therefore leadership models, or paradigms, are ways of thinking about the world that helps everyone to solve problems. Models are theories. Models don't always last forever. They are only useful (true) until they are replaced by a more useful paradigm. This is true because all models are incomplete but some are more useful than others and as we learn more about the world our models can shift. Models are supported by evidence or they are eventually abandoned because an overwhelming mountain of evidence contradicts the existing model and this makes room for the new.

In the 15th century most everyone believed the Earth was the center of the universe (or of our galaxy). Copernicus and later Galileo contradicted this belief (or theory) with a different theory, i.e. the Sun was the center of the solar system. It took many years for the world to embrace this paradigm.

Galileo suffered individual ridicule and hardship because of his embrace of the new paradigm. His book, *Dialogue Concerning the Two Chief World Systems*, defended his views and created the impression to some that he was criticizing the Pope. He was accused by the Church of heresy, forced to recant his support for his paradigm (first proposed by Copernicus), and placed under house arrest. So it goes with those who propose ideas that don't match the prevailing paradigm.

Einstein was thought to be a kook when he predicted that light would bend around the sun during an eclipse. He based his predictions on a new paradigm, the Theory of Relativity. It contradicted Newtonian physics and so the scientific community ridiculed and/or dismissed Einstein. In 1919 a team of scientists used a solar eclipse to test Einstein's theory. Overnight Einstein went from a kook to a genius. New data can replace a paradigm in an instant. Unfortunately the embrace of systems thinking over Taylor Scientific Management is taking much much longer.

Why is this model important?

The *Values and Systems Problem Solving Model* is based on research by Rob LeBow and Dr. W. Edwards Deming. Their research is complimentary and when combined creates a more robust leadership model than when taken separately. Simply stated, the combined research suggests that leaders need to begin looking for a solution to organizational problems by asking one question: *Is this problem a values issue, or systems issue?* Asking this question simplifies the search for a solution to challenging problems. It helps make a distinction between behavioral issues and complex system issues. Complex system issues influence behavior. They often cause people to behave in ways contrary to the stated organizational values.

Rob LeBow and William Simon's research correlate with Dr. Deming's research in many ways. In their book *Lasting Change*, LeBow and Simon describe how values create the context of the organization and lay the foundation for lasting changes (transformation). They asked a simple question, 'what do people want in their work environment to be more productive and to perform at the top of their game?'

> *Our team spoke to and interviewed dozens of business people, HR professionals, instructional designers, business consultants, training companies, researchers, business leaders, CEO's, organizational development specialists… After all the searching, we knew that no person or organization had a satisfactory answer. Finally we stumbled upon a research project that had begun at the University of Chicago, in which the team had collected 17 million surveys of workers in 40 countries around the world on what people wanted in their work environments to be productive, creative, fulfilled, and competitive. (Lebow, 1997)*

The answer came back as Shared Values. The respondents of this survey mentioned truth, trust, openness, honesty, respect, risk-taking, mentoring, giving credit and caring as those things they could all agree need to be in the environment. The result of an environment with these values is freedom and a lack of fear. This freedom allows employees to focus on problem-solving. They begin to realize they have the power to influence change in themselves, their managers and their processes (system).

What is a value?

A value is a fundamental personal belief that has <u>intrinsic</u> worth. For example, our founding fathers all believed freedom was a priority and a right given to us by nature (or nature's God). The "value" of freedom is described in detail in the Declaration of Independence. The Declaration of Independence acts as the foundation for our US Government. The Constitution acts as part of the structure for the Government. Values are the rudders guiding decisions because they create a priority of what is most important. Values can evolve over time as awareness and experience broadens and deepens.

Values Drive All Performance: Appreciating the Importance of Values Behaviors

Why values are so important to performance and profit (they're not just touchy-feely)

Sears suffered two "black eyes" in the 1990's. The first was when auto-repair employees in California were caught hiking their own commissions by selling customers products they didn't need. Sears mechanics charged customers for four-wheel alignments when only the front wheels could be aligned, and mechanics also made unauthorized repairs to vehicles. This was the second time in 10 years that Sears was caught bilking customers on auto-repairs.

The second was the extension of credit cards to 17 million new customers. The problem was too many of those new cardholders were barely qualified. In its zeal to attract new business and meet sales goals, Sears became a lender to too many of its riskiest customers. As the number of bankruptcies nationwide mushroomed, so did the number of unpaid accounts at Sears. By 1997 more than one third of all personal bankruptcies in the United States included Sears as a creditor.

Michael Levin, head of Sears' law department at the time, did whatever he could to assess the scope of the problem, and ultimately to understand what in its management structure, executive style, or corporate culture, had led it to commit the most serious ethical breach in its history. It was too late to avoid serious fines and a significant loss of customer trust. The deadly disease of focusing on short-term profits had trumped any other values within the Sears' foundation.

Why are values behaviors important?

Values behaviors, if consistently demonstrated by a leader, will determine the level of credibility, influence, and trust with employees. A team with aligned values set the stage for the following results:

- People have more of a reason to CARE about their work.
- Employees are more loyal when they believe their values are the same as the organization's values.
- Employees become more involved and, therefore, more creative.
- The quality and accuracy of decision-making is improved.
- Organizations with aligned values attract more resources.

Dr. W. Edwards Deming said, *"Either spoken or unspoken, if values of a company are not aligned with individual values, there is tremendous discomfort and dysfunction and **WASTE!!**"*
James Kouszes and Barry Posner reinforced Deming's thinking.

> *"Shared values are the foundation for building productive and genuine working relationships. While credible leaders honor diversity of their many constituencies, they also stress their common values. Leaders build upon agreement… There has to be some core of understanding. If disagreements over fundamental values continue, the result is intense conflict, false expectations, and diminished capacity. … Recognizing that we hold shared values provides us with a common language with which we can collaborate." (Kouszes, 1993)*

Rob Lebow & William L. Simon concur.

> *"The values of an organization are in essence not what we say they are. The values of an organization are how people behave every day. Behaviors in a Shared Values environment are judged by fellow employees, management, and the company's customers." (Lebow, 1997)*

Values are like a COMPASS

Values behaviors are like having a compass that guides you when you feel lost (during a conflict, problem, or complaint). In the 1980's, J&J managers immediately removed Tylenol from the market and stopped all production of the product after seven Chicago residents died after ingesting cyanide-laced capsules. An unknown assailant had purchased Tylenol from a local pharmacy, laced the tablets with cyanide and returned the bottles to the store shelves undetected. Unknowing customers of Tylenol purchased the product, ingested it and later died.

Despite advice from their consultants and lawyers who all predicted a disaster for their brand image if they decided to immediately remove of the product from the shelves, J&J management decided to act in the best interest of all customers and put safety ahead of profit. This demonstration of integrity, respect, and customer focus created a significant and measurable improvement in the level of trust once the problem was solved with new packaging. The consumer rewarded J&J with significant growth in both revenue and profit. Behaving consistent with values generates long-term results.

What are the key values and what are those behaviors?

Three basic values, when present and applied consistently, will increase a leader's influence, increase the ability to tell the truth, and improve long-term results. These values are; integrity, respect, and customer focus.

Integrity means doing what you say you'll do. It means keeping our word and being congruent in our actions. This means simply that words and action are aligned. They both send the same message. Because actions speak louder than words, so it follows that leaders who exhibit (behave with) integrity have the greatest influence. For example, a leader who demands that everyone be respectful of his/her time, and who then makes a habit of being late for meetings is incongruent. Expecting or demanding specific behavior from others that we don't deliver ourselves damages influence.

In the 1920s, James J. Braddock from Bergen, NJ, was a powerful professional boxer. A movie entitled Cinderella Man, released by Universal Pictures, depicts his story. There is a scene at the heart of the movie that demonstrates his strength of character, faith in himself and his commitment to values. That day his son had stolen a slab of salami from the butcher shop (when no one was watching). In the midst of the Great Depression, Braddock was out of work, like millions of others, his lights were about to be shut off from non-payment, he had no cash and no food for his two young children and was recovering from a serious hand injury that was preventing him from boxing. Braddock came home and discovered what his son had done (even though with the best of intentions) told him it was wrong. He insisted that his son bring the meat back that same day.

Respect[2] means treating others with consideration equal to what we expect for ourselves. The act of attentive listening is a great example, because we all like to feel that our opinions are important. Listening acknowledges that the other person's point of view has value. Stephen Covey calls this, "Seeking to understand before being understood". (Covey S. , 1989) Listening, before you offer your opinion, shows respect for the person and gains high marks on the leadership scale of influence.

The third value is customer focus. This includes clearly identifying each customer, serving him or her well, and continuously improving the service or product. The word customer doesn't just mean patrons. For a store manager, both patrons and employees are customers. For leaders, most of their customers are employees or internal customers. To achieve long-term results leaders must treat their employees (internal customers) with integrity and respect. This is the foundation for helping employees become more successful and for leaders to increase their influence.

The need for customer is reinforced in the work of Dr. W. Edwards Deming. Deming said that the customer is the most important part of an organization's system and therefore the customer defines quality. Knowing your customer and serving them is a principle that improves influence and long-term results.

A good example of the impact customer focus can have is an experience I had recently when dealing with the telephone company. My home office telephone was not working properly, which was causing me to run up a full flight of stairs every time I needed to answer my office line. It was maddening.

I called the telephone company to schedule a service call. The woman quoted the price for the service and then she launched right into a sales pitch, attempting to sell me additional services. I explained to her that I was not interested; I simply wanted my service fixed, but she persisted. She wasn't listening and I began to get annoyed. She wasn't listening because she wasn't interested in what I needed. Instead, she was interested in making a commission. She probably had that direction from her management. She was probably told to "up-sell" whenever speaking to a customer.

On the day of the service appointment, the telephone serviceman came to the house, and after a quick inspection of the problem, he fixed it. He then updated his work order, told me it was the phone company's fault and said there should be no charge. He added that if I was mistakenly charged, I should dispute it. I was delighted.

He treated me with respect. He focused on my needs and then told me the truth. In just those few seconds he influenced me to do additional business with the company. His influence was significantly more powerful than the influence of the customer service person. His treatment encouraged me to purchase additional services. Hers did not.

Jim Collins writes about values in his book "Good to Great". He explains how good-to-great companies place a greater weight on the character attributes of employees than on specific educational background, practical skills, specialized knowledge, or work experience. (Collins, 2001) Specific knowledge and skills are unimportant, because those can be learned. Values such as character behavior, work ethic, dedication to fulfilling commitments, are more ingrained. Dave Nassef of Pitney Bowes put it this way:

> *"I used to be in the Marines, and the Marines get a lot of credit for building people's values. But that's not the way it really works. The Marine Corps recruits people who share the corp.'s values, then provides them with the training required to accomplish the organization's mission. ..We don't just look at experience. We want to know: Who are they? Why are they? We find out who they are by asking them why they made decisions in their life. The answers to these questions give us insight into their core values." (Collins, 2001)*

To choose people based on their values is easier if you have a clear set of defined behaviors. One of the most important behaviors is the Golden Rule. The Golden Rule is a moral rule. The Golden Rule is not practiced as frequently or as intentionally as it needs to be in organizations although it is found in every single major religion throughout the world in some form or another. This moral rule is found in culture after culture. It is expressed in many forms but the main thrust is remarkably the same. (Group, May 2008)

The Greatest Rule of All: *The Golden Rule*

Confucianism: *"Do not do unto others what you would not want them to do unto you."*

Buddhism: *"Seek for others the happiness you desire for yourself. Hurt not others with that which pains you."*

Hinduism: *"All your duties are included in this: Do nothing to others that would pain you if it were done to you."*

Judaism: *"That which is hurtful to you, do not do to your fellow man."*

Islam: *"Let none of you treat his brother in a way he himself would not like to be treated. No one of you is a believer until he loves for his brother what he loves for himself."*

Taoism: *"View your neighbor's gain as your own gain, and your neighbor's loss as your own loss."*

Christianity: *"Do unto others as you would have them do unto you."*

Aristotle: *"We should behave to our friends as we wish our friends to behave to us."*

Plato: *"May I do to others as I would that they should do unto me."*

Sikhism: *"Treat others as you would be treated yourself."*

Native American Spirituality: *"Respect for all life is the foundation."*; *"Do not wrong or hate your neighbor. For it is not he who you wrong, but yourself."*

In the book the "Gold Standard: 5 Leadership Principles for Creating a Legendary Customer Experience Courtesy of the Ritz-Carlton Hotel," Joseph Michelli emphasizes how keeping the Gold Standard behaviors alive every day helps define the company, differentiate it from the competition, and create the foundation for sustainable service and continuous improvement. (Michelli, 2008)

This specific behavior gives everyone in the organization the same specific definition and expectation. This specific behavior creates the standard during good times and bad and provides a solid foundation for building trust.

Positive change comes about when it is needed because there is an awareness of these key elements of trust. The positive change is adaptive in nature. As conditions within the organization change people can use the specific behaviors as a guide for how they must continue to behave even though the conditions have changed

Why must the values be clearly described with specific behavior?

I was driving one morning to a golf outing. I was running a bit late and was behind a small car going exactly the speed limit of 25 MPH. I was feeling a bit frustrated because I wanted to make up some time and I could not pass on the two lane road with the double yellow line.

At last, to my pleasant surprise, the road was about to open up to four lanes and, in the distance I could see the Speed Limit sign which read 40 MPH. I was excited and as soon as enough space opened up I passed the slower vehicle and immediately sped to the desired 40 MPH. Perhaps I was even traveling slightly faster than 40MPH, yet I know it was only a couple miles over the limit if at all. My intention was not to speed but to merely take advantage of the new limit.

Finally cruising and making up time I was shocked to see flashing lights and to hear a siren from the Police Cruiser that had very quickly caught up to what seemed like inches of my bumper. The officer was kind enough to let me know that I had been speeding because I started the new limit (of 40MPH) prior to reaching the new speed limit sign. I always thought, and perhaps you did too, that once you saw the speed limit sign it was valid. The officer corrected me by explaining his definition. The speed limit is valid only when you actually reach the sign not when you see the sign. My definition was different from the officer's. Guess which one was seen as "correct"? My definition cost me $40 for the ticket.

The Police Officer and I had a different method of deciding "when the speed limit is in effect". Being clear on the same method would have avoided all that wasted time (I ended up being even more late than expected) and wasted money (the cost of the ticket).

Organizations need clear descriptions of values behaviors to avoid wasted time and wasted resources but it is not enough to just list the values or priorities. The values are defined by the behavior not the rhetoric. For example, whose values are these?

Our Values

Communication: We have an obligation to communicate. Here, we take the time to talk with one another… and to listen. We believe that information is meant to move and that information moves people.

Respect: We treat others as we would like to be treated ourselves. We do not tolerate abusive or disrespectful treatment.

Integrity: We work with customers and prospects openly, honestly and sincerely. When we say we will do something, we will do it; when we say we cannot or will not do something, then we won't do it.

Excellence: We are satisfied with nothing less than the very best in everything we do. We will continue to raise the bar for everyone. The great fun here will be for all of us to discover just how good we can really be.

At first glance most people guess these are from Microsoft, or GE or Shell Oil. The sad fact is these are Enron's values. Just listing the values and posting them on the wall of the conference room is not enough. We must bring them to life. This requires we define them clearly using specific behavior. This "operationalizing" of the values is critical. To operationalize means to describe using specific observable behavior.

Clearly defining the specific observable behaviors allows everyone to observe who is following those values and who is not. This enrolls everyone in the organization to influence the culture and manage the variation of the behaviors. This enables everyone to improve their ability to manage conflict and make quick decisions while knowing those decisions are in the best interest of the entire organization because the decisions and behavior are consistent with the values behavior.

...values and beliefs which reflect what members believe "ought to be" the work of the organization in the form of easily articulated ideologies, attitudes, and philosophies... (Michael J. Austin, 2008)

Start with the basics to keep it simple

Organizational leaders often attempt to incorporate too many values into their culture. The list that is too long is unwieldy, confusing, and difficult to commit to memory. Too many values in the list make the list less useful for day to day decision making. The three basic values that capture the essence of an effective culture are:

- INTEGRITY
- RESPECT
- CUSTOMER FOCUS

These three values are all-encompassing and they can easily be all inclusive. There are literally dozens of values that an organization and its people can decide to embrace. If you attempt to embrace too many different types of values the complexity increases. By using only these three to clarify everyday behaviors employees can ask what might be missing or what personal values might in conflict. With the proper questioning of employees and listening to their concerns everyone can begin see that these three values can be comprehensive without becoming too complex.

For example, when people are asked "what is the most important thing(s) in your life?" many will mention family. Family is a value. It has intrinsic worth. An appropriate balance between family and work life is an important goal in most organizations today. If you properly "operationalize" (define using specific and observable behaviors) the three values, each of your employees will be able to see how his/her family is honored and he/she can achieve balance in their lives while still working hard.

There are three steps to aligning a team on these values:

1. Use the three fundamental values as a starting point and agree on the behaviors needed to demonstrate these three values at your work place.
2. Have an open and honest discussion with employees about what they think might be missing or contradictory about the list of behaviors as compared to their personal values.
3. Use a specific standard of quality to be sure the statements meet a set of useful criteria.

LeBow's, Simon's and Deming's work all agree with the premise that people can be trusted because they already want to do a good job. They are not lacking motivation; instead they lack an environment and tools that would allow them to naturally be motivated. The University of Chicago survey data clarified by LeBow specifically mentions values such as honesty, truth and trust. (Lebow, 1997) They want the ability to offer the truth and they want to be respected.

LeBow insists people should be trusted because the trust will allow them to be great, something they already want to be. They can do without management coercion or interference to create motivation. This is an argument against the performance management and pay-for-performance policies which are methods of coercion and control and not of trust.

Shared values positively impact profit. For example, LeBow studied business and financial results for eight restaurants. Some had implemented his shared values process and others did not. He ranked them in financial performance using net income before operating expenses, performance against plan and profitability. Those with the most positive work environment (who had implemented his shared values approach) were the ones at the top of the financial performance. There was a correlation with financial performance and positive work environment.

The Values and System Problem-Solving Leadership Model helps draw a distinction between two basic types of problems namely values (behavioral interactions) and systems (the process interactions) between the interdependent parts. According to LeBow and Simon if an organization manages the variation in the values behaviors it will achieve outstanding results. In Deming's System of Profound Knowledge an organization that manages the variation in the system will achieve outstanding results. What if you combine to the approaches? In theory the two approaches combined can create even more robust results.

The Values and System Problem-Solving Model

When there is an issue, it is either a values issue or a system issue.

Values Issue	Systems Issue
Poor Behaviors:	**Poor Results:**
Breaks in integrity	Mistakes, Errors or oversights
Intentional mistake or oversight	Poor quality or performance
Showing disrespect	Poor attitude
Intentional break in policy or procedure	Lack of motivation
Blaming others	Not understanding responsibility
Making excuses	Inadequate Training
Not taking responsibility	Poor policies
Positive Behaviors:	**Positive Results:**
Keeps Agreements	Achieving desired results
Respect in all interactions	Predictability
Continuous improvement in processes that help "customers"	Managing variation

A values issue involves a purposeful break in integrity such as lying, sabotage, being disrespectful or failing to follow through on a commitment or agreement. Problems that are values issues are behavioral, which means individuals have choices as to how they can react or behave. For example, telling or not telling the truth is a choice. Being respectful in the face of disrespect is a choice. Values issues are very serious because they create an emotionally charged environment, which puts relationships at risk.

Simply stated, their research suggests that when faced with an organizational problem, leaders need to begin by asking one question: Is this problem a values issue, or systems issue?

When a problem involves a break in values, it may involve a purposeful break in integrity like: lying, sabotage, being disrespectful or failing to perform as agreed. Problems that are values-based are behavioral, which means individuals have choices as to how they can react or behave. For example, telling or not telling the truth is a choice. Being respectful in the face of disrespect is a choice. Values issues are very serious because they create an emotionally charged environment, which puts the quality of the relationships and the level of trust at risk.

In the Values and Systems problem-solving model, every problem that is not a values issue is a systems issue. Problems that result from systems issues include: mistakes, oversight, forgetting, poor training, poor quality, poor performance or lack of motivation.

More often than not, the root of a problem is due to a problem with a system, but it manifests itself on the surface as a "people" problem.

What is a system? A system is a series of independent processes that work together to achieve an aim or purpose. Think of a highway. A highway has a purpose or aim i.e. to provide an area of safe travel for automobiles from one place to another. A highway is a system because it is a series of interdependent processes that are intended to achieve an aim. Each person driving to work in the morning can be considered one part of the overall highway system. Driving an automobile is a process therefore each person driving on the highway can be considered a process. The road conditions, the traffic lights, the signs, the quality of maintenance, the design of the exit ramps are all parts of the system. Each part impacts the other parts because they are interdependent. Attempting to evaluate only one part of a system ignores the interaction of one part to another. Here is an example:

The Values and System Model enables Successful Leaders to begin to fully appreciate a system, move away from blaming people, and find innovative solutions to complex problems.

In this management model, unclear or dysfunctional processes are the real root cause of most, if not all, people problems or human conflict in organizations. Uncovering the system issue requires patience and tools. It requires thinking clearly. Too often management jumps to the conclusion that people are the cause. By embracing the Values and System Management Model, a successful leader will continue to explore ways to improve the system and will interpret emotional upsets as an opportunity to uncover serious system issues. Occasionally people can be seriously flawed and are the cause. It is rare, and when it does occur it probably means the hiring process was flawed.

In the values and system leadership model at least 94% of the time the root cause of poor values behaviors originates in the system. Leadership malpractice is when leaders focus mainly on the poor behaviors of individuals and fail to uncover the systemic causes. In the Values and System Leadership Model the broken values are most often (at least 94% of the time) a symptom not a cause and yet leadership malpractice ignores this theory. Let's take an example.

Our Rotary Club publishes a Program Book as part of the annual major fundraising event. The fund raising event is a social event that brings supporters of Rotary together to enjoy each other's company while donating to the club through certain activities such as wine tasking, auctions and raffles. Members and their friends purchase printed ads in the book to both advertise their business and/or show their support for the club. The book is distributed to all members and selected members of the community.

Those wishing to purchase and ad needed to follow certain procedures to avoid errors and improve printing quality. A physician's office submitted a hand written note with instructions about the ad she wanted. Have you ever seen a physician's handwriting? The instructions were not clear and instead of submitting a "camera ready" art the hand written note had to be typed to be submitted to the printer

The ad was submitted later than the deadline and so I did not have time to check for errors because I had to go out of town. I needed to type it and submit it without a quality check by the physician's office. I submitted it with a typo. The book was printed and distributed at the event.

The member who "sold" the ad to the physician came running up to me and he was upset. She had complained to him about the ad. She and others in Rotary blamed me for the quality of the ad. It felt disrespectful and embarrassing. Clearly in their minds I was the root cause of the error. Their reaction sounded disrespectful to me (values issue). Knowing the root cause was a combination of systems issues I did not react emotionally. Instead, I apologized and offered her a free ad for next year double the size. I also decided to change my process to provide more time to double check those ads that are submitted incorrectly.

The real root cause of the problem was the inability or unwillingness of the Physician's office to follow my instructions. Perhaps they just ignored them or perhaps the instructions were unclear and/or not even shared with the Physician's office. Perhaps the Rotary member who knew the Physician and asked them to invest did not explain the process. Perhaps he ignored my instructions. In any case, I was the one reprimanded for the error. Perhaps I should have taken extra steps to avoid the mistake and yet the system prevented me from doing that.

The reaction I received from the Rotary members reminds us that most people do NOT understand the enormous role the system plays in a mistake (94% of the time). Their reaction felt disrespectful to me. I could have become defensive and disrespectful in my reaction as well. This is where values begin to be broken. The flaws in the system cause people to go into reaction. That emotional and reactionary mode can cause disrespect and or breaks in integrity. In the Values and System Leadership Model the system flaws increase the probability that the values are broken.

In the Dallas training story the poor communication between me and the two managers caused the wasted time, poorer training process, and higher costs. Because of the waste created anyone of us might have had an emotional reaction which might have damaged the trust. By improving the communication in the system the trust is higher and the results are improved. The Values and System Leadership Model asks that everyone follow the specific values behaviors while focusing on the improvement of the system interactions. This duel model can create faster results.

As an effective leader we must begin to shift thinking or risk losing trust with employees. Embracing the Values and System Leadership Model helps us to avoid leadership malpractice while building trust and improving processes.

Part IV
The Settlement

Applying the Replacement – The Complete Performance Improvement Process (CPIP)

Chapter 9:
So What is the Difference Really?

Aim of this Chapter: To clarify the specific differences between CPIP and the typical appraisal process.

To avoid leadership malpractice and stop the injuries caused by the typical appraisal we can't just "tweak" the current process. If we are to have any chance to improve the efficacy of the typical appraisal process and eliminate the injury it is causing we must adopt a new set of beliefs about performance, redesign the elements to be consistent with those principles, and change the name. It has to be redesigned and that new design must be consistent with a leadership model that is going to perform in the knowledge economy. We must remove our worn suit of Frederick Taylor and try on the new Values and System Leadership model suit.

We must "up-grade" our leadership tools just as we would up-grade our software for a new computer. The old software no longer works well (or even at all) on our new "knowledge age" computer. We need new "leadership software" and we need to change the name so everyone knows it's different. The Complete Performance Improvement Process (CPIP) represents is the up-grade we need to transform from the typical performance appraisal.

The Aberdeen Group surveyed 400 Human Resources and Line Executives in 2010 and identified two desired outcomes from their employee performance management policies i.e. efficiency improvement and growth. (Jayson Saba, 2010) This is an enormous challenge because growing a business while improving efficiency seems contradictory. These competing execution strategies create stress on management individuals yet isn't this always challenge for executives and organizations. As long as an organization must deal with competitors in their marketplace they must find better ways to accomplish these two outcomes. As this report so correctly observes:

> *"For many organizations, one of the biggest challenges in creating a Best-in-Class performance management system is finding a way to turn the performance review process from an unfortunate distraction on the calendar to something that is deeply valued and closely adhered to." (Jayson Saba, 2010)*

CPIP accomplishes just this. CPIP enables the leader and his/her team to optimally accomplish the organization's strategic initiatives. The typical performance management process has mixed results accomplishing this alignment because its main focus is on the evaluation of the individual. CPIP focuses on the evaluation of the process(s) and the quality of the interactions between the individuals. CPIP assumes the improvement of the quality of the interactions between the parts of the system will have a greater impact on an organizations ability to accomplish strategy than attempting to improve the parts of the system. A shift in the focus from the quality improvement of the individual to the quality improvement of the interactions between the individuals (departments, teams etc.) accelerates quality and productivity improvements.

There are significant differences between the typical appraisal and CPIP. The typical appraisal damages teamwork whereas CPIP improves it. The typical appraisal disregards systems thinking whereas CPIP reinforces it. The typical appraisal ignores the need to appreciate and manage variation in a complex system whereas CPIP encourages it. The typical appraisal uses an unsophisticated blame approach to problem solving. CPIP uses a scientific learning method.

The typical appraisal encourages employees to choose safe goals easily achieved. CPIP removes barriers that enable employees to do what comes naturally, i.e. challenge themselves and to take intelligent risks. The typical appraisal (especially forced raking) creates losers and winners and pits them against one another by creating a competition for resources. It damages pride and joy in work. Deming said, *"The greatest waste ... is failure to use the abilities of people…to learn about their frustrations and about the contributions that they are eager to make."* (Deming, Out of the Crisis, 1986) CPIP creates a partnership between the leader and the employee to optimize the contribution of each.

Finally, the typical appraisal attempts to provide a way to accomplish multiple functions (communication improvement, feedback, development, promotion, pay distribution, legal protection) but it fails to do any of them effectively. CPIP optimizes the development of people, the achievement of strategic initiatives, the improvement of trust, increases in engagement, the retention of talent, the ability to adapt, and the ability to innovate. All of the key outcomes injured by the typical appraisal are achieved with CPIP.

Considering the typical appraisal is the most common management tool for improving organizational performance, a Human Resources (HR) professional might have trouble sleeping knowing they fail half the time. But, we all know HR professionals sleep just fine because when performance appraisals fail they conveniently put the blame on a manager's inability to carry out the process.

There are three claims HR professionals make against the manager. The first claim usually is the managers need more training. They claim the process, often designed or redesigned by the HR Manager, is being sabotaged because the managers are incompetent and therefore the process is often completed late not done or done poorly.

Secondly HR blames the manager for making result of the annual appraisal a surprise instead of delivering valuable feedback consistently and frequently all during the year. If there is a problem then managers should discuss it immediately and not wait.

Finally managers are accused of being too biased in their assessment of employee performance. The employee can detect this bias and therefore often objects to the rating the manager gives claiming a failure to be fair. This fear of bias causes resistance to cooperation by the employee. The fear of appearing biased often prevents the manager from telling the whole truth.

Unfortunately blaming the manager for the failure of the performance appraisal process is like blaming a driver for the poor performance of a car with two flat tires. It's not the driver. HR professionals, like most leaders, are unaware of the design flaws in performance appraisals and so they find it convenient to just blame the "driver." The irony is these design flaws are built into the process by those same HR professionals. They design the flaws into the process, watch the managers fail, then blames the managers. It's another example of insane malpractice. If it wasn't so tragic it might make a good Seinfeld episode. CPIP puts an end to this malpractice. It puts an end to this absurdity.

Two studies highlight the major Human Resource issues facing leaders today. According to a study by the Boston Consulting Group (a survey of 4,700 executives in 83 countries in July 2008) identified the top three human resource issues in the USA as managing talent, improving leadership development, and managing demographics. (Goldsmith, 2008) We can conclude that managing and retaining talent is seen as a critical success factor for the USA and the world. To accomplish this we must capture and utilize the motivation and engagement of *all* employees. We must be on the cutting edge of "management and leadership of people" technology – and to be at least as conversant with those tools as we are with our other technological advances. We must "up-grade" our leadership tools just as we would up-grade our software for a new computer. CPIP represents an up-grade for our leadership skills to address these major issues.

The CPIP has some differences and some similarities to the current typical performance appraisal process.

Here are the similarities:
- The manager and the employee will meet one-on-one.
- The manager will generate a document summarizing the meeting
- The employee completes a self-assessment form
- The ability and willingness for following the organizational values is a requirement for employment
- One formal meeting is held each year to have an in-depth conversation with each employee while the management of performance occurs all during the year

Here are the differences:
- The rating of the employee is eliminated
- It is no longer necessary to provide opinions about employee characteristics, behaviors, or traits
- It is no longer necessary for the manager to "formally" evaluate the employee on their skills of Teamwork, Leadership, Customer Focus, Continuous Improvement or Personal Learning. The manager now can facilitate agreements for improvement in each of those areas. This Evaluation is highly proactive whereas the previous can be reactive. The evaluation of the employee's performance is a partnership effort between the manager and employee
- A new set of Operational Values was created for the purpose of managing values behaviors of both employees and managers
- The manager has a self-assessment to complete
- The manager does NOT complete a report with lots of opinions about the employee. The only written document is a list of agreements that the manager and or the employee (or both) agree to complete (by a certain time)
- The manager and employee must improve their trust and the quality of their relationship

- The manager and the employee are partners in the improvement of the performance of the employee and the processes within which the employee functions
- The manager and employee may have some very open and honest conversations which will clear the air between the two people
- The manager has the ability to improve his/her behavior and performance at the same time the employee improves
- If discipline is needed it must be because there is data available to prove that values have been broken. Without data, discipline may not be possible. Data includes written memos or emails detailing breaks in values behaviors including details and dates explaining what happened and when (specific behavior).
- If values are being broken on a regular basis it will prevent the employee from receiving a merit increase (as long as there is data such as emails, letters, recordings etc.)
- Decisions about pay are made separately with a different process

If we are to have any chance to improve the efficacy of the typical appraisal process and eliminate the injury it is causing we must adopt a new set of beliefs about performance, redesign the elements to be consistent with those principles, and change the name. We must have a comprehensive approach consistent with systems thinking. CPIP does all this.

Chapter 10:
The Ability to Tell the Truth – Fearless Feedback

Aim of this Chapter: To explain how the Values and System model provides an opportunity to everyone to receive frequent and useful feedback that is NOT manager dependent.

Why is feedback needed?

There are six major reasons why effective feedback is needed. Feedback helps us to improve performance, accelerate learning, adapt to change more naturally and quickly while minimizing loss of productivity, create accountability to certain desired behaviors, improve employee engagement, and evolve.

Accelerate Learning

The ability to learn faster than your competitor is a huge advantage in the knowledge age. Feedback is a necessary element of a learning cycle. In the 1950's Walter Shewhart and Dr. W. Edwards Deming popularized this scientific learning cycle. In many business and scientific circles today it is known as the Shewhart Cycle or Deming Cycle. There are four steps to the learning cycle: Plan-Do-Study-Act. Feedback occurs in the "Do" phase of the cycle where data is collected to best understand how a process is working. It helps answer the question, "Is the process delivering the expected outputs and outcomes?" Without the feedback there can be no learning.

A key element to achieve optimum learning is creating a culture of trust. High levels of trust neutralizes the negative effects of fear. When there is high trust people are willing, by definition, to be vulnerable. The IABC Research Foundation published a study about trust and the definition they used for the study was the willingness to be vulnerable because of the presence of integrity, concern, shared objectives, and competence (Shockley-Zalabak, Ellis, & Rugger, 2000).

Because the most successful organizations are those who are able to adapt to change, the ability to give and receive useful feedback becomes a required competency in today's fast paced global economy. Receiving feedback in a fearless environment enables everyone to take positive action to adapt change. In his book, Managing Transitions, William Bridges emphasizes the need for trust in management as a building block of working with multiple simultaneous changes (Bridges, 2003). "When people trust their manager, they're willing to undertake a change even if it scares them." (Bridges, 2003). Stephen Covey confirmed this by saying trust is the highest form of motivation (Covey, 1989).

Giving and receiving feedback is a critical element for trust communication (Reina & Reina, 2006).

Adapt to change

Feedback is needed to optimize positive change. Change can't be controlled or managed. It can only be detected, anticipated, and adapted to (Wheatley, 2006). We must help people adapt to change.

"Feedback is a critical element in the ability to make rapid strategic integrated choices concerning the pace and direction of change." (Cloke & Goldsmith, 2002). The organization that can accelerate change and involve everyone to participate will create a competitive advantage. We need the mind set and the tools to accelerate adaptation to changes to remain competitive.

Fearless Feedback provides a stimulus to cause change. All change creates disequilibrium which creates motivation to adapt. Feedback provides that disruption or disequilibrium that can facilitate change (Wheatley, 2006).

Create accountability

Holding employees accountable to methods and to their agreements (commitments) is the most effective strategy for performance. Holding people accountable for results can result in unintended consequences. Feedback provides the key final step for our definition of accountability. In order to create trust we must expect employees to keep their agreements. We must expect they can be trusted to have integrity. We must expect them to do what they say they will do. When they fail to keep their agreements we must remind them and bring it to their attention. This is the role of feedback. Feedback provides confirmation that people kept their agreements. It provides confirmation that people have integrity.

Employee Engagement

Finally, feedback is important for employee engagement and retaining talent. Retaining talent and creating a culture of trust are two of the most important challenges facing leaders over the next ten years according to a 2011 study by SHRM (Society for Human Resource Management). To optimize retention and trust managers (and all employees) must know how to create employee engagement. Operating income and employee retention are higher with high levels of employee engagement according to a 2008 Towers-Watson Study. Frequent feedback is an extremely important element for creating an environment of employee engagement. An improved ability to give and receive feedback will improve the relationship between supervisors and employees. According to Gallup (Cherniss & Goleman, 2001), employee retention is directly dependent upon the quality of the relationship with the employee's immediate supervisor.

Willingly giving and receiving frequent feedback means we are invested and committed to the organization and to our relationships (Reina & Reina, 2006)

Most HR professionals believe that a manager's most important job is to give feedback to employees. Yet most managers are so poor at it which means the feedback is infrequent, poorly timed, of poor quality, or all three. Why?

Research by Watson and Wyatt reveals that 43% of employees don't get enough feedback to improve their performance. Sibson Consulting reports that HR professionals are frustrated because managers don't give constructive feedback and 58% of HR professionals give their number one feedback tool, the annual performance review, a C grade or below. Study after study point to managers who are poor at giving feedback as the major reason why performance appraisals fail.

There is no hiding the fact that we all must improve our feedback skills especially since feedback is required for learning, to improve performance, to reduce stress, and to improve employee retention and employee engagement. There are at least four important reasons (barriers) why feedback is poorly done now.

Why Are We Managers So Poor at Feedback?

First, what many managers call feedback is often not feedback at all. It is really criticism. Feedback is data from a process that is used for learning. Criticism is an opinion(s) and the typical appraisal is rife with opinions. Most managers say they are giving feedback but instead they give their opinions about the employee behaviors or individual performance. No one likes unsolicited criticism. In the book "Emotional Intelligence", Daniel Goleman explains how criticism is one of the most important tasks of a manager and also one of the most dreaded. The emotional health of employees depends upon skillfully delivered criticism. Poorly delivered feedback or criticism will damage productivity and job satisfaction (Goleman, 1995).

Criticism often causes unhelpful reactions from those receiving it including brooding, the dodging of responsibility and passive resistance to changes that need to be made. (Goleman, 1995) Fear of criticism which might lead to a loss of credibility or reputation causes people to be silent. (Kathlene Ryan, 1998) Unsolicited criticism in the form of prejudice undermines teamwork, produces hostility, isolation, and the loss of the ability to learn. (Cloke & Goldsmith, 2002) Unsolicited criticism and bias caused by structural policies such as the typical appraisal frustrates everyone and causes discomfort to both employees and managers. That frustration creates a barrier preventing the truth from being heard and the opportunity for learning.

Second, current polices require managers to be the major source of the feedback. Instead, why not give employees the ability and autonomy to collect their own data? Employees who collect their own data and can manage their own processes are more motivated and engaged. Requiring managers to give the feedback means they must be the inspector, spy, the micro-manager, or the omniscient judge. This is a very challenging, if not impossible, role to fill. Instead, why not provide autonomy and trust to employees and allow them to track their own progress with their own data on their own processes?

Third, the work environment most often discourages open and honest feedback. Any feedback (or opinions) from our managers often has consequences attached to it. For example, managers often control employee pay raises, bonuses, or performance appraisal ratings. Anything that might damage those ratings might want to be hidden by the employee. This type of environment can be threatening to useful and honest feedback.

Feedback is still typically delivered annually in the annual typical performance appraisal process. Feedback is most often delivered one direction and it needs to be reciprocal. Also, it is often stopped by fear of retribution (wrath of the manager or co-worker), being seen as something other than a team player, and/or not wanting to be the bearer of bad news.

Fourth, most managers intuitively know they cannot evaluate an individual employee without understanding how the work environment impacts the employee. Attempting to provide feedback on the behaviors of employees without studying the context within which that behavior occurs is malpractice.

Our biggest barrier to achieving optimum feedback (or fearless feedback) is the way we are thinking about people and problems. Many leaders are still stuck in the industrial age thinking while the knowledge age is washing over our organizations like a wave. Our mental models and our tools have not yet caught up with the needs in our organizations.

To give better feedback we must realize these four barriers exist and must be removed. Many HR professionals continue to be frustrated by managers who are unable and unwilling to give quality feedback and yet these four barriers continue to exist and will continue to create that frustration. All the management training in the world will not remove these barriers. The barriers are endemic in the work environment and so they must be first recognized and then removed by courageous leaders with the right management theory.

Fearless Feedback

Organizations with high quality products manage the variation in their manufacturing processes. Service companies that have high quality service manage the variation in their service processes. Every company should have a method to manage the variation of the values behaviors in organizations. "Fearless Feedback" empowers everyone to provide and receive respectful, timely, frequent, and high quality feedback about the quality of two types of interaction namely interpersonal and system. Interpersonal interactions relate to how people speak and/or behave with each other. System interactions relate to how people provide information, product, or paper within the processes they work within. System interactions relate to hand-offs within processes. Interpersonal interactions relate to how people treat each other.

With "Fearless Feedback" managers and employees can both get feedback from employees and peers. When driving if we see a police officer we slowdown to be sure we are traveling at the correct speed limit. When there is "Fearless Feedback" everyone can be a "values behavior cop." These "cops" can help manage the variation just by being present. Their presence signals the possibility for consequences if values behaviors are not followed. Buckminster Fuller once said, "Integrity is the essence of everything successful."

If employees could help each other to be "values cops" the integrity within every interaction would show it would enhance success.

According to research from the best-seller Change Anything, two out of three employees say they received negative feedback in their most recent performance appraisal and yet only one out of three of them made an effort to change behavior based on that feedback. (Kenny, 2013) What good is the feedback if it is not used? What good is a performance appraisal if one of its purposes fails?

4 Rules to Deliver the F-Word Correctly: FEEDBACK

The correct use of feedback can enhance employee engagement. The improper use will damage it severely and often irreparably. Do you deliver the F-Word correctly?

My daughter just graduated from college. We held a party for her and she was helping us prepare the house and the food. She was creating a fruit plate with a wide variety of cut fruit. She is an artist and therefore incredibly creative.

I looked over and she had used a good deal of grapes as a border for the serving plate. I asked her, *"Why are you using so many grapes when we have so many different types of fruit? I thought you were going to alternate the grapes with the pineapple, watermelon, etc."*

A few minutes passed. She was silent. I looked over at her eyes full of tears. She took my questions and observation as criticism. In a soft and humble tone she asked me, *"Would you rather do this Dad?"* I knew I had messed up. I had damaged her motivation and creativity with just a few sentences. Some of you may think she was being overly sensitive but I believe in the communication maxim, *"communication is the response I get."* I therefore must take responsibility for the unintended response I received from my daughter. I submit that leaders must embrace this communication maxim if they want to optimize and maintain employee engagement.

One of the most important skills a manager and leader must develop is the ability to know how and when to deliver feedback in order to maintain employee engagement. Here are four great rules to help you deliver the F-Word correctly.

Rule #1: Clarify the Intentions

Although the typical performance appraisal is designed with positive intentions in mind (individual and organizational improvement) it is important we shift the intentions to be more specific to achieve better results. Trust and learning are the main two intentions that managers and employees must embrace for feedback to be effective. The embrace of trust will prevent damage to the relationship while the feedback is delivered. The embrace of learning will help the person delivering the feedback to keep in mind the needs of the receiver of the feedback. Will the receiver be willing and able to take action? My daughter was unable to accept my criticism as an opportunity for learning. It wasn't clear what she could learn from the interaction and my delivery failed to maintain trust let alone improve it.

Rule #2: Feedback and Criticism are NOT the Same

As we have already explained the average manager rarely makes a distinction between feedback and criticism. This is a serious mistake. According to the Webster's II New College Dictionary feedback is data from a process for the purpose of learning and criticism is opinion and/or judgment. My daughter interpreted my comments about her fruit plate as criticism, judgment, or opinion and from her perspective she was correct.

Feedback, by definition, is direct observation or a review of data collected in a transparent and/or an "agreed upon" method. For example, regarding my daughter, I could have said, "You put 42 grapes around the entire perimeter of the fruit plate." While doing this I must also be aware of my tone of voice. It should be neutral because data is also neutral.

Another example: if someone is late I could tell him/her, *"We were scheduled to meet at 2 PM and it is now 2:30 PM. You are 30 minutes later than I expected."* If you really want to deliver feedback keep this idea in mind: it is observable and the tone is neutral. Without these factors in mind it can quickly become criticism and can harm engagement.

Rule #3: Deliver Criticism Only with Permission

Sometimes we need to deliver criticism. Sometimes we must give our opinion. If you are going to do so, When it's delivered let's name it an opinion. If it is an opinion and our intentions are positive (either to improve trust and/or improve learning) we must ask permission prior to delivery to avoid a negative response. With my daughter I could have asked, *"May I give you my opinion about the fruit plate?"* It's not wrong to deliver criticism but how and when we do it is important. The result we receive may not be what we expected or what we desired. My daughter had tears because she took my criticism to heart. It hurt her feelings. Hurt feelings will most certainly damage engagement and motivation. I wanted her to hear my opinion but instead she shut down. I can blame her for being overly sensitive or change my approach, ask her permission, and then deliver my opinion in a neutral tone.

Rule #4: Help Employees Manage Their Own

Employee engagement is improved when employees have control over their own performance feedback. The best leaders help employees to find (or create) ways to track their own progress. The best leaders avoid manager dependent feedback. Manager dependent feedback (or opinion) means the employee must wait to hear from the manager about how he/she is doing. Manager dependent feedback does not enhance employee engagement because the employee feels controlled and/or dependent upon the all-knowing all-powerful manager.

The best leaders willingly arrange for employees to track their own progress. This sense of freedom creates ownership and responsibility. In the industrial age learning was mostly dependent upon how fast managers could solve problems. New policies and procedures were created mostly by management and needed to be implemented by the employees. Management used command and control and the Taylor Scientific Management Theory to accomplish this. In the Industrial Age it's management who knows best. They were responsible for creating the policies and procedures and then holding people accountable to those using Management by Objective or MBO (performance appraisals and pay-for-performance policies). Feedback took the form of corrections to the policies and procedures created by management. Feedback was therefore manager dependent.

Organizations must become more like "Self-Organizing Systems much like Social Networks." The Internet and mobile phones are accelerating the development of social networks. Networks are communities of people who have certain things in common and they want to communicate quickly, consistently and frequently. Each Community is connected to other communities through individuals who share those common connections. People love social networks because they feel connected and a sense of belonging. Social Networks help people share their interests, passions, values, priorities, with others of like minds.   Facebook is a great example of people who want to stay in touch with friends. LinkedIn is another example of business people who want to network to learn or find work.

These networks are voluntary, chaotic, complex, self-organizing, and innovative. Organizations who want future success must embrace the paradox of needing to be predictable in product and service while embracing the complexity, voluntary nature, and chaos of a network. Members of networks are naturally already engaged. That is why people opt-in-to social networks. Organizations that adopt the right methods of leadership will naturally create a network type of environment and that will naturally create employee engagement.

To shift thinking and behaviors from the old industrial model to the new social network (systems thinking) world leaders must influence employees to "opt-in." This means treating employees more like volunteers than like slaves. (Cloke & Goldsmith, 2002) Chaotic, diverse high change environments that allow flexible work hours, mobility, work-life balance, and collaboration are now needed to optimize trust and learning. Many leaders are unprepared to know how to create these environments.

Chaos and disequilibrium are necessary for networks to continuously learn. Organizations must get comfortable with this disequilibrium in order to continually adapt to change. Leaders must be expert facilitators of chaotic environments while simultaneously managing trust. Fearless feedback enables social networks to adopt these principles and adapt to change.

The Evolution of Feedback

Since the 1950's, and especially since the 1980's, when Japan surpassed the USA in quality improvement (thanks in large part to Dr. W. Edwards Deming) organizational leaders have come to realize the need and responsibility to manage a system. A system is a series of interdependent processes that are in existence to achieve an aim or purpose.

Because of this realization methods of giving feedback also had to experience an evolution. The nature and method of delivery of feedback needed to evolve from the management of individuals to the ability to manage a system. The chart below shows the evolution.

The Evolution of Feedback

	The Age of the Artisan and Apprentice	The Industrial Age	The Knowledge Age
Interpersonal Interactions Feedback Characteristics	Paternalistic and omnipotent relationship	Paternalistic, authoritarian, and omnipotent relationship	Partnerships based on trust and exploration of what is best
System Interactions Feedback Characteristics	"This is the way I have always done it and this is the right way!" The "expert" is always right.	"This is the way we need to do it because this is the most efficient way we have designed! This is the right way." The "boss" is always right.	"This is what we want. Let's experiment using the PDSA Learning Cycle to find an even better way to help all our stakeholders.

In the book "The Leadership Challenge", Kouses and Posner offer evidence of how feedback improves both performance and the ability to manage hardship (stress). In a study of soldiers who had to do a day long march, those who received the most accurate and frequent feedback consistently outperformed those who received little or inaccurate feedback (Kouses & Posner, 1995).

Feedback has changed over the years in both its purpose and scope because of the evolution of the economy. The evolution away from paternalistic, omnipotent management creates a need for more frequent feedback loops. This helps us accelerate our decision making and response to change. We must accelerate our decision making in every part of the system in order to respond to change faster than our competitors. We must accumulate knowledge faster than our competitors. The paternalistic, authoritarian, and omnipotent model is too slow.

Interpersonal interactions can come from anyone in an organization. In most organizations it is the employee's manager who is formally responsible for giving feedback to the employee. This is a manager dependent process that can contribute to the creation of a sluggish bureaucracy. Interpersonal interactions enable people to communicate effectively with integrity and respect. For example if someone is disrespectful they often are unaware of the effect it has on others and they need to hear about it in order to stop it in the future. When they break integrity they also need to know it in order to stop. Employees need to understand how their behavior impacts the performance of others. Every employee needs to behave with respect and integrity at all times or performance will suffer.

The White Flag®

How to create awareness, coaching opportunities, and accountability to values behaviors.

The White Flag® Origin: A sign of negotiators, neutral parties, or surrendering parties

The White Flag® is an international sign of truce ceasefire, and/or request for negotiation. It is also often associated with surrender, since it is often the weaker military party which requests negotiation. Showing a white flag signifies to all that an approaching negotiator is unarmed, with intent to surrender or a desire to communicate. Persons carrying or waving a white flag are not to be fired upon, nor are they allowed to open fire.

The use of the flag to surrender is included in the Geneva Convention. The improper use of a white flag is forbidden by the rules of war and constitutes a war crime of perfidy[2]. There have been numerous reported cases of such behavior in conflicts, such as fighters using a white flag as a ruse to approach and attack enemies, or killings of fighters attempting to surrender by carrying a white flag.

The White Flag® Process enables everyone to provide safe and fearless feedback about values behaviors. Employees can give feedback to each other and to management using The White Flag® process. The White Flag® is a metaphor for *"Truce! Don't attack me, I*

---

2   *It is prohibited to kill, injure or capture an adversary by resort to perfidy. Acts inviting the confidence of an adversary to lead him to believe that he is entitled to, or is obliged to accord, protection under the rules of international law applicable in armed conflict, with intent to betray that confidence, shall constitute perfidy.*

have valuable information and I am just here to help." The American Red Cross uses a similar symbol. When they go into a dangerous area of conflict, they are always displaying their "red cross on a white background". This prevents them from being attacked and allows them to help the wounded.

Here is how the White Flag® Process works (figure 1). When an employee or manager observes behavior that is inconsistent with the standard described in the values behaviors, they are encouraged, even obligated, to approach the person assuming they are unaware of what they did. They ask, *"Are you willing to hear feedback about the values?"* If there is too much emotion, they wait for a better time. If the employee says yes, then they state what they saw and explain how it does not fit the agreed upon values behaviors. In other words, they provide data about what happened and the reactions that were the results of the behavior. They say, "I just wanted to let you know." They provide any clarification if needed. They say, "Thank you!"

In one of my clients two managers were competing for a promotion. They were both qualified but only one could be chosen. After the decision one found himself reporting to the "new" manager. It was quite uncomfortable for both. They were both upset. The new manager was afraid the employee would sabotage the performance of the department. The employee thought the "new" manager as a bit incompetent and therefore could not be trusted.

The behaviors began to slip. Their interpersonal interactions began to be more and more brief and curt. The strain of the relationship was beginning to damage the performance of the entire department. The "new" manager decided it was time for an open and honest discussion. It was time for new agreements to be made with clear expectations of behaviors and clear agreements for action. The "new" manager decided to have a White Flag® meeting with the employee. They were able to talk through the issues related to this difficult change in authority. They are making huge gains in results for the team. Without the White Flag® Process, or something like it, it is less likely they would have been able to have an open and honest discussion and solve the problem themselves.

The White Flag® enables feedback in a safe and caring environment for the purpose of learning. There are two purposes for the White Flag®: building trust and/or enhancing learning. It's not for the purpose of evaluating the employee. It is not to criticize. Instead it's for the purpose of providing insight to the employee on any deviations to the standard. Receiving The White Flag® feedback creates a culture of accountability to values behaviors which leads to performance improvement. The feedback provides employees with an opportunity to learn immediately. Because most employees (or managers) who deviate from the operational values are unaware how their behavior impacts others, the immediate feedback gives insight into how to change now. There is no delay. There is no need to wait until the manager tells them during an annual (or mid-year) performance evaluation.

Another unique feature of the White Flag® Process is the manager doesn't always have to be the one to provide the feedback. Anyone can give the feedback if they observed the behavior. Employees can give feedback to each other. Managers can give feedback to each other. Employees can give feedback to managers.

Managers therefore don't always have to be watching because employees can observe each other. Employees willingly ask for feedback themselves and willingly provide it to each other because it is safe to do so and they see how the feedback can enable them to contribute toward creating an environment of integrity, respect, customer service, trust, and learning.

Everyone wants feedback. Any responsible adult will want to learn how to improve their interactions. Conversely, anyone unwilling to listen and learn is being irresponsible and possibly does not belong in the organization. Very often, irresponsible employees will quit when they know they will be held accountable to these values behaviors. Often these employees are those causing the most wasted management time on performance issues. The values behaviors are a high standard to meet and the White Flag® Process leaves no place to hide from that standard.

Figure #1

The White Flag ®
Values Feedback Process

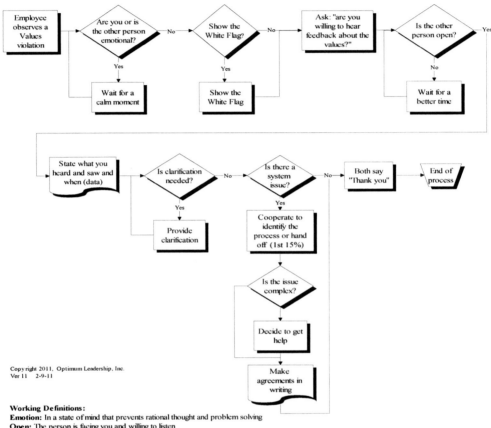

Working Definitions:
Emotion: In a state of mind that prevents rational thought and problem solving
Open: The person is facing you and willing to listen
The White Flag: Allows a person to approach another without being attacked (without argument or being defensive)
Data: Only what happened without editorial comments, judgment or opinions. *What I heard and saw you do was... Your tone was ... (descriptive word) and your body language was ...I just thought you would like to know.*
Clarification: A restatement of what happened (data) in different words.
Descriptive words: Non-evaluative..i.e. *stiff, sharp, harsh, quiet, rigid* etc. Not: *Good, bad, wrong* etc.
Make agreements: May include one of four types of system issues: 1) A complex process that requires a project team to create improvement; 2) Simple process that requires new agreements; 3) A policy exists and needs to be reviewed; 4) A new process is needed because none exists.

The most important element needed for the White Flag is a list of clear operational values behaviors. Ideally these behaviors are created with the entire senior leadership team, a contingent of key influential employees and a contingent of management staff. An example of those behaviors follows.

Optimum Leadership, Inc. Operational Values

Integrity:

- Communicate openly, honestly and responsibly: Say what you mean and mean what you say. ...and don't say it mean (tone of voice).
- Make only agreements[3] you intend to keep.
- Act upon your agreements to the best of your ability.
- Communicate when you can't keep agreements to those who need to know.
- Admit when a mistake is made and look at the system[4] as a team for a solution (no blame, make no excuses, no complaining).

Respect:

- Treat others as we would like to be treated
- Communicate directly, calmly and professionally (the absence of profanity, sarcasm and condescension)
- Listen attentively and congruently[5] without interruption and paraphrase to confirm understanding (stop, look, listen and confirm)
- Acknowledge the value of different perspectives and demonstrate it by our actions

Customer[6] Focus:

- Ask clarifying questions to be sure you understand what customers need.
- Make suggestions and recommendations that may better suit their needs
- Always keep your customer informed (as defined by the customer)
- Acknowledge requests promptly (as defined by the customer)
- Anticipate customer "wants"
- Treat all customers with respect and integrity
- Continuously explore ways to make more and more "higher quality" agreements with customers (continuous improvement)

Once the values are created the employees need to see them, understand them, appreciate why they are important, and embrace them. Ideally the employees will see how the values

---

3   *Agreement: An activity that is specific, measurable and time sensitive.*
4   *System: A series of interdependent processes that achieve an aim.*
5   *Congruent: Words, tone of voice and visual body language match to form a consistent message.*
6   *Customer: Anyone with whom we interact, provide information or services.*

behaviors will improve the entire environment. To achieve this outcome it is important to have a process that is customized for the specific organization. Here is one example.

Draft Script for introducing the Signing of a Values Poster:

We have worked hard over the past few months with Wally Hauck to redesign our performance management system and implement the Complete Performance Improvement Process (CPIP). As a part of this process, we have adopted a set of organizational values that are critically important to the foundation of RMI, and in this context, we are asking everyone to live these values to help create an environment of trust and performance. The management team has learned that they must make a commitment to demonstrate this behavior at all times to achieve these goals.

*We have created this poster with the values printed on it and we are all ready to sign it. If you sign the values poster that means YOU are willing to receive feedback on the values from others (using the White Flag®). If you don't sign the poster you may still receive feedback from others using the White Flag® but a signature makes it official that you are proactively seeking that feedback so that you can improve your relationships, your influence as a leader, and your personal growth as a leader. A signature means you are willing to learn what you are doing now that may not be consistent with the values. It shows a high level of commitment and responsibility to the values and a high degree of maturity and confidence because you may learn new things about yourself. At a later time everyone will be asked to not only receive feedback about the values but to also give feedback as well. The leadership team of the organization must sign the poster because they **must** be willing to receive feedback first. Only then can they expect others to be completely committed to the values. Gandhi once said: "We must become the change we seek." Signing the poster means you are willing to become the change by having others help you. We all have things we do unconsciously that can hurt relationships and productivity. You are leading the change when you sign. We understand that some may not be ready to sign right now. There must be room for those who are not ready to sign. The safer an organization is the more signatures will appear on the values poster. If you don't feel safe to sign please don't. We want the number of signatures on the posters to be a leading indicator of improved productivity and an improved environment of "A Culture of Trust".*

If you have specific concerns and are willing to verbalize those now, we will be happy to listen and begin to address your concerns. This is another step in our journey toward a culture of trust, pride, and productivity.

Thank you all for your participation."

Why is The White Flag® Process Important?

The White Flag® is a predictable tool to increase trust, reduce fear, while treating everyone with dignity even when they make a mistake. Most importantly The White Flag® accomplishes what the typical appraisal never could, i.e. immediate feedback for the purpose of learning. It provides data to employees and motivation for personal transformation. Personal transformation can only come from consistent insight and honest feedback. The typical appraisal fails at this miserably.

It helps leaders to instantly become aware of their behavior and its impact

Self-awareness is one of the key elements of emotional intelligence. (Goleman, 1995) A leader must be self-aware to be effective. The White Flag® is a tool that can help management become self-aware. According to Ryan & Oestreich in their book _Driving Fear Out of the Workplace_, abrasive, abusive, and/or ambiguous behavior of managers can contribute towards fear. (Kathlene Ryan, 1998) In Oestreich's studies the majority of managers were unaware they contributed to fear and intimidation of employees. Ryan and Oestreich also pointed out other systemic causes of the fear such as poorly managed personnel systems and perceptions of management (management beliefs and culture). The authors recommend eliminating the fear with a method(s) that addresses all four key causes of fear namely: 1) Abusive/abrasive behavior; 2) Ambiguous behavior; 3) Personnel systems and 4) Management perceptions and beliefs. (Kathlene Ryan, 1998) The White Flag® Process used in conjunction with the CPIP can help with all four of these requirements.

> _"While we know that some managers consciously intimidate their employees, most do not. We are confident that the greatest percentage of intimidating behaviors are committed unconsciously by managers who have no idea how their behavior is affecting others. Moreover, given the legacy of mistrust... many employees expect to experience repercussions even though there may be no immediate evidence that they actually will occur." (Ryan & Oestreich, 1991)._

A few years ago I had just finished conducting two-day training for a team of Senior Leaders in a Human Resource Department. We had just finished creating the operational values behaviors document. Under the Respect Section it read: _"Treat others the way you would like to be treated"_.

I received a call from one of the participants. He was very upset. He had just over heard a "yelling match" that two of the other participants had in the hallway where everyone could hear their heated exchange. It included loud voices, inappropriate tone and accusatory language. All behavior that was clearly inconsistent with *"treating others the way they would like to be treated."*

When the two participants were reminded of their agreement (The White Flag® was used) they were incredulous. Neither had any idea they had created fear in those who had observed them. Apparently they were used to treating each other in that very same manner. It was a habit for them. There was no disrespect between them because they both were able to work through differences often in that manner. For the observers however, this behavior was clear disrespect. Their outbursts disturbed and caused fear. The behavior was appropriate for them but inappropriate for the others. Their behavior had to change now because a new standard had been created and they were receiving feedback from their colleagues about it. They were becoming more aware of the impact they were creating.

> *"In interview after interview, the pattern was the same, regardless of the level of the person being interviewed. The quality of the relationship a person has with his or her direct supervisor is a key determinant of the fear or lack of fear- that person experiences at work." (Kathlene Ryan, 1998)*

It is the lack of awareness that prevents a change in management behavior and is a barrier to transformation of the organization.

The White Flag® Process enables managers to trust employees to fix their own performance problems and /or "prevent" performance problems from occurring. The White Flag® provides a method to hold everyone accountable to the values behaviors. Accountability is defined as an awareness of what needs to be done (expectations), an understanding of the process that must be used, an agreement to follow the agreed upon process, and consequences (or feedback) if they don't keep their agreement and/or if the process fails.

The White Flag® Process helps an organization to manage the variation in values behaviors

Managing the variation in values issues is an important skill for successful leaders for two reasons:

1. Behavior consistent with values is a predictor of performance improvement. In other words the better employees behave consistent with values the higher the level of performance.

2. Addressing values issues immediately enables everyone to uncover system issues that are creating the waste and the increased costs in the organization. Addressing values issues immediately can uncover opportunities for significant improvement in organizational performance.

As with any process, for the White Flag® to work best it requires certain ground rules to be followed.

Ground Rules for Using the White Flag®

*   It is unacceptable to allow behavior that is inconsistent with the values to continue without respectful feedback– *"We teach what we allow."*
*   Feedback must be delivered in person and one-on-one (no telephone unless no other option is available due to geographic issues and no email no group meetings)
*   Always be calm during the meeting
*   Always be sure the other person is calm and get permission first before proceeding, *"May I give you feedback about the values…?"*
*   Describe the situation using the description of specific behavior and not opinions (avoid criticism or judgment language): *"Here is what I heard you say.. here is what I saw you do…"*
*   Refer to the Operational Values standard if necessary to clarify the behavior needed and the behavior observed
*   Keep your tone of voice helpful, warm, friendly, and empathic
*   Use statements that begin with "When you did *this*, I felt *this*…   "
*   Always ask questions when you do not understand or disagree (do not judge, no criticism)

- Always ask for a new agreement on how to change the process or system (hand-off) in the future, e.g. *"Are you willing to agree to …?"* or… *"I am willing to do this… will that work for you?"*
- Always confirm the agreements with helpful neutral language in an email after the meeting: *"Here is what we agreed….thank you."*

Use the White Flag® to identify the system issues that need to be corrected and which were the contributing factor(s) or cause of the break in values.

When it is determined that there is a system issue this process can be used to decide on the next action step(s)

Improving a System Issue

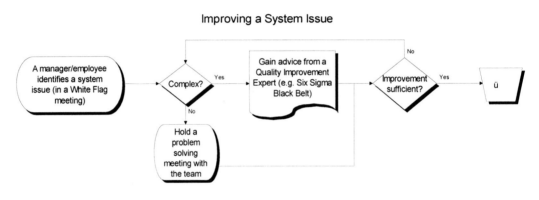

Copyright Optimum Leadership, 2012

Bullying and Fearless Feedback

Bullying and employee engagement don't mix. Bullying is one person intimidating or threatening another in a disrespectful, dominating, or cruel manner. Bullies tend to put performance results ahead of all other considerations including respect and trust. Bullies think about themselves and not about others. Aggressiveness is action without regard to others. It's an "I win and you lose" strategy. Assertiveness is action with a "win-win" strategy. Employee engagement can only grow in a culture that discourages and prevents bullying while encouraging collaboration, respect, and effective relationships with win-win communications.

Causes of bullying are complex. The first set of factors relate to the psychological needs and flaws of the bully. According to author Susan Coloraso bullies tend to have specific attitudes and behaviors including blaming others for situations. They lack the willingness to take responsibility for their actions or their miserable situations. They lack emotional intelligence traits such as the ability to sincerely understand how others might feel and the ability to express empathy. They tend to be narcissistic focusing all their concern about themselves and not about others.

Bullies also believe competition is an important strategy for success. They have difficulty with collaboration because they feel superior and others are seen in an inferior position. For them, aggression is the way to success.

Women and men can both bully although men have a higher tendency toward physical abuse and women use more psychological abuse such as passive aggressive manipulations.

The second set of factors that cause bullying is the lack of an effective response from the workplace system. Dr. W. Edwards Deming said 94% of all results come from the system. Bullies are mostly allowed to continue without feedback and/or consequences for their poor behaviors. Although the root causes of bullying stems from the experiences, and probably the parenting, of the bully, it's the responses (or lack of) of the system that keeps the behaviors alive.

Organizations that are unprepared and/or unwilling to create consequences for bullying behaviors will be victimized by those same bullies. Unfortunately some leaders give "lip service" to a set of organizational values that discourage bullying behaviors. Instead of confronting the poor behaviors immediately and consistently, leaders can instead ignore (or downplay) the behaviors and place more value on the results bullies are able to achieve. The results achieved by the bully often trump the willingness of the leaders to have a confrontation.

In 2011 Jerry Sandusky was accused, tried, and convicted of 45 of 48 counts of child molestation. Sandusky was a longtime assistant football coach at the revered Pennsylvania State University. Evidence revealed during the trial and the FBI investigation concluded that the head coach, the University President, the vice-president and the athletic director all played a part of cover up the activities of Sandusky. (Dedman, 2012)

Although Sandusky's behavior was revealed in an incident in 2011 it took up to 10 years for his behavior to be formally confronted. In 2010 Penn State was ranked 3rd in the nation for total revenue generated by their football program. Over $50 million in profit was cleared by Penn State from the football program in 2010. The main point in the FBI report by Louis Freeh concluded that the University acted in such a way as to avoid bad publicity. (Dedman, 2012) In a statement after reading the report the President of the University explained, "It has become clear to me that I need to reconsider our community's leadership culture." Without a clear method for confrontation the results achieved by the bully often trump the willingness of the leaders to have a confrontation.

We teach what we allow. Bullies learn their behaviors. They are not born as bullies. They were possibly allowed by parents, or even encouraged with subtle messages, to continue their tactics. The only way to change is to stop the subtle messages and confront the poor behaviors directly and respectfully.

Besides respectful confrontation organizations should also evaluate the hiring process to ensure bullies are not allowed to slip through the "hiring cracks."

A system of effective Fearless Feedback will go a long way toward reducing the probability of bullying. This must start with the senior leadership. Senior leaders must make it clear that results with bullying are unacceptable even if the results are financially profitable. Leaders must take a stand. Financial results achieved with bullying tactics must be evaluated in the context of the cost to employee engagement. The costs associated with low employee engagement levels are much more difficult (if not impossible) to measure than financial results. The bullying will either stop or be significantly reduced if the system is set up to provide respectful and immediate feedback to bullies and if they are given the choice to either change their behaviors or move on.

Bullying and employee engagement don't mix. Senior leaders must decide if results from employee engagement are more valuable than short-term results with bullying. If senior leaders pay lip service to respect and win-win solutions but then avoid respectful consequences for bullying, things won't change and employee engagement will suffer.

System Interactions are the second type of feedback required to achieve optimum employee engagement. These interactions provide information about how well employees are working with and within their processes. Employees influence their processes and their processes influence their performance. How well an employee interacts with his/her processes will determine the quality and speed of their work and the satisfaction of their customers (either internal or external).

Employees should be able to receive frequent feedback from their processes. Their manager may need to give them feedback on the quality of their interpersonal interactions but feedback from the processes should not be fully dependent upon the employee's manager. The employee, if they understand how to study a process, can arrange to collect their own data.

Managing variation in Systems Interactions

> *"If you can't describe what you are doing as a process, you don't know what you're doing."*
>
> *Dr. W. Edwards Deming*

The quality and the speed of organizational learning are strategic advantages. As stated numerous times before this is more true today than ever before because our economy is a knowledge economy. For example, Google is an organization that makes information and knowledge more accessible. The capitalization of Google is worth more than the capitalization of any of the three domestic automakers.

The faster an organization learns the more profit it will attract. Furthermore, how an organization chooses to learn will depend upon its approach to handling problems. Does the organization have a proactive process to identify the type of problem and the correct way of handling that problem? Reactive organizations lack this conscious process and therefore usually just ignore (absolve) the problems or only react to them when they arise. Learning organizations know how to identify the most important problems, know when to take action and they have a process to dissolve the problems.

Knowing how to manage the variation in processes (or system issues) is a needed competency for leaders in the knowledge economy. The ability to handle a system issue requires an understanding and appreciation of these five success factors:

1. The ability to take responsibility for a problem and decide to dissolve it (prevent it from happening again).
2. Appreciating the concept of optimization and having the willingness to accept responsibility for optimization of the system.
3. Understanding and appreciating the concept of variation.

4. Understanding and appreciating the four types of problems often encountered by a leader

5. Understanding and appreciating the standard process improvement tools

Many leaders thrive on solving problems. Some leaders enjoy exaggerating the seriousness of a problem just to look good when they provide a solution. This type of behavior is consistent with Frederick Taylor Scientific Management because it confirms managers are omnipotent and omniscient. At worst, some leaders create problems in order to have the opportunity to swoop in and "save the day" with dramatic flair. The personal thrills of the situation and/or the rewards offered to solve the problems are often the motivations behind this behavior.

The discipline for modern knowledge leader is to become a facilitator for problem solving. Knowledge leaders are able to put ego aside and commit to identify and dissolve problems that will make a significant positive difference for the employees, the organization, and the customers. The optimum leader has the commitment and the skill to identify those problems that must be dissolved and he/she knows the difference between resolving, solving, and dissolving a problem.

The Four (4) Ways of Handling a Problem (or System Issue)

1. **<u>Absolve</u>** yourself of it - "It's not my problem."
The problem is ignored or is left for someone else to address it.

2. **<u>Resolve</u>** it - remember what worked before with a similar problem, modify as appears necessary, and do just enough to satisfy the present situation (do the minimum so it will go away for now).

Action is taken to address the problem in the short term (e.g. the fire is put out).

3.   **Solve** it - do study and research to find the best solution to the problem.

The problem is evaluated and action is taken to either detect the fire more quickly or to "put out the fire" more quickly (e.g. new fire detectors and sprinkler system are installed).

4.   **Dissolve** it - both solve it and prevent its reoccurrence - change the system or process so the system or process no longer has the problem - this is the Deming process improvement approach.

Innovative solutions are implemented to prevent the fires (e.g. replace combustible materials with fire-retardant ones)

Resolving a problem is similar to putting out a fire. All effort is directed to putting out the flames and eliminating all danger, and/or destruction.

Solving a problem means some effort is put forth to identify some factors to prevent the reoccurrence or to minimize the destruction in case it happens again. For example, instead of just putting the fire out, the fire department team might insist that the buildings have smoke detectors or sprinkler systems installed.

Dissolving a problem means it will not occur again. This requires study, knowledge, and prediction. This requires effort, the most effective way of thinking about a problem, and the correct tools. For example, a fire department might insist that fire-retardant material is used to replace the material that caught fire in the first place. Some significant change is needed to prevent the reoccurrence.

Most organizational cultures are great at resolving and solving problems. They are great at reactionary problem solving. In order to dissolve a problem one must have the right theory, the right tools, and a strategy focused on optimizing the system over time and not focused on short-term results..

What is Optimization?

Optimization is an orchestration of a system. It is not a state of being. In fact, a powerful metaphor for optimization is an orchestra. An orchestra has each of its parts coordinating with the whole. No one musician is attempting to "out-play" another or to stand-out above the rest. They each play a role to contribute to the beautiful outcome of the music which provides joy to the audience.

Because optimization is not a state of being it can never be fully achieved. There is always room to improve regardless of how much progress is made. Optimization is an approach or strategy not a condition. Another over used phrase is "continuous improvement" but optimization is a more sophisticated approach than just "continuous improvement" because a process can be improved but it might not optimize the system. For example, we can continuously improve gas mileage by reducing vehicle weight to save fuel costs. In so doing, we may, at the same time, inadvertently reduce vehicle safety especially in a crash. This is the opposite of optimization. This is improving the parts without consideration for how the whole is impacted.

Optimization takes into account all factors important to a customer experience. To optimize a system one must collect data and that data can help identify the variation thereby enabling the leaders to better manage that variation. The management of variation is all about probabilities not certainties. The key is to work on the system to improve the probability that customers will be delighted with the entire experience of the product.

What about mistakes?

Managing variation in a system is not just about finding mistakes and fixing them. In an organization where people will be evaluated using performance appraisals it is highly probable they will hide serious mistakes knowing they might be punished if those mistakes are discovered. There are at least two problems here. First, hiding mistakes increases costs and damages the customer experience and loyalty. A delay in the discovery of a mistake can damage a relationship with a customer. An unhappy customer will buy less in the future and will possibly tell others why the product(s) must be rejected. An unnoticed mistake can cause the symptoms to worsen and therefore increase the cost of repair. Just as untreated cancer can cause an increase in cost of healing or even death, an undetected mistake will damage the entire system.

There is another problem when discussing people's mistakes during a performance appraisal meeting. If the mistake was one that another person could have made then correcting or punishing that person still does not solve the problem and does not prevent it in the future. Very often the cause of an airline accident is determined to be "pilot error". This determination does little to help prevent the accident from occurring in the future because pilots are well-trained and their actions are often guided by policy and procedure while being assisted with instruments and technology.

The key to preventing the accident in the future must be a change in the process that enables the actions of the pilot to be influenced by the system and not rely entirely on their memory, their experience, and/or their reactions. The proper approach to avoiding serious errors in the future is to help make behaviors more "system dependent" and less "person dependent". An example of a system-dependent method of preventing errors (not a memory-dependent method) is the little window that pops up on your computer when you delete a file. It asks, *"Are you sure?"*

Improving a system requires to use of the learning cycle, often called the Shewhart Cycle (Deming, The New Economics - Second Edition, 1994) to improve key processes. The Learning Cycle enables organizations to improve, individuals to develop a sense of pride in their work, reduces waste and the loss created by that waste. Learning is also the most powerful long-term intrinsic motivator for employees.

Waste and loss created by too much variation in poor processes can drain a business of its precious resources and prevent it from properly servicing both its employees and its customers. Waste and loss lead to disloyalty of both employees and customers and this loss can drive a company out of existence.

Any variation in processes can add waste. Toyota has identified eight different types of waste that need to be managed.

Types of Waste

- Waste from doing more than needs to be done when it needs to be done (over production): e.g. *If you prepare for a meeting that ends up being rescheduled it is waste.*
- Waste from waiting time: e.g. *I must wait for information to be sent to me before I can act.*
- Transportation waste: e.g. *travel time to a location does not add value.*
- Processing waste: e.g. *activities that prevent you from finishing your work on-time without defects and without interruption or any other type of activity that interrupts concentration).*
- Inventory waste: e.g. *If I purchase office supplies I don't want to over purchase and yet I want to buy enough to achieve the right discount.*
- Waste of motion: e.g. *If I have to complete a task (or set of tasks) can I do it in a way that avoids unnecessary activity or motion?*
- Waste from product defects *e.g. do we have time to do it over but don't have time to do it right the first time? How do we handle defective products or services?*
- Waste of under-utilization of people skills *e.g. are we using all of our skills and talents to promote the Speaking profession?*

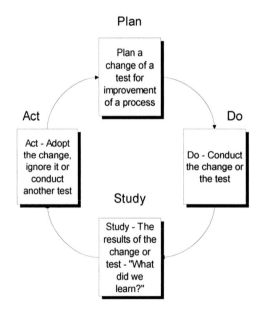

The interactions in a system are very complex. For example, your body is a complex system. Your heart needs the muscles to be in good shape so you can exercise and keep your heart in good shape. Yet the heart must be in good shape to begin with if the muscles are to be exercised.

The Four Types of System Issues

As we have learned in previous sections, if it is a values issue, address it with the White Flag® Process. The White Flag® will enable you to uncover the real issue located somewhere in the system.

If it is a system issue then you can ask, *"Is this an important issue such that it must not happen again?"* If so, *"Which type of issue is it?"* For purposes of creating the correct strategy to address (or dissolve) the problem it is useful to identify the type of problem. A leader can ask the following questions to identify the specific type of problem and therefore identify the specific strategy that will work best.

Is it a simple and easy change in the system and is it simple enough so you can make new agreements to clarify and dissolve the issue?

This is the easiest type of change to make and it often does not require bureaucracy to fix it. Avoiding bureaucratic control is essential to keep organizations nimble and easily adaptive to changing circumstances and customer demands.

Does it require a reminder of a current Standard Operating Procedure (S.O.P) or policy? Are you authorized to communicate and take action to review that policy with employees? Does the policy need to change to dissolve the issue?

Often others have already experienced the same problem and a policy has already been established with the intention of preventing it from occurring. For example, an employee may misunderstand how to notify a supervisor or Human Resources when he/she intends to take a personal day and this could result in a conflict. A simple reminder about the policy will suffice to help everyone follow the policy next time. Perhaps an improvement in the communication process of that policy would also help. For example, the policy might be covered explicitly in the New Employee Orientation.

Does it require a new process? (There is no process to handle this).

Very often a problem surfaces because there is no clear process (or there are multiple processes) for the same objective. For example, if a new product is created by marketing, the sales department needs a clear process to present it to existing customers or new customers. Often sales department management will delegate the decision about how, who, and when to sell the new product to each of the individual sales representatives. This will create inconsistent results across the entire sales force. It may cause frustration and mistakes which will then result in lost sales or higher costs.

In these types of situations a new process must be developed and the team must come together to create the process. If it is a simple process that falls within the responsibility of the sales function, the sales manager(s) and his/her team can create the process on their own.

Is it a complex process? For example, does it involve interactions between departments or an interaction between the customer and certain department (e.g. a customer complaint)? Does it require an improvement team because of the complexity?

Often a problem has been ignored because it is complex and cuts across departmental lines. This creates a barrier because no one manager and/or team can, or wants to, takes full responsibility for the improvement. This requires managers and teams to work together to form a process-improvement team. Often a lack of clarity in one department causes the other department to experience poor performance. For example, the marketing department may expect sales to achieve a certain sales goal for a particular product; yet, marketing has not provided a thorough product-training process. In this example, the marketing manager and sales manager would need to cooperate to form a process-improvement team.

One of my clients is a medical practice. They provide radiology services to patients. The scheduling department receives calls from patients and/or referring physician offices to schedule the patients for various types of scans. Each scan can be unique because the patient is unique yet the amount of time needed for each scan is often the same. This can cause the schedule to fall way behind or to create gaps in the day. The ability to understand the complexity of the individual patient's case requires a great deal of education and experience. Often the scheduling person does not have that level of education or experience. The scheduler can therefore schedule the patient incorrectly. This creates a "ripple" effect through the entire organization. This is a great example of a very complex problem that requires a cross functional team who can continuously improve the predictability and productivity of the technicians, schedulers, and the patients.

To help decide which type of problem you are facing, a leader can begin by asking the following questions. The more "no" answers to these questions the higher the probability it is a type #4 issue (a complex process) and there is a need to form a process-improvement team to dissolve it.

Key Questions to Uncover System Issues and to identify complexity

- Do we know where in the process the problem (issue, mistake, upset, conflict) occurred? Do we know where the variation originates (what is the first 15% of the process)?
- Do we have a flow chart of the process?
- Do we know who the customer is (who is being served by the process)? Do we know who the supplier(s) is? Do we have agreements and standards from the supplier?
- Do we know what the customer needs? How do we know?
- Do we have data for the customer? What type? How old? In what form? Do we have data for the supplier? What type? How old?
- Do we know how to solve this problem?
- Do we already have a team effort to dissolve this problem?
- Can we be sure this will not return, or is it isolated?
- Is it a low or high priority to prevent this from happening again?
- Do we know who can help us answer some of these questions?

If a process improvement team is needed they will probably need to understand how to use the basic quality tools. Without these tools the process improvement efforts is less predictable and more laborious.

The seven (7) basic quality tools

1. Brainstorming: To gather information on a given subject from a group of people in a non-threatening environment. Successful brainstorming allows people to be creative (does not restrict ideas in any way); generates excitement in the group; equalizes participation; and expands the ideas often resulting in new and original solutions to problems.

2. Cause-and-Effect / Fishbone Diagram: The purpose is to identify all of the causes of a problem (the effect) and organize them in order to get a deeper understanding of the problem and to dissolve it. A fishbone or cause-and-effect diagram can also help you focus on the area(s) offering the best opportunities for improvement.

3. Data Collection: Use working and operational definitions to collect data so that it will be as consistent, useful, and undistorted as possible. Operational definitions are used to define the measurement process to reduce variation in data collected.

4. Analyzing data: Control Charts – The purpose is to measure the variability of a system or process over time, determine whether the outcome is predictable, and filter out the system's or process' noise (common causes) from signal (special causes); Run Charts - To show the variability of a system or process over time. Every process exhibits some variation.

5. Flowchart: To provide a picture of a process, which allows you to understand it and see opportunities for improvement.

6. Histogram: A histogram is a graphic method of displaying numerous data in a form that indicates the central tendency, the spread along the scale of measurement, and the relative frequency of occurrence of the various values. The purpose of a Histogram is to graphically view process performance and variability

7. Pareto Chart: To focus attention on the areas of potential improvement that offer the greatest potential return on time, effort, and resources invested. A Pareto chart shows which issues to work on first. A Pareto chart is a graph or picture of the sources of problems in order from most- to least-important. It is based on the principle of "the vital few and trivial many"; that is that 80 percent of the trouble comes from 20 percent of the problems. The 80-20 rule.

A leader can begin to evaluate his/her process improvement skills through the lens of their ability to use the seven basic quality improvement tools. Guessing at answers to problems is the same as pretending to be omnipotent. Furthermore, whenever a manager decides on his/her own to answers to complex problems they are missing an opportunity. They miss an opportunity to align the employees and therefore may damage their engagement. They miss an opportunity to gain knowledge. If their answers are incomplete and/or unsophisticated they may actually make things worse.

When a problem involves complex system issues it must be studied using tools that can help a leader reach an aligned decision with those who are most impacted by the process and with those who must sustain the changes. As more people learn how to use the tools, the leader can delegate more of the problem-solving responsibility to those who will take full responsibility for results.

Leaders are responsible for helping everyone to improve the quality of the interpersonal interactions and the system interactions. The White Flag® Process can help uncover the root causes of problems in the interpersonal interactions. The basic quality tools can help uncover the root causes of problems with system interactions. These two approaches help create a culture that can provide timely and quality fearless feedback for the purpose of learning and trust building. These approaches take the focus off the criticism of the individual and place the focus on the improvement of the quality of the interactions.

Chapter 11:
The Complete Performance Improvement Process (CPIP)
How does the CPIP work to improve accountability without rating individuals? Does it raise the standard of performance or lower it?

Aim of this Chapter: To explain the CPIP process and how it can be implemented.

CPIP is designed to create an environment that will optimize the probability of open and honest communication. It is also designed to optimize performance of the individual and the organization but instead of using control techniques it utilizes intrinsic motivation and influence to improve accountability. The design allows for the injury of the typical appraisal to be eliminated while the value is optimized.

CPIP provides the opportunity (the vehicle) to create a high trust environment which will optimize the opportunity for the manager and employee to cooperate, synergize, and innovate to accomplish the goals. Instead of the manager grading (evaluating) the individual, the two become a team to achieve the S.M.A.R.T. Goals faster and faster with higher quality. They work as a team to adapt to ever changing conditions (either internal or external). They avoid blame and criticism and innovate to optimize energy and resources (especially time resources).

The strategic initiatives must be made clear to all employees. As we discussed in an earlier chapter, the strategy of the organization is part of the foundation. Without a set of strategic objectives the manager and employee have nothing to work toward and have nothing to build their objectives upon.

With higher trust, they can better synergize to create S.M.A.R.T. Goals. S.M.A.R.T. is an acronym and stands for **S**pecific, **M**easurable, **A**ligned with strategy, **R**ealistic, and **T**ime sensitive. They can also identify a process(s) to accomplish those goals. From the process they can identify agreements that must be completed in order accomplish the S.M.A.R.T. Goals. Agreements are the nucleus of performance. The better each employee keeps agreements the higher the performance. As the quality of the agreements improves the quality of the performance improves.

One purpose of CPIP is therefore to facilitate high quality agreements that an employee and manager can complete which will move the organization forward toward the accomplishment of the strategy.

If agreements are broken this may become a values issue. When an agreement is broken and that lack of action is not accompanied with a responsible adjustment in the goal or responsible communication of the problems (or barriers) preventing accomplishment of the agreements this becomes a values issue (inconsistent with the operational values behaviors). These breaks in values must be documented. This documentation data can be used to confront the employee with their poor performance. High performance therefore is defined as the willingness and ability to identify and keep challenging agreements. These agreements are aligned with the process(s) which will accomplish the S.M.A.R.T. Goals which lead toward the accomplishment of the department strategy and the organizational strategy.

Because the employee is given lots of autonomy in the choice of the S.M.A.R.T. Goals, autonomy regarding the method to achieve the goals, and autonomy on the agreements they make, there is lots of ownership and responsibility. There is also lots of motivation or engagement. As part of the exercise to identify their S.M.A.R.T Goals it's often useful to ask them what frustrates them at work. Working toward removing their frustrations is also a very motivating exercise.

One client of mine is also using the CPIP to develop open and honest dialogue between peers in different departments. Because the purpose of CPIP is to improve the quality of the interactions the tool can be applied wherever interactions occur. Often organizations and leaders suffer from what is often called the silo mentality. The silo mentality is an attitude that occurs when managers in different departments do not cooperate or share information on a timely basis. Often they can even compete for that same information or resources and will hoard to prevent the other from achieving the goals. A silo mentality reduces efficiency, increases costs and prevents customer service improvements.

By using the CPIP between peers in those different departments my client has been able to break down the barriers between the departments and share the knowledge necessary to improve the communication and productivity. The Human Resource Manager told me that she had always wanted to break down these barriers but until the CPIP became available she did not have a mechanism to get things started. CPIP was the catalyst for peer managers to begin to cooperate across departments.

The Complete Performance Improvement Process (CPIP)

What are the steps?

There are four big steps in the *Complete Performance Improvement Process* the replacement for the typical performance evaluation:

1. Create a Strategy and Organizational Goals
2. Prepare for the meeting – collect data and complete the forms
3. Conduct the meeting – share data – make agreements
4. Review the entire process and make improvements

The Complete Performance Improvement Process (CPIP) 4 Step Procedure

---

Step #1: Agree on Strategy Initiatives. Create goals and objectives that must be improved to achieve the Strategy and communicate those goals and objectives to all employees, i.e. improvement in:

- Revenue, Profit, Speed, Internal Communication, Processes, Quality, etc.

Step #2: Prepare for the meeting:

A. Set the Environment

- Ask employees to agree on specific Values behavior (see Values)
- Ask employees to be willing to give (and receive) feedback to you (from you) and each other regarding values behavior (White Flag®) when they see values being broken
- Explain "the grade" or rating is now eliminated

B. Complete the Forms

- Manager and employee complete the Relationship Self-Assessment (purpose is to uncover values issues)
- Manager and employee complete the System-Opportunity Check List (purpose is to uncover opportunities for improvement in the system)
- Manager prepares to receive White Flag® feedback by completing the Values Coaching Process forms

Step #3: Conduct the meeting:

A.   Improve Trust and the Relationship

- Manager asks for White Flag® Feedback – Creates a safe environment and makes the manager "vulnerable" (Manager uses White Flag® Coaching Process Self-assessment to be prepared)
- Manager asks permission and then gives White Flag® feedback (concrete examples and facts only and without emotion)
- Manager and employee discuss the results of Relationship Self-Assessment forms and the gaps in their answers

B. Identifying opportunities for system improvement

- Manager and employee discuss the results of the System-Opportunity Check List

C. Make agreements - Accountability

- Manager and employee make agreements to move toward the measurable goals (as a team)
- Manager confirms agreements with dates and sets new meeting date based on how long it will take to achieve agreements. There is follow up on those agreements (accountability).

Step #4: Improve the process:

- Managers discuss how to improve the CPIP process by sharing what happened and making suggestions for improvement
- Employees and management discuss (as a team) changes to improve the process

Step #1 is to agree on measurable goals and communicate those goals to employees. Any job may have a different set of goals yet those goals must be in the context of the bigger goals (or strategies) of the organization. Employees who understand how their jobs connect with the "big picture" goals of the organization are much more likely to make good decisions, care about quality, care about customers, and care about their co-workers. In other words, clarifying the strategy and the goals is the first of many steps toward engagement. As stated in an earlier chapter the clarification of strategy is part of the foundation for engagement (House Metaphor).

Strategic Initiative

The preferred words to use for a description of how "aligned action" occurs in organizations is: *Strategic Initiative, Objectives, Process, Tasks and Agreements*. A Strategic Initiative is a BIG GOAL for the organization that the leadership believes will help it achieve the purpose of the organization. For example, "creating a culture of trust" is a strategic initiative. CPIP assists leaders to improve trust and every organization should have a strategic initiative to improve trust because that strategy will predictably improve performance over the long-term. Trust is like the oil in the engine of action in an organization. It facilitates action. Trust helps an organization achieve its purpose more quickly and with less waste.

Another example of a strategic initiative is to "improve customer service". A leader can easily explain how an improvement in customer service will create a competitive advantage, increase revenue, and help the organization achieve its purpose. The customer service example can help to further clarify how CPIP can work.

Objective or Goal

Once a strategic initiative is clarified, a goal or goals can be set (the term *objective* can be used interchangeably). A goal is something toward which effort is directed. All factors may not be under the control of the person who chose the goal. For example, increasing productivity in a particular department is a goal that can support the strategic initiative of improving customer service. This goal is dependent upon the support and cooperation of other departments. All factors are not under the control of the employee who set the goal. He/she certainly cannot control others' behaviors and cooperation in the different departments. For that matter one could argue they also cannot control the behaviors and cooperation of those in the same department.

> *"If you do not know how to ask the right question, you discover nothing... What we need to do is learn to work in the system, by which I mean that everybody, every team, every platform, every division, every component is there not for individual competitive profit or recognition, but for contribution to the system as a whole on a win-win basis."*
> *Dr. W. Edwards Deming*

Ideally the strategies, objectives (goals) are set in cooperation with the teams within and between the departments to avoid any competing interests. Once goals are created they must be communicated to all those who may need to help achieve them.

Process

A process is a series of steps. A process is like a recipe for a gourmet meal. It is a series of actions dedicated to achieve an extraordinary outcome. The process of responding to incoming customer orders is a process that is part of the customer service strategy. CPIP is designed to assist department teams to have open and honest discussions about how to design and improve the processes for achieving goals. Full cooperation with complete honesty is needed to perform optimum processes to achieve the goals of the organization. It is desired to achieve goals with the least amount of resources and minimum waste.

Task

A Task is a step in a process. Answering an incoming call from a customer is a task. A task is only one step in a process. The CPIP is designed to put the full focus, resources and energy of the manager and employees on achieving the goals (objectives) tasks and agreements all of which will lead to the achievement of the strategic initiatives.

Agreement

Agreements are commitments to complete a specific task by a certain time. An agreement is a specific, measurable and time sensitive task where all factors are thought to be under control. For example, the sales department manager may decide that the process of transferring information to the customer service department for all new orders, if improved, could help improve customer service. He/she therefore might ask a small team of sales people to identify the current process, identify key tasks and agreements that all salespeople must perform in order to improve the quality and speed of the information on new orders.

The CPIP is designed to discuss these processes, tasks and agreements. This discussion requires a good understanding and appreciation for a system and a clear understanding about how to study and improve a process.

Step #2 Prepare

In part A of the CPIP the employees are made aware of the operational values. They are also informed about the White Flag® Process. It is also made clear that the employee will no longer receive a formal rated by the manager (or by anyone else).

Complete the Forms

In part B both the manager and the employee complete the Relationship Self-Assessment Check List and the System Opportunity Check List. The purpose of these forms is to enable the manager and the employee to assess the current quality of the relationship between the manager and employee and the quality of the relationship between the employee and the system within which he/she works. The completion of the forms prepares them to work together as a team to improve the processes, assign the tasks and make the necessary agreements to accomplish the goals.

Imagine yourself as the manager and you and your employee are going to have a CPIP meeting. You complete the Relationship Self-Assessment on your own. You rate the trust level between yourself and the employee a 3 (out of 5). When you get into the meeting you may find the employee also rates trust a 3. Therefore, the two of you probably have the same perspective and therefore no conflict. At this point however you and the employee may want to improve that level of trust because a 3 is an average rating for trust. An average rating is probably not enough to ensure optimum performance.

If, on the other hand, the employee rates the trust a 1 while your rating is still a 3, the two of you obviously need to discuss the gap. The size of the gap is just as important as the rating. The purpose is to have a quality discussion about the relationship using the data and the perspective of both the manager and employee. Each has a valid perspective and each perspective must be honored especially if the quality of the interaction is going to be improved.

The quality of this discussion will provide an opportunity to improve trust, strengthen the relationship and provide a greater probability of identifying those processes, tasks, and agreements that will move the organization closer to the strategic objectives. The data is discarded after the conversation because it has served its purpose (a quality conversation).

The second form (and the 5th action in Step 2) in Part B is the System-Opportunity Check List. The purpose of this form is to help the manager and employee to understand how the system is impacting the employee performance. Does the employee have all the tools that they need? Do the employee skills match his/her job responsibilities? To demonstrate how this form works, as the leader, if you don't think the skills match the job responsibilities, but the employee thinks they do, a discussion about this must occur. The expectations of the employee and the manager are out of sync. This can lead to poor performance, mistakes, poor quality, and poor customer service. Again, the gap is just as important as the rating itself.

In summary, Part B in Step#2 is really a pre-check list that can uncover some values issues and some systems issues so they can be addressed in the CPIP meeting. These check lists make the meeting more productive and valuable.

The 6th action is where the Manager prepares to receive White Flag® feedback by completing the Values Coaching Process forms. The purpose of the Values Coaching Process is to help the manager reflect on their current personal values behavior and be fully aware of any possible challenges that might arise during the meeting with the employee. Full preparation can help prevent a defensive reaction and unnecessary conflict during the meeting. The Value Coaching Process is described in more detail in a later chapter about Special Tools.

Step #3 The Meeting

Now that the forms are complete, a meeting can be held. There are three parts, A, B and C in conducting a CPIP meeting. In Part A, the bullet point is geared to improve the trust in the relationship. This is where the manager asks for White Flag® feedback first.

The White Flag® process provides an opportunity for feedback. It also improves trust because the manager makes him/herself vulnerable thereby actually increasing trust instantly with the employee and giving him/her more influence.

The second bullet point is where the manager gives White Flag® feedback with concrete examples of specific values behavior. The third bullet point under Part A is where a manager and employee discuss the results of the Relationship Self-Assessment. They discuss any gaps that they need to close or any scores that are too low and need improvement. This requires some skills to be sure the sensitive issues are discussed and resolved. It requires a firm adherence to the values behaviors and some skill of active listening and providing empathy.

Opportunity for System Improvement

Part B is for the manager and employee to identify opportunities for system improvements. The System-Opportunity Check List explores system factors that can either help or hinder employee performance. For example, are the employee skills aligning with his/her responsibilities? Part B is about systems improvement and the check list provides a way to discuss factors that may need to be changed to make any significant improvement in the individual performance or the employee.

Make Quality Agreements

Part C provides an opportunity for the manager and employee to identify the processes, tasks and agreements that must be addressed. This requires the skills of listening, appreciating a system, and process improvement tools. The agreements are the culmination of the entire meeting. The goal is to make high quality agreements that can make a significant and measurable difference in the performance of the entire organization and move it closer and faster toward the achievement of the strategic initiatives.

The high quality agreements accomplish a number of important outcomes. First, these agreements move the department and the organization closer to the achievement of the goals and strategies. Second, agreements that are challenging, but not too challenging, provide intrinsic motivation to the individuals. (Csikszentmihalyi, 1990)

The agreements will include a completion date. The completion dates are critical because they can trigger a new meeting with the employee in order to create new agreements. This is another unique feature of the CPIP. The frequency of meetings and feedback is customized specifically for each employee. The meetings are held based on feedback from the system and from the employee. The frequency of meetings is not determined by a bureaucratic policy designed to control behaviors. The CPIP is not "married" to any specific time frame like the typical performance evaluation (one year).

Step #4 CPIP Improvement

Step #4 is about improving the entire CPIP. Most often managers and employees have little or no influence over how the typical Performance Evaluation process is conducted. The Human Resource and Legal Departments are often in charge of the entire process and prevent any changes in an effort to either be fair to all or to attempt to protect the organization from legal challenges that can arise when an employee leaves or is removed for poor performance.

The CPIP is a process and therefore it can be improved. Step #4 is all about the manager(s) asking for the opinions of their colleagues and the employees to identify changes to the CPIP that will provide greater trust, better agreements, greater truth and greater learning. By changing the CPIP process the managers and employees feel autonomy and continue to own the process. They take personal responsibility for making it work.

"Follow effective action with quiet reflection. From the quiet reflection will come even more effective action."
Peter F. Drucker

Relationship Self-Assessment – Leader

Note: This form is to be completed for the sole purpose of preparing for the Agreements Meeting. It is to be destroyed after the meeting (no record is kept in the file).

(Completed by leader to prepare for the Agreements Meeting – one of these is needed for each meeting)

Directions: **Circle the number in the column that best describes what you have observed in your organization.** If the rating is below 3 please make notes to explain in preparation for the meeting. **Assessment Statement**	Strongly Disagree	Disagree	Somewhat agree	Agree	Strongly Agree	Don't Know	**Notes**
1. My employee trusts me.	1	2	3	4	5		
2. I trust the employee.	1	2	3	4	5		
3. My employee treats others with the utmost respect and integrity.	1	2	3	4	5		
4. My employee works as a team player without being asked or expecting incentives.	1	2	3	4	5		
5. My employee shows they care about quality by continuously improving what they do without being asked or expecting incentives.	1	2	3	4	5		
6. My employee continuously makes suggestions without being asked or expecting incentives.	1	2	3	4	5		
7. I promptly evaluate and implement their suggestions.	1	2	3	4	5		
8. My employee is proactive in his/her approach to work (not reactive).	1	2	3	4	5		
9. When my employee makes a mistake he/she lets the appropriate people know without hesitation.	1	2	3	4	5		
10. My employee and I are aligned on the purpose and vision of the unit/section.	1	2	3	4	5		

Relationship Self-Assessment - Employee

Note: This form is to be completed for the sole purpose of preparing for the Agreements Meeting. It is to be destroyed after the meeting (no record is kept in the file).

(Completed by employee to prepare for the Agreements Meeting – one of these is needed for each meeting).

Directions: **Circle the number in the column that best describes what you have observed in your organization.** If the rating is below 3 please make notes to explain in preparation for the meeting. **Assessment Statement**	Strongly Disagree	Disagree	Somewhat agree	Agree	Strongly Agree	Don't Know	Notes
1. My leader trusts me.	1	2	3	4	5		
2. I trust the leader.	1	2	3	4	5		
3. My manager treats others with the utmost respect and integrity	1	2	3	4	5		
4. My manager works as a team player without being asked or expecting incentives.	1	2	3	4	5		
5. My manager shows he/she cares about quality by continuously improving what they do without being asked or expecting incentives	1	2	3	4	5		
6. My manager continuously makes suggestions without being asked or expecting incentives.	1	2	3	4	5		
7. I promptly evaluate and implement their suggestions	1	2	3	4	5		
8. My manager is proactive in his/her approach to work (not reactive).	1	2	3	4	5		
9. When my manager makes a mistake he/she lets the appropriate people know without hesitation.	1	2	3	4	5		
10. My manager and I are aligned on the purpose and vision of the unit/section.	1	2	3	4	5		

System Opportunity Checklist for Leaders

Note: This form is to be completed for the sole purpose of preparing for the Agreements Meeting. It is to be destroyed after the meeting (no record is kept in the file)

Directions: Please circle the number on the scale that best describes your opinion. The Manager completes this based on his/her perception. Employee completes this from the perspective of how they see it. If the answer is below "5" or there is a significant gap between Employee rating and Manager rating, please provide data (examples) with names of processes.

Rating	Statement	Notes
1 2 3 4 5 6 7 8 9 10 Completely Somewhat Completely Disagree Agree Agree	1. The employee skills and education match his/her current role/job responsibilities.	
Rating	**Statement**	**Notes**
1 2 3 4 5 6 7 8 9 10 Completely Somewhat Completely Disagree Agree Agree	2. The employee is clear about what is expected of him/her in his/her role/job responsibilities.	
Rating	**Statement**	**Notes**
1 2 3 4 5 6 7 8 9 10 Completely Somewhat Completely Disagree Agree Agree	3. The employee is clear about the Values and what is expected of him/her in following the Values	
Rating	**Statement**	**Notes**
1 2 3 4 5 6 7 8 9 10 Completely Somewhat Completely Disagree Agree Agree	4. The employee has all the resources they need to perform their role/job responsibilities.	
Rating	**Statement**	**Notes**
1 2 3 4 5 6 7 8 9 10 Completely Somewhat Completely Disagree Agree Agree	5. The employee has a clear career plan that will help them achieve what they want.	

Rating										Statement	Notes
1 2 3 4 5 6 7 8 9 10 Completely Disagree / Somewhat Agree / Completely Agree										6. The employee is continuously learning in their current role/job responsibilities	

Rating										Statement	Notes
1 2 3 4 5 6 7 8 9 10 Completely Disagree / Somewhat Agree / Completely Agree										7. Managers in the Organization follow values with him/her.	

Rating										Statement	Notes
1 2 3 4 5 6 7 8 9 10 Completely Disagree / Somewhat Agree / Completely Agree										8. Their fellow workers follow values with him/her.	

System Opportunity Checklist for Employee

Note: This form is to be completed for the sole purpose of preparing for the Agreements Meeting. It is to be destroyed after the meeting (no record is kept in the file)

Directions: Please circle the number on the scale that best describes your opinion. The Manager completes this based on their perception. Employee completes this from the perspective of how they see it. If the answer is below "5" or there is a significant gap between Employee rating and Manager rating, please provide data (examples)with names of processes.

Rating										Statement	Notes
1 2 3 4 5 6 7 8 9 10 Completely Disagree / Somewhat Agree / Completely Agree										1. My skills and education match my current role/job responsibilities.	

Rating										Statement	Notes
1 2 3 4 5 6 7 8 9 10 Completely Disagree / Somewhat Agree / Completely Agree										2. I am clear about what is expected of me in my role/job responsibilities.	

Rating										Statement	Notes
1 2 3 4 5 6 7 8 9 10 Completely Disagree Somewhat Agree Completely Agree										3. I am clear about the Values and what is expected of me in following the Values	
1 2 3 4 5 6 7 8 9 10 Completely Disagree Somewhat Agree Completely Agree										4. I have all the resources I need to perform my role/job responsibilities.	
1 2 3 4 5 6 7 8 9 10 Completely Disagree Somewhat Agree Completely Agree										5. I have a clear career plan that will help me achieve what I want.	
1 2 3 4 5 6 7 8 9 10 Completely Disagree Somewhat Agree Completely Agree										6. I am continuously learning in my current role/job responsibil-ities.	
1 2 3 4 5 6 7 8 9 10 Completely Disagree Somewhat Agree Completely Agree										7. Managers in the Organization follow values with me.	
1 2 3 4 5 6 7 8 9 10 Completely Disagree Somewhat Agree Completely Agree										8. My fellow workers follow values with me.	

CPIP Agreements Meeting Agenda

Item		
Section I: Discuss Values and make agreements:	45	Minutes
• Welcome and thank you • Discuss Gaps in Relationship Self-Assessment Checklist (if necessary Manager asks for White Flag® Feedback – celebrate successes and discuss opportunities and Manager gives White Flag® feedback - celebrate successes and discuss opportunities)		
Section III: Objectives	45	Minutes
• Discuss career aspirations: Are you happy where you are? Do you aspire to another job here? Elsewhere? How can I help you? • Discuss objectives (strategy-goals-objectives) • Discuss Gaps in System Opportunity Checklist • Make agreements to achieve objectives and to address issues identified on checklist		
Section III: Review agreements	5	Minutes
Adjourn	95	Minutes

The key outcome of the CPIP meeting is the list of agreements. A form was created to assist the manager and employee about the key elements of an agreement and to assist in the recording of those agreements. As we have stated, the agreements confirm the action steps and create the accountability. Agreements are like the nuggets of value that come out of the CPIP. The ability to facilitate high quality agreements is a skill leaders must continuously improve in order to make CPIP successful.

Meeting Agreements

— This is the only page retrained

Date of Meeting: _____
Staff Person: _____
Manager:_____

Agreements:

Who ?	Objective	What is the agreement[1]?	When?	Completed?

To assist the manager with improving the quality of the CPIP meeting a check list has been created.

CPIP Meeting Quality Improvement Checklist

Facilitate the meeting:

- I started the conversation with subjects important to the employee and to the employee's communication style
- I reinforced the importance of the values behaviors and asked for White Flag® feedback from the employee. I acknowledged any concerns without being defensive and without shame. I made agreements for improvement.
- I asked permission to give White Flag® feedback to the employee and delivered it appropriately and respectfully.
- I facilitated agreements necessary for the employee to improve values behaviors.
- I suggested agreements I can make to improve my values behaviors.
- We reviewed all necessary S.M.A.R.T. Goals/Objectives.
- We created or made agreements to create processes to achieve S.M.A.R.T. Goals/Objectives
- We made agreements to improve or to implement processes
- We recorded the agreements
- We identified system barriers that were preventing performance improvements
- We made agreements to take action to either remove or to begin to remove each of the barriers
- We discussed the career aspirations of the employee for purposes of succession planning, development actions and promotional decisions
- We discussed any training needed or desired and made agreements
- We set up a next meeting date based on agreements created

Confirm the agreements:

- The agreements made during the meeting were confirmed in writing
- The agreements confirmed were accurate and had specific dates (they met the definition of agreement)

Follow up:

- We reviewed all agreements and made new agreements.
- I confronted any broken agreements using the White Flag® and recorded any values issues.

- I admitted any broken agreements that I had. I took responsibility without shame or excuses. I made new agreements.
- We reviewed the status of the S.M.A.R.T. Goals/Objectives and made new agreements.
- We identified system barriers preventing performance improvements.
- We made agreements to take action to either remove or to begin to remove each of the barriers.
- We set up a next meeting date based on agreements created

One of the biggest challenges today for leaders and Human Resources managers is to cascade the strategic objectives through the organization and to ensure people are working on their objectives. The Society for Human Resources Management (SHRM) conducted a study in 2010. The researches wanted to identify, through a survey, the top challenges for the next 10 years. They identified four main challenges including *Getting and Making the Most of Human Capital, To Attract and Keep the Best Talent, Cultivate a Culture of Trust, Open Communication and Fairness, and to Keep a Clear Line of Sight Between Employees' Work and Organizational Objectives.* (Management, 2010)

CPIP helps leaders to accomplish the clear line of site if certain success factors are put in place.

As a review, the key success factors that must be in place in order for CPIP to work optimally and the strategic objectives are cascaded throughout the organization are as follows:

1. The big objectives are clearly stated and the senior management team is aligned on those objectives.

   a. The big objectives are clearly stated and the senior management team is aligned on those objectives such that there is little or no compromise. Although some senior managers may feel daunted by the strategy they are in agreement that the achievement of the strategies will create success for everyone and will not contradict their personal values.

2. There is a high level of trust between the senior leaders and the staff.

3. The organization appreciates how the "flow of action" will facilitate the adoption of the goals throughout the organization.

a. The flow of action includes the creation of S.M.A.R.T. Goals (Specific, Measureable, Aligned with strategic initiatives, Realistic, and Time sensitive); the identification of a process to achieve the goals; the facilitation of agreements to accomplish tasks needed to complete the process.

4. Managers and/or employees must be willing and able to create goals which, when accomplished, will move the organizations forward toward the achievement of the strategic initiatives. This is more of an art than a science.

a. S.M.A.R.T. Goals (Specific, Measureable, Aligned with strategic initiatives, Realistic, and Time sensitive).

5. A clear set of operational values that everyone has committed to following.

6. A clear set of outcome measures (or score card) that let's everyone know how the organization is doing and to see the connection of how they are impacting the measures with their efforts to achieve their goals.

a. These outcome measures should be calculated and reported with full transparency.

b. Typically these outcome measures are for financial results (revenue and/or profit); customer retention, satisfaction and/or growth; effectiveness or efficiently of key processes (cycle-time or quality); Employee retention, engagement or development and learning.

7. Managers and employees have the following skills or are taking action to develop these skills and abilities:

a. How a system works and how to create and understand a process(s)

b. Create S.M.A.R.T. Goals – Specific, Measureable, Aligned with strategic initiatives, Realistic, and Time sensitive

c. Create a process to achieve the S.M.A.R.T. Goals

d. Project management skills to facilitate the achievement of the process(s)

e. Facilitate agreements to achieve the process steps. Influencing skills.

f. Confront inappropriate behaviors (inconsistent with values behavior) when things go wrong. They can use the White Flag® process.

g. Ask questions to uncover root causes of process problems

h. Willingness to hold people accountable to their agreements and document when agreements are continuously broken

To ensure proper planning by the manager a checklist for how the manager effectively implements the CPIP is included here.

Prepare and Plan:
- The strategic objectives for the organization are clear.
- I have identified objectives and S.M.A.R.T. Goals for our function with my manager.
- I know which of my objectives and S.M.A.R.T. Goals the employee can best impact.
- I am aware of the communication style of the employee and of my communication style and how it might impact the meeting. I am able to adapt to the employee's communication style and prepared a set of words and actions to use to do so.
- I have honestly completed the Relationship Self-Assessment and have made notes with data to support my ratings.
- I am prepared to receive White Flag® feedback from the employee and I am ready to listen and acknowledge any perspectives that claim I may have broken values with the employee.
- I have honestly completed the System Opportunity Checklist and have made notes with data to support my ratings.
- I have scheduled 2 hours if this is my first CPIP with this employee (1 or 1-1/2 hours with others).
- I have scheduled the meeting in a neutral, quiet, private, and safe space if necessary.
- I prepared a list of agreements I want the employee to make with me.

Facilitate the meeting:
- I started the conversation with subjects important to the employee and to the employee's communication style
- I reinforced the importance of the values behaviors and asked for White Flag® feedback from the employee. I acknowledged any concerns without being defensive and without shame. I made agreements for improvement.
- I asked permission to give White Flag® feedback to the employee and delivered it

appropriately and respectfully.

- I facilitated agreements necessary for the employee to improve values behaviors.
- I suggested agreements I can make to improve my values behaviors.
- We reviewed all necessary S.M.A.R.T. Goals/Objectives.
- We created or made agreements to create processes to achieve S.M.A.R.T. Goals/ Objectives
- We made agreements to improve or to implement processes
- We recorded the agreements
- We identified system barriers that were preventing performance improvements
- We made agreements to take action to either remove or to begin to remove each of the barriers
- We discussed the career aspirations of the employee for purposes of succession planning, development actions and promotional decisions
- We discussed any training needed or desired and made agreements
- We set up a next meeting date based on agreements created

Confirm the agreements:
- The agreements made during the meeting were confirmed in writing
- The agreements confirmed were accurate and had specific dates (they met the definition of agreement)

Follow up:
- We reviewed all agreements and made new agreements.
- I confronted any broken agreements using the White Flag® and recorded any values issues.
- I admitted any broken agreements that I had. I took responsibility without shame or excuses. I made new agreements.
- We reviewed the status of the S.M.A.R.T. Goals/Objectives and made new agreements.
- We identified system barriers preventing performance improvements.
- We made agreements to take action to either remove or to begin to remove each of the barriers.

- We set up a next meeting date based on agreements created

To help the manager to better prepare for the CPIP it is sometimes beneficial to assess his/her current opinions about the employee.   Although the manager opinions are not recorded as a permanent record he/she can still acknowledge the existence of the opinions and use them to make decisions about how to facilitate the CPIP in order to accomplish the ideal outcomes. The outcomes, as mentioned many times before are improved trust, learning and an improvement in the quality of the interpersonal and system interactions.

If a manager holds certain negative opinions about the employee he/she is obligated (in the CPIP process) to uncover the root causes of those opinions and address them respectfully. To assist the manager this four situation model was created.

The Four Major Situations

#2	#4
The Leader and the Employee have high trust.	The Leader and the Employee have high trust.
The employee is performing poorly in his/her job	The employee is an excellent performer in his/her job
#1	#3
The Leader and the Employee have low trust.	The Leader and the Employee have low trust.
The employee is performing poorly in his/her job	The employee is an excellent performer in his/her job

Situation #1:
Low Trust and Low Performance Description

You are concerned about meeting with this person because you know you will have a challenging conversation. Your employee may be new or you may be new to the role of his/her manager. Most likely you have not had enough opportunity (or the right opportunity) to work out your differences. Lincoln said, "<u>I don't like that man. I must get to know him better.</u>" The CPIP meeting will provide the opportunity to get to know him/her better. Be prepared for this meeting to be longer than others (possibly 2-3 hours).

Action Steps:
1. Be sure to complete both forms (The Relationship Self-Assessment and the System Opportunity Checklist) and of course, be sure to ask the employee to complete the forms as well.
2. Some of the differences may be caused by the differences in style. It is useful to familiarize yourself with his/her communication style.
3. In the beginning of the meeting be sure to get him/her talking.
4. If he/she is reluctant to talk begin asking questions about them such as: *"How are you feeling about your job?"* or *"How are you feeling about our organization?"* *What is it like to work here?"* *"Do you feel supported here?"* *"What do you really want?"* *"How can we help you get what you want?"*
5. Be sure to use active listening and L.E.A.D. with Trust when responding. You will need this employee to make changes in behavior. The best way to do that is to be willing to listen for changes YOU can make first and make agreements to help them get what they want.
6. You may want to consider using the *Values Coaching Process* before discussing the System Opportunity Checklist if trust is truly an issue.

Situation #2:
High Trust and Low Performance Description

You are concerned about meeting with this person because you know you will have a challenging conversation especially about performance. The good news is the high trust will help you to have the conversation more quickly and with higher quality. Your employee may be new to the job or they may not be clear about the expectations or the process within which they must operate. Also, there may be competing objectives. For example, they may need to work faster because they are falling behind and their quality may be suffering. The conflict between workload and quality of work may be causing poor performance.

Action Steps:
1. First be sure to complete both forms (The Relationship Self-Assessment and the System Opportunity Checklist) and of course, be sure to ask the employee to complete the forms as well.
2. In the beginning of the meeting confirm the strength of your relationship and reinforce that because of the high level of trust, whatever challenges there are will be addressed together as a team. Reinforce that the system is causing the challenges and reinforce your commitment to their success.
3. Begin the system opportunity discussion portion by asking questions such as: *"How are you feeling about your job?" or "Do you have all the support you need?" What is it like to work here?" "Do you feel supported here?" "How do you feel about your performance?" "Do you think we agree on the expectations of the work you need to do?"*
4. Be sure to use active listening and L.E.A.D. with Trust when responding. You will need this employee to make changes in behavior. The best way to do that is to be willing to listen for changes YOU can make first and make agreements to help them get what they want.
5. Because trust is high, it may not be necessary to use the Values Coaching Process step.

Situation #3:
Low Trust and High Performance Description

You are concerned about meeting with this person because you know you will have a challenging conversation especially about the relationship. You are also concerned because the performance is high and you don't want to do anything to jeopardize that while you know that the trust must improve to sustain the performance. The good news is that there is much for you to learn about how and why the quality of work is so high. Your employee is probably not new to their job and yet you might be new to your management position. You might not know them well yet and it is possible you just need to get to know them better to improve the relationship. Or, perhaps your relationship has suffered due to a clash in communication style or some other system conflicts. In any event, you realize that the trust level must improve to sustain the performance level.

Action Steps:

1. First be sure to complete both forms (The Relationship Self-Assessment and the System Opportunity Checklist) and of course, be sure to ask the employee to complete the forms as well.
2. Some of the differences may be caused by the differences in style. It is useful to familiarize yourself with a style instrument so your can be prepared to address the differences.
3. In the beginning of the meeting be sure to get them talking.
4. If they are reluctant to talk begin asking questions about them such as: *"How are you feeling about your job?"* or *"How are you feeling about our organization?"* *What is it like to work here?"* *"Do you feel supported here?"* *"What do you really want?"* *"How can we help you get what you want?"*
5. Be sure to use active listening and L.E.A.D. with Trust when responding. You will need this employee to make changes in behavior in order to improve the relationship. The best way to do that is to be willing to listen for changes YOU can make first and make agreements to help them get what they want.
6. You may want to consider using the *Values Coaching Process* before discussing the System Opportunity Checklist if trust is truly an issue or if you have had emotional conflicts in the past with this employee.

Situation #4:

High Trust and High Performance Description

You are generally excited about this meeting because the relationship and the performance are both solid. Your only concern might be to be sure he/she is able to keep up the good work and you don't want to do anything to jeopardize that performance. There is much for you to learn about how and why the quality of work is so high and, because the relationship is solid, there will probably be a free flow of ideas with open and honest communication. Your employee is probably not new to their job. You both probably share the same expectations for his/her job and the processes within which he/she works are probably clearly defined and supported.

Action Steps:

1. First be sure to complete both forms (The Relationship Self-Assessment and the System Opportunity Checklist) and of course, be sure to ask the employee to complete the forms as well.

2. In the beginning of the meeting reinforce the strength of the relationship by discussing the Relationship Self-Assessment results. Reinforce how the two of you can make a real difference in the entire department if you can synergize

3. In the System Opportunity Checklist discussion, begin asking questions such as: *"What is making you so successful?"* or *"How can we share your success with others?"* *"What do you really want?"* *"Where do you see yourself in the future?"* *"How can we help you get what you want?"*

4. Be sure to use active listening and L.E.A.D. with Trust when responding. Be sure to listen for ways to improve the entire organization by sharing what they are already doing. See if you can synergize to tackle other challenging issues facing the department. Take advantage of their expertise and your relationship with them to solve challenging problems facing the entire department.

5. Consider asking the employee to play a coaching role with other employees.

6. Think about how he/she can maintain their level of challenge by taking on more or different types of work.

7. Use the Communication style instrument to identify the opportunities for the employee to continue to utilize their strengths in other situations.

To help new managers to better understand and appreciate how CPIP works and how it is different from the typical appraisal a list of frequently asked questions is included here.

Frequently Asked Questions about CPIP and How It is Different

How does CPIP help us to reinforce Ethics (ethical behaviors)?

The foundation of CPIP is based in the operational values behaviors. Values behaviors (either defined or undefined) influence the performance and improvement in any organization. Ethics (and ethical decisions) are based on sound principles of judgment where people make the right decisions with the right principles when no-one is watching or coaxing them. The values behaviors are reinforced throughout the CPIP and so ethical behavior is encouraged and reinforced with the use of CPIP. It is reinforced in all interactions, i.e. toward the employee and toward the manager. With CPIP the manager is held accountable (with White Flag® feedback) to the values behaviors with the same vigor as employees are held. This creates a sense of fairness where the manager gains credibility by his/her ability to follow values behaviors before giving feedback to the employee to follow those same behaviors. This avoids the possibility of a double standard i.e. managers have privileges that employees don't enjoy.

How does CPIP increase the inspiration of employees?

The forms used in CPIP include key questions based on employee engagement criteria. (Csikszentmihalyi, 1990) CPIP collects subjective data about the current status of the employee's engagement (emotional connection with work) from both the employee's perspective and the manager's perspective. The purpose of CPIP is to create a safe environment to share the truth about this criterion. When the manager and employee share the truth, discuss it, and then make good decisions (as partners) to improve the conditions within which the employee works, this inspires both the employee and manager to improve trust, learning, and performance. A learning environment is a motivating environment.

How does CPIP improve attendance?

CPIP alone will not help improve attendance. It must work in conjunction with the values behaviors and the responsibility (by everyone) of providing immediate feedback with the White Flag® when values behaviors are violated. Failure to arrive to work on time (or at all) is a values issue when it is inconsistent with values behaviors. For example, when an employee doesn't show for work and never calls that is different than someone who calls in and has a legitimate excuse. Very often showing up for work on-time is an unspoken and sometimes unwritten agreement the employee makes with the employer but it is still an agreement the employee is expected to follow. A pattern of breaking that agreement is often a sign the employee is not interested (engaged) in remaining employed. If the employee is sending a message (either spoken or unspoken) *"I don't want to work here anymore!"*, why not help them quit?

CPIP is a planning session to improve the quality of the interpersonal (relationship) interactions and the system interactions (hand offs). CPIP training requires the use of both types of actions: 1) delivering immediate feedback (and facilitating agreements) every day and 2) creating synergy between two employees to solve problems once per year in the CPIP. The immediate feedback holds employees accountable to their agreements. Showing up ready for work is an agreement and individual responsibility that the employee must manage as a working adult. The use of the White Flag® and CPIP reinforces adult behaviors. The two work together as a system of performance management.

Leaders often define a "poor performer" as one who is unable or unwilling to achieve results (meet the goals). This is an unsophisticated definition because it does not include the impact the system might have on the employee's ability to achieve the goals. CPIP uses a different definition. A poor performer is an employee who continuously breaks his/her agreements. In this definition it is assumed the system has an influence on an employee's performance. An employee (manager) who continually breaks values behaviors and/or fails to give/receive feedback using the White Flag® when values behaviors are broken is also a poor performer.

How does CPIP improve accountability?

I could copy and paste the answer from the previous question here. Being accountable and/or responsible means you are clear about your individual responsibilities and you make an agreement to fulfill them with a predictable process and there are consequences (feedback) when those obligations or agreements are not met. If the process fails then the values behaviors apply, i.e. the employee must immediately notify those who need to know and new agreements are made. The employee is obligated to admit mistakes and take action to correct them. CPIP is about creating a safe environment to uncover root causes of poor performance (system issues) and make agreements to remove those root causes. This environment is the height of accountability where adults work with adults, leaders work with leaders, and those who behave like "victims or children" are no longer welcome.

If there is no grade for the employee in CPIP how does one document good or great performance?

CPIP provides a greater opportunity to document great performance because it removes opinion and bias from the equation and replaces them with data. CPIP requires agreements that are made to be confirmed in writing. This written record of agreements provides the foundation for how an employee is able to follow values behaviors. This record therefore demonstrates employees' ability to work with respect, integrity, and a focus on customer needs with every single action. Any breaks in agreements are recorded and therefore become a permanent record. A pattern of intentionally broken agreements becomes a record of poor performance. Conversely, a record of the pattern of agreements kept provides a history of high performance and great accomplishment. The employee (in conjunction with their partner-manager) identifies goals aligned with the strategy of their department and those goals are aligned with the strategy of the organization. Those employees who develop skills to identify key processes, tasks and agreements to accomplish those goals are the high performers. They can be asked to create a record of their accomplishments and confirm that record in writing so their history of high performance is recorded. This history provides a rich and informative story about how well an employee is performing and it is much higher quality than a grade provided by a biased manager.

A separate process where employees (peers) can acknowledge immediate and surprise appreciation has been shown to boost employee engagement and performance. One such process is called The Appreciation Process and it can supplement the CPIP. The events of appreciation can be recorded and kept in the employees' performance record to show how well the employee is able to create high quality interactions with peers and customers.

How does CPIP help employees (managers) to document poor performance?

The answer to this question is very much related to previous questions above. The use of the White Flag® (providing immediate feedback on values behaviors) is essential to document patters of poor performance. According to W. Edwards Deming 94% of mistakes is a result of a failure in the system within which an employee works. Mistakes blamed on the employee are a form of malpractice because blame is inconsistent with values and with systems thinking.

Instead, the manager and employee should work as a team (a partnership) to uncover the root causes of those "system" mistakes and make agreements to avoid them or reduce in the future. The mistakes may just be common cause variation from the process itself.

Following values behaviors is an individual responsibility. The proper use of the White Flag ®, along with proper documentation of agreements made and broken, provides a record of poor performance and this leads to a high level of accountability. This method also creates a sense of fairness across the entire culture. Everyone is expected to follow values and everyone (even the bosses) must be held to that same standard. There is no double standard with the use of CPIP and the White Flag®.

How do we make decisions about promotions (or other job changes) without the typical grade in the typical performance appraisal?

If you relied on the performance appraisal grades to make decisions about promotions then a new process is needed to make those decisions. This new process can be much more transparent and can create an atmosphere that is fairer. The use of a grade in a performance appraisal, by a biased manager, damages trust and credibility. A team of managers and employee is best able to create this new process and then promote it throughout the organization. It must be customized to the organization. It will have certain characteristics. It must be clear, measurable, based on data, based on how the organization can be optimized over-time. Many organizations who use the typical appraisal process award promotions based on bias, luck, and/or politics. This often damages employee engagement. A better process can be created.

How do we distribute pay raises if we don't have a grade on a performance appraisal?

A new process is needed for pay distribution. Just as the decisions for promotion will be more transparent, decisions about pay will also be more equitable with a transparent process. Studies show that pay decisions based on biased performance appraisal scores, and or forced distribution, damage engagement, innovation, and performance. The article mentioned earlier describes how Microsoft has damaged its innovative thinking process with its dysfunctional distribution of pay. (Eichenwald, 2012) This subject will be addressed in more details in Chapter 13.

Chapter 12:
More Tools to Manage Variation in Values Behaviors

Aim of this Chapter: To explain more tools to help leaders to continuously manage trust and to address special situations especially during the CPIP meetings.

The CPIP meeting often uncovers some challenging situations. Often the truth is allowed to emerge for the first time and it can be a bit ugly or uncomfortable. Once the truth comes out the relationship can heal but it is much like opening a closet full of junk that has never been cleaned out. Opening the door just a bit can release all the junk and it comes pouring out uncontrollably.

It is not enough to wait until an incident occurs. We want everyone (especially leaders) to be proactive in reinforcing the values behaviors because that will lead to a safe and trusting environment which will lead to improved innovation. The White Flag® is useful but it is not proactive. It is reactionary. The White Flag® may also need to be used in a very emotional situation and that makes it challenging to manage the communication.

To be proactive and manage the variation in the values behaviors there are six additional tools. These tools are designed to be used in conjunction with the Complete Performance Improvement Process (CPIP). They are:

1. L.E.A.D. with Trust
2. The Values Coaching Process
3. The White Flag® Coaching Process
4. The Bridge to Accountability and De-selection
5. Coaching and Trust-Building Checklist
6. Corrective Action and Dismissal by Managers

All these tools work as a system. This listing here must not be interpreted as a list in priority or importance.

L.E.A.D. with Trust: Achieving High Performance with Influence in Challenging Times

Leaders are able to accomplish more by influencing others instead of attempting to control others. When a leader has influence, he or she has the ability to create trusting environments giving others the freedom to make the right decisions without inspection or control. They can trust without observation. Today, more and more managers have less and less control over people and less and less time to tell them what to do. Instead, leaders need the full cooperation and trust of peers and employees to accomplish goals and execute strategic objectives.

The top three issues facing organizations in the next ten years are (SHRM and Globoforce, 2012):

- Attracting and retaining high quality talent
- Creating cultures of trust and employee engagement
- Execute strategic goals more quickly and effectively and with less resistance

To manage these issues leaders need to develop their influencing skills. That is exactly what L.E.A.D. with Trust can deliver.

Question #1: What should I do if I want or need to improve my relationship and trust with my employee?

Answer #1: The Values Coaching Process can be used here. Ask for White Flag® feedback from your employee and make agreements to improve your values behaviors first before you ask employees to improve their values behavior. Complete the Values Coaching Process self-assessment form and ask your employee for White Flag® feedback. You will also be coaching your employee on how to give White Flag® feedback at the same time you are re-building the trust.

Question #2: How can I be sure I am helping employees to follow values and how can I know I am helping them improve their processes?

Answer #2: Use the Process for Following and Coaching Values behaviors. Employees want to do a good job and they sometimes make mistakes and nearly all the time these mistakes are unintentional. Make new agreements with the employee to avoid any confusion or misunderstandings.

Question #3: What if an employee is disrespected (another employee broke values with the employee) and the employee complains to you about the situation, what do you do?

Answer #3: Use the White Flag® coaching process to uncover why this employee was unwilling or unable to use the White Flag® and encourage them (coach) to use it (or to forget about the broken value). Perhaps they need extra coaching from HR also. The White Flag® Coaching process can help with that too.

Question #4: What if an employee and a manager are not getting along (no trust and the relationship is severely damaged) and the employee has poor performance (the manager is complaining about the employee's performance to the Human Resources Department)?

Answer #4: Use the Bridge to Accountability process to uncover why the employee was unwilling or unable to rebuild trust and create a plan of action. Human Resources must help facilitate a plan of action or help the employee de-select. Often the manager (and or other employee) has contributed to the dysfunction by also breaking values. This is why HR needs to facilitate this interaction.

Question #5: What if an employee continuously breaks values with the manager (or with another employee)? What do you do?

Answer #5: Use the White Flag® Process. Document the repetitive behavior and clear violations in values behaviors such as broken agreements. After each offence, facilitate a new agreement that clearly states the behavior you are looking to see next time and refer to the values behaviors as examples of the behavior you seek. When those agreements are broken, this must be documented clearly (ideally in an email) summarizing what the agreement was, what happened instead, and what the new agreement is. A document trail is collected over-time.

Question #6: What if an employee is performing poorly and does not have the competency to do the tasks detailed in the agreements he or she sets?

Answer #6: The CPIP is designed to uncover this situation and create a plan for improvement. The System Opportunity Check List is there to uncover areas of improvement (e.g. employee skills, resources needed to do the job, tools needed to do the job etc.). Facilitate agreements with the employee that you both believe will resolve the competency issues. Allow HR to help you with options that will enable the employee to improve. If the employee is willing to improve their behaviors, the manager can facilitate agreements to help him/her improve. If the employee is unwilling they are probably de-selecting (ready to quit). Help them de-select and use the White Flag® and Bridge to Accountability processes.

The Values Coaching Process

The Values Coaching Process is the most effective proactive tool to prevent unnecessary destructive conflict and to increase trust between manager and employee. The purpose of this process is to help a manager/leader to understand how to modify his/her communication with specific employees and therefore improve the trust and quality of the relationship.

The Values Coaching Process can be used to improve the relationships between employees especially between a manager and employee. The manager completes the Values Coaching Process self-assessment form which includes introspective questions about each of the values behaviors. The manager is asked to truthfully assess their past behaviors with the employee and identify possible weak spots where he/she may have damaged the relationship. The Values Coaching Process Self-Assessment form prepares the manager to hear the feedback from the employee. The Self-Assessment is used to uncover areas of strength and weakness. It allows the manager to be more open to what could be termed sensitive feedback.

If the relationship between the employee and the manager is strong and has a high level of trust, the Values Coaching Process preparation and discussion will be uneventful and will confirm that an open and honest discussion can occur. However, if trust is low, then the relationship has probably been damaged and needs repair. The Values Coaching Process will begin to open up the dialogue to get the issues "out on the table" and then they can be addressed.

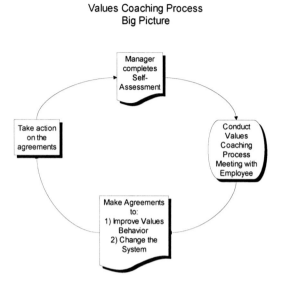

Values Coaching Process
Big Picture

Step #1:

Manager completes Values Coaching Process Self-Assessment:
- Identify what they are doing well (values behaviors)
- Identifies areas for improvement
- Identifies barriers preventing improvement
- Manager provides a blank copy of the Values Coaching Process Form and explains how to use it for self-assessment and in preparation for Meeting #2. Manager asks employee to complete the form for their own use

Step #2:
- Values Coaching Process meeting:
- Manager explains importance of values and importance of the meeting (Big Why)
- Manager requests and receives White Flag® feedback
- Manager uses PI and L.E.A.D. with Trust tools to optimize meeting and maintain relationships
- Manager and employee uncover system issues that require action
- Manager and employee make agreements (an agreement is a specific, measurable, and time sensitive task using a predictable method)

Step #3:

- Take Action on Agreements:
- Manager and employee keep agreements
- System improvements made
- When the employee is ready, the process is reversed
- After 3 months the next meeting is held (maximum time) and the process is repeated starting with the self-assessment

Values Coaching Process

Self Assessment Form

Name: _____	Date of Planning: ___/___/___	Dept: _____
Job Title: _____	Supervisor: _____	

Instructions: *Please briefly state examples of how you are living the following values, how you would like to improve, and any barriers prevent you from living the values.*

Use the spaces provided to record your answers.

Integrity

- Communicate openly, honestly and responsibly, in a professional manner (without condescension, sarcasm or profanity)
- Make only agreements you are willing and able to keep. Communicate when you cannot keep agreements to those who need to know.
- We take responsibility for our own actions and the quality of our work.
- We use our mistakes to create a safe learning environment. When we make a mistake we admit, take action to correct it and work together to prevent it from recurring.
- When we see a mistake from others, we communicate it respectfully and work with other to correct it and prevent it from occurring in the future.

Agreement: A specific, measurable, attainable, realistic, time-based arrangement.

How am I currently living with integrity?
How can I improve my ability to live with integrity:
What barriers are preventing me from living with integrity:

Respect
- We treat others as we want to be treated - with dignity and professionalism. For example, we encourage, acknowledge and are considerate of others opinions and perspectives and demonstrate it with our actions.
- We communicate effectively:
- We listen attentively without interruptions and paraphrase to confirm understanding.
- We communicate directly and professionally any issues/concerns first with the person involved and no one else (no gossip).
- Our words, tone of voice and body language match to form a consistent message.
- We welcome a creative exchange of ideas and opinions and are non-judgmental (no criticism).
- We will ask clarifying questions if we disagree or do not understand (avoiding criticism or judgment)

How am I currently behaving with respect?
How can I improve my ability to show respect?
What barriers are preventing me from behaving with respect?

Following and Coaching Values behaviors

Use the Process for Following and Coaching Values behaviors when an employee is inconsistent with values behaviors and change is needed. Employees want to do a good job and they sometimes make mistakes and nearly all the time these mistakes are unintentional. This process enables a leader and employee to make new agreements with each other to avoid any confusion or misunderstandings and to resolve inconsistencies.

The Process of *"Following and Coaching Values Behaviors"*

- An interaction occurs between employee that either goes well or does not go well
- Employee determines if values behaviors were violated and which value it was
- Employees identify agreements that need to be made to resolve the issue and to take action
- Employee(s) use the White Flag® process if necessary to identify system issues and agreements
- If the system issue is not clearly identified then the employees can identify what kind of system issue exists and agree on a strategy for action

    Type 1 = Simple process that can be fixed immediately with new agreements

    Type 2 = A current procedure that needs review and agreements previously made need to be reinforced

    Type 3 = A process that needs to be created by an improvement team (and/or with the Six Thinking Hats[7]) because it has not been completely defined and it impacts multiple employees and/or departments

    Type 4 = a complex process that requires a team effort and/or needs to be modified or improved with the Six Thinking Hats process
- Employees make agreements
- If this is a pattern of broken values it must be documented with clear history of behaviors (document in a memo or email) and the employee must be notified that the documentation exists

The Bridge to Accountability

Often a Human Resource department is contacted after the relationship between a manager and an employee has already been badly damaged. The Bridge to Accountability process brings a manager and the employee (and/or another employee whom is a colleague) back to the basic elements of respect and integrity in order to begin to repair a damaged relationship. The purpose of the Bridge to Accountability is to restore and

---

7   *Edward DeBono Six Thinking Hats Process, http://www.edwdebono.com/*

renew a relationship between a manager and employee (as long as it is not damaged beyond repair) so that it is effective and sustainable.

The Bridge to Accountability helps managers and employees to understand:

- The importance of maintaining values
- The accountability portion of the Values and System Model
- A tool for holding employees accountable while maintaining an effective relationship
- How to create effective expectation plans (or performance plans) employees are willing, not forced, to implement
- How to redirect employees positively by communicating SPECIFIC and CLEAR expectations
- How to transition into a focused discipline strategy
- To help Managers redirect employees positively by communicating SPECIFIC, and CLEAR expectations
- How to help employees DE-SELECT if they just cannot or are not willing to meet expectations

The Bridge to Accountability Steps:

- Manager decides if he/she has a disciplinary issue and needs help
- Manager creates a tentative plan with HR (brings any data from poor performance or values issues)
- Human Resources evaluates the data and asks manager if employee and/or manager needs or wants professional counseling
- Human Resources facilitates a "Forgiveness Meeting" (script available)
- Human Resources facilitates agreements to resolve conflicts and move forward to improve trust and performance of processes
- Human Resources facilitates "Agreements Meeting" (script available)
- Human Resources facilitates a de-selection of employee if necessary (employee chooses not to cooperate and makes it clear he/she does not wish to work with the organization any longer). Sometimes an employee is sending a clear message through his/her actions (or in-actions). The behavior clearly demonstrates he/she is unwilling or unable to perform his/her work (the message is sent without saying the words, "I quit..."). Leaders need a process to uncover that message quickly and definitively.

Coaching and Trust Building Checklist

The Coaching and Trust Building Checklist is a list of behaviors showing how an Optimum Leader wants to treat all co-workers in order to optimize learning and minimize fear.

The checklist is to allow a leader to interact with all co-workers (including employees, managers, and/or colleagues) to optimize learning and productivity. The coaching enables anyone to create an environment of optimum trust while delivering optimum feedback without criticism, and optimum learning using the Plan-Do-Study-Act Learning Cycle. The process helps focus attention on process improvement and away from flaws in the personnel.

Coaching and Trust Building Skills Check List and Feedback Form

Relationship Check List	Yes	No	N/A
Demonstrates Integrity			
1. Words, tone and body language all match to form a consistent message			
2. Gives away credit for good work (even if they played a role)			
3. Stays on the subject at hand (ability to focus)			
4. Acknowledges or asks permission to change the subject (respect)			
5. Confirms understanding with closed end questions			
6. Maintains composure even in the face of challenging statements or issues (remains calm and non-defensive in words and tone)			
7. Takes responsibility for their contribution of poor work			
Expresses Concern			
8. Expresses appreciation to others for good deeds or kind words			
9. Does not interrupt (allows venting and respectfully interrupts)			
10. Asks permission to ask questions			
11. Asks questions when disagrees or does not understand			
12. Uses proper words:			
• Avoids trust destroying words (try, but, should, vagaries etc.) • Uses trust building words (I will, I can, Names, I understand etc.) • Makes every comment using non-judgmental phrases and gestures • Speaks clearly (easy to understand) • Is courteous (thank you, please, I appreciate)			
13. Is able to read body language (is aware of congruence or a lack of)			
14. Avoids defensive tone and language			
15. Expresses empathy when appropriate			

16. Uses supportive physiology			
• Uses confident, calm, welcoming, and non-threatening posture and gestures • Maintains eye contact when listening and answering and presenting • Avoids distracting mannerisms • Uses supportive (non-defensive) facial expressions • Maintains effective volume and pace of voice to the end of sentences • Uses appropriate speed and volume in voice • Matches and mirrors participants to create rapport			
17. Implements proper use of questions with positive impression (non-manipulative and not condescending)			
18. Listens effectively to comments and questions (rephrase, paraphrase, recap and doesn't interrupt)			
19. Uses only self-effacing humor (does not use humor at another's expense)			

Coaching and Trust Building Skills Check List and Feedback Form continued

Demonstrates Competence	Yes	No	N/A
20. Is able to explain the big picture of a situation before explaining details			
21. Makes effective use of common ground or metaphors to explain their points			
22. Uses stories and metaphors effectively to make their points			
23. Delivers the outcomes needed or expected or more			
24. Is knowledgeable on necessary subjects			
25. Is aware of limitations and acknowledges them			
26. Focuses attention on one subject at a time until a clear course of action or agreement is made			
27. Is able to problem solve, brainstorm and create innovative solutions			
28. Uses data to make decisions			
29. Is willing to implement decisions and ideas other than their own			
30. Is able and willing to ask "why" questions			
31. Is willing to take time to find root causes to problems			
32. Willing and able to customize a message to match communication style differences			
33. Wants to continuously learn and wants others to learn as well (demonstrates learning is a priority)			
34. Has the discipline to follow policy and procedure while still continuously looking for improvements			
Aligns Common Objectives			
35. Explains "why" actions must be taken (doesn't demand or over use authority)			
36. Facilitates challenging agreements consistent with vision, values, mission and goals			
37. Is aware of the need to avoid compromise if possible and changes agreements to achieve outcomes and avoid compromise if possible. If it is not possible, they tell the truth (don't give in)			
38. Suggests and makes agreements that capture the essence of the discussion			

Corrective Action and Dismissal Process for Managers

Purpose of the Process:

To empower managers to make decisions about corrective actions, discipline of employees and dismissal of employees

Intended Outcomes:

- Managers are empowered
- Managers are accountable for managing the variation in values issues and system issues in their teams and departments
- Associates and managers are following values behaviors
- Reduced dismissals that create legal challenges or wasted time

If corrective action or termination is not done is there a high probability:

Consideration-Question	Yes	No
The situation will create a perception of favoritism (e.g. other associates will perceive the associate is being treated differently because others have received a corrective action for the same behaviors)?		
The situation will create an environment that encourages continued poor performance by the associate in the future (are we teaching what we are allowing)?		
The situation will create an environment that will deflate or discourage other associates (e.g. other associates were significantly impacted by the behaviors)?		
The situation will damage the supervisor/manager credibility and/or the credibility of our company with other associates (e.g. other associates were significantly impacted by the behaviors, values were clearly broken)?		
The associate continues to break values and has received White Flag® feedback in the past continuing to demonstrate a pattern of unacceptable behavior?		
The associate continues to ignore or not follow a policy or procedure even after receiving either clear verbal or written communication that communicates consequences of failure to comply?		
The associate continues to break agreements. (The choices are within their control and are not a system issue outside of their control)?		
If you were the associate and given corrective action would you feel you'd been treated fairly?		

Note: Please provide data to any or all of the items for any "yes" answer (e.g. personal observation, documentation from others, and documentation from the associate).

Chapter 13:
Stop Pay-for-performance Too

Aim of this Chapter: To make a case against pay-for-performance and explain how it damages employee engagement especially if it is linked to the typical performance appraisal.

ADD - **Use story of "outstanding" vs. Truly exceptional.. owner of dealership complained it could not be reached and the language was faulty and accused them of manipulating so they did not have to pay the bonuses.**

Story of Dr.'s who were not willing to be engaged in the ee initiative.. interviewed them and they said… pay scale was ineffective and "the concerns raised are a key to the company survival and ability to thrive.

Without a correction in this arena I am afraid it may not prosper as well as it might otherwise."

The typical manager is using enslavement policies because that is how we have all been taught to think about people and problems. We have been taught a theory of motivation that is wrong. Perhaps you are thinking, *"How arrogant! How can 90% of very smart managers be wrong?"* They can be wrong for the same reason Galileo was criticized and put on house arrest until his death for claiming the sun is the center of the universe (Copernicus' theory). 90% can also be wrong for the same reason Einstein was called a kook by most of his scientific colleagues when he, using his new Theory of Relativity, made a prediction that light from the sun would be bent by gravity during a solar eclipse. Obviously both Galileo and Einstein have been exonerated and proven to be courageous innovators who communicated a new theory in the face of strong resistance.

We have been taught a pair of theories that are no longer useful for creating optimal engagement: B.F. Skinner with his theory of Behaviorism and Frederick Taylor with his theory of Scientific Management. If we want optimal enslavement these theories work well. If we want optimal engagement, we need new theories.

B.F. Skinner made popular our current addiction to pay-for-performance. Using animals in his experiments he "proved" that behavior is simply an outcome of genetics and rewards and those rewards could motivate. He then made the claim that the same is true for humans. WRONG! Humans are much more complex and are motivated by much more than a simple reward. Alfie Kohn, in his landmark work, <u>Punished by Rewards,</u> lays out a solid argument against pay-for-performance. (Kohn, 1993) Kohn argues that pay-for-performance creates many unintended consequences such as diminished interest in the task, a reduction in the focus on the customer, a diminished focus on quality, competition instead of cooperation etc. The unintended consequences created are the opposite needed for engagement.

I attended a marketing conference promoted by a medical association. I was one of the featured speakers on leadership and performance management. Each year the association featured a competition for the best marketing programs. The membership voted for 1st and 2nd place prizes for each of the type of marketing expertise. At this particular conference one particular marketing organization won 90% of the awards. The organizers of the competition were a bit embarrassed. After the award ceremony the conference organizers decided to award three levels of prizes for the next year in order to avoid the embarrassment and to spread the awards more fairly. Contingent rewards create competition, a lack of fairness, and damaged relationships yet we continue to apply them. We are addicted to a pay-for-performance workplace.

People addicted to alcohol and cocaine will continue to use these substances even though they experience the damaging results. I believe HR professionals do the same with pay-for-performance policies. They see the damage yet they don't make the connection and they don't change behavior. It takes courage and persistence to change this policy. I think it is time we stop this addiction.

Every research study I have ever read shows money is **not** the top motivator. At best, it is forth behind challenge, making a difference, personal achievement, enjoyment, etc. Yet, managers continue to use rewards to improve performance. Again, we are addicted to a theory that has limits and holds us back from achieving engagement. Pay-for-performance's mantra, "Do this and you will get that" is a just another method of control. Control is enslavement not engagement.

Even pay-for-performance sales compensation plans are not meeting expectations. Of all the plans that one might think will work well it is sales performance plans but that is not what some sales experts say.

> *"Too often, companies fall into the trap of thinking that sales underperformance is primarily a compensation issue. Many companies fail to do the hard*

but strategic work of segmenting customers to identify those offering the greatest value to the company," says Larry Montan, a partner in Deloitte and Touche's human capital practices. "Even companies that have segmented customers frequently have not organized their sales force and compensation programs to drive behavior that supports strategic objectives such as selling into new channels, pushing new products, or targeting the most attractive customers. Instead, basic compensation programs continue to reward sales reps for selling any products, rather than those that are a tougher sell but more strategically important to the future of the company."

Fifty-six percent of companies surveyed see room for improvement in their sales compensation plans. Seventy-nine percent have made six or more changes to their plan in the past two years, yet dissatisfaction persists.

Another example of our addiction became apparent when I made a presentation at a Society for Human Resources Management Conference (SHRM) which included an argument against pay-for-performance. At the beginning of the presentation I asked the audience of HR professionals if they wanted to hear something new and exciting. They enthusiastically said YES! They claimed to always want something new. When I presented a model of leadership that did not include pay-for-performance they revolted. They weren't ready for their addiction to be attacked.

Pay-for-performance helped Frederick Taylor install his Scientific Management in the minds of virtually every manager, teacher, professor, and parent. In the late 1800's and early 1900's, during the explosion of the industrial age, many immigrants had low skills and did not speak English. Pay-for-performance was the perfect solution to the question, *"How can management quickly 'motivate' people to work in factories and do what they need to do?"* Taylor studied the job tasks and then bribed the factory workers with pay-for-performance to do it his way (because his way was the most efficient). It worked beautifully because the tasks were clearly described, simple to do, and required neither problem solving skills nor critical thinking.

One thing led to another and schools adopted the behaviorist model for education. Design the curriculum and bribe the children with grades to get them to study what we want (not necessarily what they want). Pay-for-performance works, but it only works to a point. As long as the tasks are clear and mindless, improvement can be seen. When problem solving or complex critical thinking is required pay-for-performance's efficacy begins to run into trouble. Furthermore, the long-term effects of pay-for-performance begin to show their destructive nature. Incentives will have a detrimental effect on both performance and motivation when the task begins to become interesting to the person (employee and/or student) and it requires effort to uncover a solution that is not immediately apparent. (Kohn, 1993)

The very popular pay-for-performance policy is consistent with malpractice because it's designed to control employee behaviors in order to achieve specific results.

People want to be rewarded for their hard work and they should be. However, when leaders make the individual rewards contingent on specific individual goals and/or behaviors this policy crosses the line into malpractice. Leaders think this policy will increase employee engagement but it instead violates the engagement psychology. The use of contingency pay-for-performance to achieve organizational results is akin to the use of bloodletting leeches by physicians in the 1700's to cure heart disease. It was once thought to be effective but it is now completely outdated in the "new" knowledge age. These typical pay-for-performance policies violate employee engagement and natural law because they:

- Attempt to control behaviors (e.g. they limit options)
- Send a message of distrust (i.e. employees would not work on the right things with the right effort without a reward)
- Limit innovation (there may be a better result employees could work toward)
- Ignore interdependence (achieving a goal in one area of an organization might cause waste in another area)
- Increase the probability of dishonesty to achieve a specific goal to receive a specific reward (e.g. people often cheat if they think they need to do it to achieve their individual goals and if they think they can get away with it)

An alternative reward system consistent with systems thinking and aligned with engagement natural law will instead:

- Align with a larger purpose and or the compelling mission of the organization and not just the individual needs of the single employee

- Allow for choice in methods for completing tasks and accomplishing the individual goals
- Give employees opportunities to be challenged and to optimize the use of their strengths
- Enable employees to track their own progress with control over their own feedback without dependence on the biased ratings usually issued by managers
- Demonstrate clear progress toward a win-win set of outcomes for both the individual and the organization.
- Share profit increases (because of the collective accomplishments) with a clear specific method and without biased judgments about individual performance e.g. who is more responsible for a winning no-hitter baseball game, the pitcher who throws the ball, the catcher who reads the batters and calls the types of pitches, or the teammates who field the grounders and fly balls?

This alternative reward system optimizes intrinsic motivation and increases employee engagement. It minimizes the control created by contingency based policies.

Leaders who want to increase employee engagement must design their pay-for-performance policies consistent with employee engagement psychology. Otherwise, regardless of their good intentions, they are undermining the very thing they are trying to accomplish i.e. engagement and sustainable improved performance. They will be practicing leadership malpractice.

Contingent vs. Surprise

A new General Manager at an auto dealership was faced with low employee engagement. He wanted to boost morale. After a very satisfactory sales year he decided to express his appreciation with a surprise bonus for every employee. He had about $4,000 in the budget. That averaged about $100 for each and every employee.

He went to the bank and obtained 40 crisp $100 bills. He met with each employee one-on-one. He shook their hands and expressed his sincere appreciation for the work they were doing every day and told them the $100 was only a small token of his depth of appreciation. This action made a lasting impression on the employees. Their morale and engagement was immediately increased. The General Manager's management team told him how much everyone appreciated this action. A surprise demonstration of appreciation is more powerful and more respectful than a contingency reward.

Human Resources managers have difficulty seeing a world of high performance and optimum accountability without the pay-for-performance policies. They insist that top performers must be paid according to their results. Most are addicted to this policy and, the sad fact is, it doesn't work. Here are at least five compelling reasons why pay-for-performance policies are so damaging.

Unintended Consequences

Pay-for-performance policies create unintended consequences. Those consequences often are so damaging that they outweigh the expected benefits. I donate blood to the American Red Cross whenever I can. I normally just show up at a collection center at a convenient time in hopes I will not wait long. After experiencing long waits in the past an appointment sounded preferable and when the call center operator asked me if I wanted to set one I said yes.

What I didn't realize is the Red Cross uses pay-for-performance to "motivate" their call center operators. The operators are paid a fee for each appointment they schedule. I know this because I asked one of the operators because my first appointment did not go well. I arrived on-time but was told there were too many appointments made too close to each other and the walk-ins needed to be alternated between the appointments so as to not turn anyone away. I ended up waiting over an hour. With the best of intentions American Red Cross management instituted a policy that didn't just damage their customer satisfaction. It created incredible frustrations and a loss of trust in the entire organization.

Limits autonomy and damages engagement

Pay-for-performance is a method of control. Control is the opposite of freedom. Without freedom people are hesitant to take risk and to be innovative. Pay-for-performance damages innovation and creativity. Furthermore, in his book "Why We Do What We Do", Edward Deci explains how pay-for-performance rewards causes people to lose intrinsic interest in the tasks they are being paid to do. If policies that control behavior damages both innovation and interest in the task can we conclude they can also damage performance? (Deci, 1995)

Reduces innovation and problem solving

Second, pay-for-performance policies ignore factors that come from the system. Ignoring system issues prevents innovative and significant performance improvements. For example, a sales person who makes huge bonuses might be benefiting from his/her specific assigned territory. Why should he/she continuously make those large bonuses when the client mix is the major contributing factor? Furthermore, if the client mix is the major reason for the performance success, why can't the other sales people develop their territories to match that client mix? These questions rarely get asked or answered because the sales person will protect their position or risk losing their competitive edge against his/her fellow sales people.

Encourages unethical behaviors

Pay-for-performance bonus policies very often encourage unethical behaviors. These behaviors are difficult to prevent especially when the bonuses or the stakes are large.

In 1992 the California Department of Consumer Affairs investigated Sears Roebuck for performing unnecessary auto repairs for their customers. Auto repair employees were under pressure from senior management and supervisors to meet stretch goals to increase in the number of repairs and corresponding revenue. (Friedrichs, 2010)

Sports enthusiasts continue to be disappointed by their heroes. One of the most disappointing was Lance Armstrong. Accused of using performance enhancing drugs Armstrong denied all allegations for years. Finally he stepped forward and admitted his drug use. Two major reasons were given for his denial. He claimed others were doing it too and that prevented him from effectively competing unless he too participated. Companies with whom he held his lucrative endorsement contracts encouraged him to deny the charges if he was to keep the endorsements going.

One of the most disturbing ethical breaks involves our children. In July 2011, 178 teachers and administrators in Atlanta schools cheated to boost test scores for the students and avoid penalties by the No Child Left Behind policies.

Damages relationships

Irena Sendler was a heroin during World War II. She smuggled Jewish infants out in the bottom of the tool box she carried. She managed to smuggle out and save 2500 kids/

infants. She would load the children into the tool box and burlap bags. She trained her dog to bark and distract the Nazi soldiers who would inspect her truck before she left her work.

Ultimately, she was caught, however, and the Nazi's broke both of her legs and arms and beat her severely. Irena kept a record of the names of all the kids she had smuggled out so after the war, she could attempt to locate any parents that may have survived.

In 2007 Irena was up for the Nobel Peace Prize. She was not selected. Al Gore won instead for his work on global warming. Barack Obama won the following year for his work organizing ACORN.

There was disappointment experienced by many when Irena did not get win the Peace Prize. Many felt her contributions were much more effective in promoting peace than the other two winners mentioned. Those who feel this disappointment are biased. Bias often plays a major role in the awarding of prizes.

When managers make judgment calls about the contribution of an individual they increase the probability that others will be disappointed. By expressing their opinions and/or biases about one person they can solicit negative reactions from others. When attempting to motivate everyone by rewarding only a few, management an actually make morale worse for the majority. These negative reactions can damage relationships between the winners and losers and between the losers and management. With the best of intentions management creates the opposite effect they were seeking.

Is there a replacement for pay-for-performance?

Any decisions about how to distribute pay or bonuses must be separated from the CPIP discussions in order to avoid unintended consequences which can lead to the damage of openness and honesty. Instead of attempting to pay for individual performance why not adopt a different policy that better matches the CPIP paradigm? Because individuals in an organization are interdependent the quality of the interactions between the individuals will affect the performance of the organization. Therefore individuals who consistently fulfill their individual responsibilities (as defined by the following of values behaviors) can become qualified to receive bonus pay. Those who do not are disqualified from receiving a bonus. This can be documented using the White Flag® process.

Once an individual is qualified he/she can then receive a portion of a bonus pool that can be generated by some formula of profitability. Their portion can be defined by the percentage of total salary expense that their salary represents. For example, if a qualified employee's salary represents 1% of the total salary expense in an organization, he/she can therefore receive 1% of the total bonus poll generated by the organization. A policy like this helps avoid any bias by management and avoids competition between employees.

Chapter 14:
An Amazing journey – Organizational Democracy, Self-Management, and Self-Organizing Systems

Aim of this Chapter: To describe an alternative organizational model that is consistent with natural law and matches best with Deming's System of Profound Knowledge.

The Flocking Birds

Leaders can and must learn from nature to predictably improve results. Nature operates on principles that don't change. Leaders get into trouble when they ignore natural principles and operate based on bias or short term thinking. A good metaphor for this type of principled decision-making is flocking birds.

It is a most mystifying phenomenon. As a group, they have no leader to tell them when to turn left or right, or when to slow down or to speed up; yet as a group, they change direction as effortlessly as a single organism. How is this possible? It is possible because, flocking birds naturally follow three basic principles: first, they fly in the same general direction as their closest neighbors; second, they fly at the same average speed as their closest neighbors; third, they fly at the same average distance from their closest neighbor and avoid colliding with them at all costs. Following these three basic principles, they are able, as a group, to respond to their fast-changing environment with rapid, precise adjustments.

Flocking birds are a "self-organizing system". Organizations can achieve the same agile capabilities if the leader clarifies the vision and the organizational objectives, and teaches clear effective principles. In doing so, the leader establishes trust and increases his/her influence, while empowering each individual to make the right decisions at the right time. In the presence of a clear vision, clear objectives and sound principles, individuals participating in a self-organizing system learn how to adjust to a fast-paced environment. Like the birds, people will respond quickly, appropriately and in the best interests of the "flock", without needing a controlling authority to tell them what to do.

This metaphor suggests a different role for leadership that the one many organizations embrace now. This model requires a high level of trust and rejects an emphasis on control. It requires a deep understanding and an embrace of natural principles. It requires an ability to facilitate the understanding of these principles to others so they can be followed without excessive supervision.

When our Founding Fathers wrote the Declaration of Independence they started with articulating principles of nature and Nature's God. Our founding is based on these principles and our success is as well. At the time there was nothing like this on earth. There was no organization on earth that adopted these principles to form a government of, by and for the people and that strayed so far from the typical monarchy model. There is an opportunity to learn from this historical experiment. There is an opportunity to form organizations based on sound principles and sound theory and one consistent with nature. The United States began to stray from this approach starting sometime in the late 19th century and some would say it is time to return to this more successful model of how to lead a country, an organization, a school etc.

Organizational Democracy: A New Model of Leadership

Some hierarchical organizations are collapsing around us. The Greeks are protesting. Libya hunted down and killed Gaddafi. Egyptians threw out Mubarak. The Post Office is losing money and is reorganizing to reduce services to reduce costs. Nearly every state and municipality is financially challenged and some have even declared bankruptcy. Even our beloved USA is severely stretched financially with $16 trillion of debt and growing.

Why is this happening? One could make the case that faltering of the global economy is the major cause. It might be deeper than that. Our command and control leadership model is failing and we are witnessing the symptoms of the past 150 years of its implementation. Possibly, we are witnessing its demise.

Could our command and control leadership be a reason why about 70% of planned change efforts fail to achieve the intended outcomes? Planned change efforts are often doomed from the beginning because the responsibility for creating change lies at that top and is forced on those who "must be changed." The principles of this type of change are that 1) management knows best, 2) people don't know what they need (management does), 3) people don't like change and so they must be changed through bribes or threats. These principles are contrary to natural law and so people resist, feel confused, and feel stressed.

Some say this model could lead to chaos if no one person is in charge. There is a difference between chaos and positive chaos. Chaos usually is a disorganized and confusing situation. Positive chaos is self-organizing based on principles.

Positive chaos operates under a specific set of principles. It embraces a high level of trust and clarity. Positive chaos means people are willing to adapt to change as it happens based on their own perceptions and decisions (experiments based on the learning cycle) to serve a higher purpose consistent with principle. With positive chaos people don't have to be forced to change via threats, bribes of other controlling means. They willingly change their actions and procedures as needed because they understand why the change is needed and they have the ability to make those decisions. They have autonomy. They are trusted. They have the skills to match the challenges they face. They are given the choice about how to change to serve their internal and external customers. There is stress in positive chaos but the stress is positive because it stems from the desire to meet a challenge. The challenge is to accomplish what is best for the customer and the organization and employees are able to fully deploy their skills and their cognitive energy to meet these challenges.

In an organization that embraces Deming's Theory of Profound Knowledge, employees have a greater probability of experiencing positive chaos. The employees are entrusted to follow specified processes. They understand the unambiguous connections to their customers and what their customers need. They continuously look for ways to make the pathway to their customer simple, direct and improved. Their actions for change are made in accordance with the learning cycle of plan, do, study, and act. Knowing and utilizing this method fosters trust throughout the organization. Employees and management don't always understand what changes are coming from their fellow employees but they can be certain the changes are consistent with principles which will deliver the best for the organization, the best for the people, and the best for the customer. This is positive chaos in action.

In our world of accelerated change the only change that will endure is the one ruled by positive chaos. Only those principles of providing autonomy, trust, and expecting people to respond positively by applying their skills to the challenges they face will keep us competitive.

What we have now

We have been taught an authoritarian leadership model for at least 150 years. The industrial age brought the need for mass production. In this model only managers knew how to solve problems and how to direct and discipline workers. In this model workers were thought to be mindless and naturally lazy and that meant they needed to be controlled and incented by managers to get them to work. The main forces keeping people working, according to the industrial age manager, was the carrot and stick.

The need for mass production denied the need for a worker's mind. Policies such as pay-for-performance and performance reviews were refined to ensure workers kept working. In preparation for the factory workforce schools were modeled after factories. Curriculums were created to give the key skills needed to work in factories. Curiosity in schools was unnecessary and even discouraged. Students instead only needed to fit within a certain model of behaviors. They were tested according to certain standards and certain curriculum. This model is no longer working.

What we need

Growing up I would often receive "hand me down" clothes from my brother. They were often too large at first and eventually I grew out of them. Although they were useful for a while I eventually needed to discard them because they just did not fit. The same is true for our hierarchical command and control management model. We have outgrown it.

We are transitioning into the knowledge economy where mass production is making way for customization. Being managed by others is making way for self-management. Being told the answers is making way for creating our own solutions. We now need every heart and every brain to be engaged to solve the complex problems in today's knowledge economy. We now need everyone to be capable of self-management.

We can see evidence of success of this model in the extremely popular social networks. Social networks are self-organizing and self-managed systems. Social networks such as Facebook and Linkedin are examples of self-management and optimum freedom of choice. People in these social networks are free to opt-in because they share the same interests and objectives. They organize based on these interests and principles.

Planned change vs. Self-organizing change

We tend to view chaos as negative, something to be avoided. We see chaos as confusing, scary and, stressful because we are off balance. Our current mind-set in organizations seems to be avoidance of feeling off balance, or out of control and yet in nature being off balance leads to growth and adaptation to environmental changes. (Wheatley, 2006) To achieve employee engagement leaders in our knowledge based economy must embrace chaos and make decisions that ensure the chaos is positive not negative. Positive chaos is an outcome of a clear set of principles which are embraced and acted upon with autonomy. Positive chaos requires clear principles that are aligned with natural law and the autonomy to act.

Positive chaos puts decisions in the hands of employees optimizing the chance for change to be initiated and to be sustainable. The typical appraisal prevents autonomy and therefore stops change from taking hold.

Organizations need to be more like social networks. Organizational Democracy will take many of the same characteristics of a social network. Optimum freedom of choice within a context of specific principles will begin to define an Organizational Democracy.

How we can begin to create Organizational Democracies

The House Metaphor helps explain how an organizational democracy might be organized and implemented. The House Metaphor guides us to create the solid foundation first. Agreeing on solid principles is essential. Three principles that provide an excellent start are:

First, the context is the most important element of performance. Leaders must take responsibility to create a context that allows for optimum freedom and encourages self-management with positive conflict (not negative conflict). This requires a solid foundation with a clear vision, mission, and values along with a clear understanding of self-management and how it can change the role of managers and employees.

Our Founding Fathers understood this. The Declaration of Independence clarified the specific (natural rights) principles upon which we are bound if we are to protect our rights. All men are created equal. The government must be of, by and for the people. The inalienable (natural) rights of life, liberty, and the pursuit of happiness are to be protected. These can be protected if we follow the principles. Furthermore, the Constitution was designed to fulfill the principles outlined in the Declaration. The Constitution was designed to carry out the principles and keep the government from going beyond its responsibilities. Organizations can follow the same strategy.

Careful thought is required for this foundation. Each of the elements of the foundation plays an essential role in the success. Alignment of the senior leadership team is critical. Our founding fathers took over 100 days of vigorous debate to align on a document they could sign as our Constitution. The process of aligning on the foundation is a critical step to create an organizational democracy. It must not be rushed because any "crack" in the foundation, in the form of a lack of alignment, will cause harm later. The alignment must be achieved with the vision, mission, values, management theory, and strategy. Without this alignment the tendency will be to fall back into the hierarchical autocratic model where a small group of people become appointed to make most of the important decisions. This defeats the purpose for creating the organizational democracy.

The vision tells the organization what it hopes to become in the not too distant future. The mission tells everyone why the organization exists. The values explain how everyone will behave along the journey. The management theory will provide a way to think about problems. The strategy tells everyone where to focus their energy.

Second, in an organizational democracy, the quality of the interactions is more important than the quality of the individuals. Managers and employees must accept the joint responsibility to manage the quality of their interpersonal interactions and their system interactions. System interactions refer to how processes work. Everyone must understand how to manage the variation in their processes and in their connections between organizational functions. They must be able to understand how to study and improve processes which work between people and between functions.

CPIP is a tool that can assist in the creation of the key elements of the structure in the House Metaphor. An organizational democracy will require self-organizing teams that manage the variation in key processes. These teams will be responsible for selected processes. These processes will include both self-management processes and operational processes. Self-management processes might include the hiring of members, the selection of leaders, the resolving of conflicts, the improvement of processes. The CPIP can be used to develop trust and learning within the team and between the teams. This can allow team members to choose their own leaders. Just as we vote for our representatives in the Congress and the Senate why not elect the leaders who will lead out self-managed teams?

The operational processes might include production processes, customer service processes, and financial reporting processes, etc. The point is the self-organizing teams will know their responsibilities and their roles and their job will be to manage the variation in those processes for the purpose of serving their customers (internal and external).

With the existence of CPIP these teams can now manage the quality of the interpersonal interactions and the system interactions. This allows for optimum trust and effective relationships. Everyone must accept the responsibility to manage the variation in trust because trust is a key component of self-management and organizational democracy. Everyone must begin to understand how to create trust and how to repair trust while they manage the variation in the operational processes and the self-management processes.

The structure must also include an opportunity for all team members to learn and to use the quality improvement tools. If the teams are to self-manage they must be able to solve their own problems. The basic quality tools enable teams to identify and address problems without relationship damaging conflict. When conflict occurs members of self-managing teams can learn conflict resolution strategies and tools that enable them to keep the conflict productive and not destructive.

Third, organizational democracies require multiple feedback loops. These feedback loops are not manager dependent. They are managed instead by the team members. The feedback loops provide the self-managing team members the opportunity to best manage the quality of the interactions, trust, and learning. Feedback is about collecting and reporting of data and minimizing the use of opinions or criticism.

A client wanted a better way to manage a call center team. The manager notices how the team members were disengaged. Senior management wanted the calls to be answered quickly and they wanted minimum wait time in the call queue if a caller had to be placed on hold waiting for a customer service representative. The CEO often (weekly) reviewed the call answer time and the hold/wait time for the team. Whenever the times were creeping up he would remind the manager to speak with her team to get the times lower. Whenever the times were low he would encourage even more improvement. After a number of months of these reminders and encouragements the manager noticed a lack of improvement and a lack of motivation.

A different approach was needed. A self-organizing approach (organizational democracy) was needed. Feedback loops were needed and autonomy of decisions was needed to optimize learning, trust, engagement, and improvement.

A "dashboard" of performance data was created. The call center staff was presented with this "dashboard" once per week. It was posted where everyone could see it. The team members could take time to think about the results. Once per week they met to discuss the results and discuss how they could improve them (as a team). By getting the employees more involved in learning how to make things better and tapping into their creative ideas for improvement they became more engaged they improved the "dashboard" scores too. Everyone, the CEO, the employees, the manager, and the customers were all happier.

CPIP offers a tool that can facilitate the self-management. CPIP can be used to improve the quality of the interactions between team members, managers, and members of other teams. The typical appraisal does provide the opportunity for self-management. It is the wrong vehicle to move us from organizational teams to team organizations. (Cloke & Goldsmith, 2002) We need a new tool to help us make the transformation to organizational democracy. CPIP is that tool that helps self-managed teams to adapt quickly to the dynamic changes occurring in our knowledge economy.

Works Cited

Accountemps. (2012). *Survey Finds Wide Discrepancy in Perceived Value of Perforamnce Assessments.* Menlo Park, CA: Accountemps.

Achievers Intelligence. (2012). *Insight Into Today's Workforce.* Sanfrancisco, CA: Achievers.

Aquayo, R. (1990). *Dr. Deming: The American Who Taught the Japanese About Quality.* New York: Simon & Schuster.

Blessing - White Research. (2011). *Global Employee Engagement Report 2011.* Skillman, NJ: Blessing-White Research.

Board, C. A. (2003). *Columbia Accident Investigation Board.* Washington D.C.: National Aeronautics and Space Administration.

Bridges, W. (2003). *Managing Transitions.* Cambridge, MA: Perseus.

Cherniss, C., & Goleman, D. (2001). *The Emotionally Intelligent Workplace.* NY, NY: Jossey-Bass.

Christine Porath, C. P. (2013, January - February). *The Price of Incivility.* Retrieved January Sunday the 27th, 2031, from hbr.org: http://hbr.org/2013/01/the-price-of-incivility/ar/2

Cloke, K., & Goldsmith, J. (2002). *The End of Management.* Sanfrancisco, CA: Jossey-Bass.

Coens, T., & Jenkins, M. (2000). *Abolishing Performance Appraisals: Why They Backfire and What to do Instead.* San Francisco, CA: Berrtt-Koehler.

Covey, S. (1989). *7 Habits of Highly Effective People.* NY, NY: Simon and Schuster.

Dannel P. Malloy. (2012). *2012 The Year for Education Reform: The Time Has Come for Change in Connecticut's Schools.* Hartford, CT: State of Connecticut Department of Education.

Deming, W. E. (1986). *Out of the Crisis.* Cambridge, MA: Massachusetts Institute of Technology.

Deming, W. E. (1994). *The New Economics - Second Edition.* Cambridge, MA: Massechusettes Institute of Technology.

Eger, J. M. (2010, October 28). The 4th Grade Slump can Last Forever. *Huffington Post.*

Eichenwald, K. (2012, July 3). Microsoft's Lost Decade. *Vanity Fair.*

Gladwell, M. (2002, July 22). The Talent Myth. *The New Yorker*, pp. 28-33.

Goleman, D. (1995). *Emotional Intelligence.* NY NY: Bantam Books.

Hauck, W. (2008). *THE IMPACT ON TRUST BY THE PERFORMANCE APPRAISAL INTERVIEW AND POLICY A Dissertation.* Milford CT: Wally Hauck.

Kathlene Ryan, D. O. (1998). *Driving Fear Out of the Workplace.* San Francisco: Jossey-Bass.

Kenneth Cloke, J. G. (2002). *The End of Management and the Rise of Organizational Democracy.* San Francisco, CA: Jossey-Bass.

Kenny, J. (2013, January 9). *HR and Employment Law News.* Retrieved January 9, 2013, from www.blr.com: http://hr.blr.com/HR-news/Performance-Termination/Performance-Employee-Appraisal/Study-Only-one-in-three-workers-makes-changes-base

Kouses, J., & Posner, B. (1995). *The Leadership Challenge.* San Francisco, CA: Jossey-Bass.

Mowbray, J. (2002, October 28). Visas for Terrorists. *National Review,* pp. 32-37.

Murphy, M., Burgio-Murphy, A., & Young, J. (2007). Washington DC: Leadership IQ.

Pamela Shockley-Zalaak, S. M. (2010). *Building the High-Trust Organization.* San Francisco and still have time to do frequent working : John Wiiey & Somes.

Reina, D., & Reina, M. (2006). *Trust and Betrayal in the Workplace.* San Francisco: Berrrett-Koehler.

Russell L. Ackhoff, D. G. (2008). *Turning Learning Right Side Up.* Upper Saddle River, NJ: Wharton School Publishing.

Salary.com. (2006-2007). *Perforamnce Review Survey.* San Francisco, CA: Salary.com.

Scott Keller, C. A. (2012). *The Inconvenient Truth About Change Management: Why it isn't working and what to do about it.* New York, NY: McKinsey & Company.

Senge, P. (1990). *The Fifth Discipline: The Art & Practrice of The Learning Organization.* New York: Double Day/Currency.

Shockley-Zalabak, P., Ellis, K., & Rugger, C. (2000). *'Measuring Organizational Trust.* San Franciso, CA: IABC Research Foundation.

SHRM and Globoforce. (2012). *Employee Recognition Survey.* Southboro, MA: SHRM/Globoforce.

The Hay Group. (2003, March Volume 2, Issue 1). Performance Management: Painful Event or Productive Dialogue. *Hay Insight Connections,* p. 2.

Tribus, M. (1990, February 1). *The Germ Theory of Management.* Retrieved December 3, 2012, from Systemsthinking.co.uk: http://www.systemsthinking.co.uk/The_Germ_theory_of_Management.pdf

Verespej, M. (2003, May 12). Human Resources - A Call for Civility. *IndustryWeek.com*, p. http://www.industryweek.com/columns/asp/columns.asp?ColumnId=743.

Watson Wyatt. (2004). *WorkUSA 2004: Performance Management Summary.* Washington D.C.: Watson Wyatt.

Wheatley, M. (2006). *Leadership and the New Science.* San Farancisco, CA: Berrett-Koehler.

William J. Bellows, P. (2003). Conformance to Specifications, Zero Defects,and Six Signma Quality - A Closer Look. *International Journal of Internet and Enterprise.*

Zappe, J. (2012). *Business Leaders Pin Blame on HR For Worsening Shortage of Talent.* NY NY: TLNT.

CPSIA information can be obtained at www.ICGtesting.com
Printed in the USA
BVOW040134130713

325601BV00005B/11/P